St. Helena Library
1492 Library Lane
St. Helena, CA 94574
(707) 963-5244

The Broken Road

The Broken Road

From the Iron Gates to Mount Athos

PATRICK LEIGH FERMOR

Edited by Colin Thubron and Artemis Cooper

NEW YORK REVIEW BOOKS

New York

THIS IS A NEW YORK REVIEW BOOK
PUBLISHED BY THE NEW YORK REVIEW OF BOOKS
435 Hudson Street, New York, NY 10014
www.nyrb.com

First published in Great Britain in 2013 by
John Murray (Publishers), an Hachette UK Company
Maps drawn by Rodney Paull

Title page and chapter opener drawing by John Craxton
Photograph on p. x from the Patrick Leigh Fermor Archive,
reproduced by permission of the Trustees of
the National Library of Scotland.

Library of Congress Cataloging-in-Publication Data
is on file at the Library of Congress.

Hardback ISBN 978-1-59017-754-9
Ebook ISBN 978-1-59017-756-3

Set in Adobe Garamond 11/14 pt
Printed in the United States of America on acid-free paper.

10 8 6 4 2 1 3 5 7 9

In memory of Joan

Contents

Maps

Patrick Leigh Fermor at the Rila monastery, Bulgaria, autumn 1934

'I must have been an uncouth spectacle with long, unkempt and dust-clogged hair bleached to a shaggy tow and a face burnt to the hue of a walnut sideboard by the sun; rumpled clothes, a rucksack and a carved Hungarian walking-stick; also – I blush, now, to set it down, but honesty compels it – a scarlet and yellow braid belt bought in Transylvania, a steel-hilted dagger and a brown kalpack from the fair in Berkovitza.'

Introduction

There is something poignant and mysterious about incomplete masterpieces. The pair of books that preceded the present volume – *A Time of Gifts* and *Between the Woods and the Water* – remain the magnificent two thirds of an unfinished trilogy. They are unique among twentieth-century travel books. Forty and fifty years after the event, their journey – and its prodigious feat of recall – reads like the dream odyssey of every footloose student.

The eighteen-year-old Leigh Fermor set out from the Hook of Holland in 1933 to walk to Constantinople (as he determinedly called Istanbul). But it was only decades afterwards that he embarked on the parallel journey – the written one – looking back from maturity on his youthful rite of passage. *A Time of Gifts* (1977) carried him through Germany, Austria and Czecho-slovakia. *Between the Woods and the Water* (1986) continued across Hungary and into Transylvania and left him at the Danube's Iron Gates, close to where the Rumanian and Bulgarian frontiers converge. He was still five hundred miles from his destination in Constantinople.

The literary completion of this epic would have been a triumph comparable to that of William Golding's sea trilogy or, in a different genre, to Evelyn Waugh's *Sword of Honour*. But there, at the Iron Gates, Leigh Fermor's remembered journey hung suspended. Impatient readers gathered that he had succumbed to writer's block, frozen by failed memory or the task of equalling his own tremendous style.

But on his death in 2011 he left behind a manuscript of the final narrative whose shortcomings or elusiveness had tormented him for so many years. He never completed it as he would have wished. The reasons for this are uncertain. The problem remained obscure even to him, and *The Broken Road* is only its partial resolution. The book's fascination resides not only in the near-conclusion of its youthful epic, but in the light that it throws on the creative process of this brilliant and very private man.

At the age of eighteen Paddy (as friends and fans called him) thought himself a failure. His housemaster at King's School, Canterbury, had memorably labelled him 'a dangerous mixture of sophistication and recklessness', and he had been sacked from most of his schools. His parents were separated, his father – a distinguished geologist – was far away in India, and although Paddy toyed with entering the army, the prospect of its discipline irked him. Instead, he longed to be a writer. In rented digs in London's Shepherd Market, between wild parties among the remnant of the 1920s Bright Young People, he struggled with composing adolescent verse and stories. But in the winter of 1933, he wrote, gloom and perplexity descended. 'Everything suddenly seeming unbearable, loathsome, trivial, restless . . . Detestation, suddenly, of parties. Contempt for everyone, starting and finishing with myself.'

It was then that the idea of a journey dawned on him – a solitary walk in romantic poverty. An imaginary map of Europe unfurled in his mind. 'A new life! Freedom! Something to write about!' As 'a thousand glistening umbrellas were tilted over a thousand bowler hats in Piccadilly', he set out with a parental allowance of a pound a week and a copy of the *Oxford Book of English Verse* and Horace's Odes in his rucksack.

His walk up the Rhine into the heart of Middle Europe, down the Danube and across the Great Hungarian Plain to Transylvania, became a counterpoint of nights in hovels and sojourns in the castles of kindly aristocrats. But above all, as he travelled – exultantly curious – through the landscapes and histories of the unfolding continent, this was a young man's introduction to the riches of European culture. The journey took him a year. But it was over forty years before he began to publish it.

Other matters intervened. For four years after he reached Constantinople, he lived in Rumania with his first great love, Princess Balasha Cantacuzene. It was during this time that he first began to write up his youthful walk, but 'the words wouldn't flow,' he wrote, 'I couldn't get them to sound right.' And none of this first effort survives.

Then came the war, and his period as an SOE officer in occupied Crete, culminating in his legendary abduction of General Kreipe, divisional commander of the island's central sector. It was not until 1950 that literary success arrived, with a travel book on the Caribbean, followed by a novel and the resonant account of his retreat into monasteries, *A Time to Keep Silence*. Above all, his travels in Greece, where he settled with his wife Joan Eyres Monsell, yielded two books – *Mani* and *Roumeli* – that celebrate not the sites of classical antiquity but the earthy, demotic *Romiosyne*, the folk culture of the land he had come to love.

Late in 1962 the American *Holiday* magazine (a journal more serious than its name) commissioned Paddy to write a 5,000-word article on 'The Pleasures of Walking'. With no presentiment of what he was starting, he plunged into describing his epic trek. Nearly seventy pages later, he was still only two thirds of the way through – just short of the Bulgarian frontier, at the Iron Gates

– and the discipline of compression had grown unbearable.
Enormous seams of memory were opening up. Between one
sentence and another he threw off the constraints of an article.
Those first seventy pages were set aside, and when he resumed
the narrative, writing at his journey's natural pace, he was
composing a full-scale book – from Bulgaria to Turkey. Now all
the stuff of his walk – the byways of history and language, the
vividly etched characters, the exuberantly observed architecture
and landscape – came swarming on to the page. On New Year's
Day 1964 he wrote to his publisher, the loyal and long-suffering
Jock Murray, that the narrative had 'ripened out of all recognition. Much more personal, and far livelier in pace, and lots of
it, I hope, very odd.'

So, ironically, the last stretch of his journey – from the Iron
Gates to Constantinople – was the first part of his walk that he
attempted to write in full. He wanted to call the book 'Parallax',
a word (familiar to astronomy) that defines the transformation
that an object undergoes when viewed from different angles. It
was a measure of how acutely he felt the change in perspective
between his younger and older selves. Jock Murray, however,
balked at the title as too opaque (he thought parallax sounded
like a patent medicine) and it was tentatively renamed 'A Youthful
Journey'.

In the mid-1960s, with the manuscript still incomplete, Paddy
put it aside and became absorbed with his wife Joan in the creation of their home in the Peloponnese. When eventually he
returned to the project in the early 1970s, he realized that he
must start all over again, from his journey's beginnings in Holland,
and that there would be more than one book. For the next fifteen
years he laboured over the Great Trudge, as he called it, to produce
the two superb works that carried him to the Bulgarian border.
The manuscript of 'A Youthful Journey', meanwhile, handwritten

on stiff cardboard sheets, languished half-forgotten on a shelf in his study, enclosed in three black ring binders.

The spectacular success of the first two volumes drastically increased public expectation for the third. *Between the Woods and the Water* had ended with the irrevocable words: 'To be Concluded', and the commitment was to dog Paddy for the rest of his life. By the time he returned to 'A Youthful Journey' – which began at the Iron Gates, where *Between the Woods and the Water* ended – he was in his seventies; the text itself was some twenty years old, and the experiences remembered were over half a century away. This early manuscript was written in prolix bursts, barely edited. It lacked the artful reworking, the rich polish and some-times the coherence that he had come to demand of himself. The slow, intense, perfectionist labour by which the first two volumes had been achieved – even their proofs were so covered in correc-tions and elaborations that they had to be reset wholesale – seemed a near-insuperable challenge now. And other events weighed in. With the death of Jock Murray in 1993, and of Joan in 2003, the two people who had most encouraged him were gone. The long ice age that set in was perhaps as bewildering to Paddy as to others. Even the help of a psychiatrist did little to ease him.

One of the astonishing facts about *A Time of Gifts* and *Between the Woods and the Water* is that they were written from memory, with no diaries or notebooks to sustain them. Paddy's first diary was stolen in a Munich youth hostel in 1934, and those that succeeded it, along with his picaresque letters to his mother, were stored during the war in the Harrods Depository, where years later they were destroyed unclaimed. It was a loss, he used to say, that 'still aches, like an old wound in wet weather'.

Yet curiously the absence of corroborating records may have been liberating. To a writer of Paddy's visual gifts, memories and associations would mount up together in vivid feats of reimagining. 'While piecing together fragments which have lain undisturbed for two decades and more,' he wrote in a reflective passage of *The Broken Road*, 'all at once a detail will surface which acts as potently as the taste of madeleine which made the whole of Proust's childhood unfurl. The haul of irrelevant detail, interlocking trains of thought and associations, and the echoes of echoes re-echoed and ricocheted, is overwhelming . . .' Without the constraints of a day-to-day logbook, these retrievals could develop less into a literal narrative than into memory-spurred recreations. Acts of poetic licence and conflation were, he admitted, all but inevitable.

In 1965, just after he had laid aside the unfinished 'A Youthful Journey' in order to build his Peloponnesian home, he was commissioned to write an article on the Danube, from its source to its end in Rumania's Black Sea. Communist Rumania, at this time, was easing open to the West, and he seized the opportunity of revisiting Balasha Cantacuzene. It was the first time he had seen her since leaving for the war in 1939. He met her secretly, at night, in the little town of Pucioasa, in the attic flat she now shared with her sister and brother-in-law. He was shocked by the toll that the past quarter century had taken, but moved to see her again. In 1949, already stripped of almost all their possessions, they had been evicted from their estate with just a quarter of an hour to pack, and she had thrown into her suitcase Paddy's fourth and final diary, which he had left behind with her. This precious remnant he took home to Greece. Written in faded pencil, the Green Diary, as he called it, carries his life forward to 1935 after his walk was over, and is appended with sketches of churches, costumes, friends, vocabularies in Hungarian, Rumanian, Bulgarian and Greek, and the names and addresses of almost everyone he stayed with.

But strangely, although the diary covered all his walk from

the Iron Gates to Constantinople and more, he never collated it with 'A Youthful Journey'. Perhaps its callowness jarred with the later, more studied manuscript, or their factual differences disconcerted him. The two narratives often diverge. Whatever the reason, the diary – which retained an almost talismanic significance for him – did nothing to solve his dilemma.

In 2008, while researching Paddy's biography, Artemis Cooper came upon a typescript of 'A Youthful Journey' in the John Murray offices in London. Paddy had never allowed her access to the manuscript in its black ring binders, and had forgotten that years ago he must have sent a copy of the unfinished work to Murrays; but now he asked for the typescript to be sent to him. He was in his early nineties. He had developed tunnel vision and could read only two lines of text at a time. But Olivia Stewart, a devoted friend after his wife's death, typed it up in an enlarged font size, along with the diary.

Now Paddy began painfully to revise once more, reading the typescript with a magnifying glass and correcting it in black fountain pen. Given his perfectionism, it was an all but impossible task. The whole narrative, he once said, needed 'unpicking', and if he had possessed the time and stamina he might have rewritten much of it wholesale. He was still editing, in a shaky hand, until a few months before his death.

It is this typescript, checked against the original manuscript of 'A Youthful Journey', that forms *The Broken Road*. It was mostly written in the onrush of creation between 1963 and 1964, with haphazard slips of grammar, style and punctuation, very different from Paddy's finished prose. Occasionally he hurled together data with the clear intention of clarifying it later. A few passages he expressly wanted cut.

As Paddy's editors and literary executors, we have sought, above all, to bring lucidity to the text, while minimizing our own words. There is scarcely a phrase here, let alone a sentence, that is not his. In attempting to preserve his distinctive style, we have respected the structure of his often elaborate sentences, with their train of subordinate clauses. We have retained his characteristic punctuation, his occasional lists and his long paragraphs. Provisionally he broke the text into many numbered sections; we have separated it instead into eight chapters, mostly titled geographically, as was his custom. The footnotes (a handful are his own) are mainly inserted for the elucidation of history and the translation of languages (whose occasional, exuberant guesswork we have generally corrected in the main text).

Finally, we must take responsibility for the book's title. *The Broken Road* is an acknowledgement that Paddy's written journey never reached its destination. (It stops short at the Bulgarian town of Burgas, fifty miles from the Turkish frontier.) The title recognizes, too, that the present volume is not the polished and reworked book that he would have most desired: only the furthest, in the end, that we could go.

Paddy's decision to write about his teenage walk seems almost preordained. He had a natural empathy with his boyhood; he remained, in a sense, oddly innocent. In *The Broken Road*, his generosity of heart, his youthful bravura and occasional swankiness go hand in hand with an indulgent estimate of others and an intense gratitude for any kindness shown. But these are tempered by unexpected intimations of vulnerability, with hints of depression and homesickness. The book is franker and more self-revelatory than it might have become with varnishing. Faithfully he records his boyish delight in the high society of Bucharest – the naivety of an idealizing teenager – and his occasional prejudices.

Yet the youth encountered in these pages is recognizably the protagonist of *A Time of Gifts* or, for that matter, of *Mani*. The mature man's interests and obsessions are already in place: his fascination with the dramas and quirks of history and language, the delight in costume, folklore, ritual, the excitement at changing landscapes. However uneven the text, there are passages that are as purely characteristic as any he wrote. Who will forget the dog that trots beside him in the Bulgarian dusk, barking at the moon as it rises again and again over the switchback hills? Or the migrating storks that cloud the Balkan skies, or the gabbling barber's apprentice who plagued him through northern Bulgaria, or the fantasy – a conceit which only Paddy could fashion – of an intermarried human and mermaid people surviving the second Flood?

Paddy's exuberance, of course, was not reflected in the Europe through which he was walking. The Austro-Hungarian empire had disintegrated only fifteen years earlier, and its old rival, the Ottoman empire, was still a living memory in the southern Balkans. The post-war Paris peace treaties had left a tinderbox in their wake. Bulgaria, 'the Prussia of the East' (as the Greek premier Venizelos dubbed her), had fought alongside Germany, and was now so stripped of territory as to feel dangerously bereft. A land of rural poverty, whose independent Orthodox Church was rife with nationalism, it retained an old Slavic bond with Russia. Rumania, on the other hand, had sided with the Allies, and had been rewarded with a huge extension of its frontiers as a bulwark against the Bolsheviks.

These two countries where Paddy's journey ends – Bulgaria and Rumania – were culturally very different, but they were both agrarian and poor, largely composed of small-holdings, and their ruling classes were no longer landed aristocracy. In Bulgaria this class had scarcely existed, while the Bucharest *haut monde* with whom Paddy fraternized were increasingly beleaguered in a world which was passing to a young and fragile bourgeoisie.

In retrospect it seems as if the whole continent through which he travelled was sleepwalking towards disaster. The Balkans were still in the grip of the Great Depression, and of deep peasant misery. The twin behemoths of Nazism and Bolshevism were already looming huge. In Germany Hitler had come to power the January before, and many of those whom Paddy encountered – the dashing aristocrats, the Rumanian Jews, the Gypsies – seem marked, in retrospect, by foreboding.

Although it was Paddy's intention to end his journey at Constantinople, his only writings on the city were diary jottings with no mention, inexplicably, of Byzantine or Ottoman splendour. His real love and destination became – and remained – Greece. Just eleven days after reaching Constantinople his surviving diary records him leaving for Greece's religious heartland, the monastic state of Mount Athos. On 24 January 1935 this diary ceases to consist of impressionistic notes and becomes a fully written record, which ends only as he leaves the Holy Mountain. And here – beyond Constantinople – we have chosen to end the present volume.

Uniquely the Athos narrative was written virtually on the spot. Paddy was just twenty years old at the time of its composition, and later he corrected and recorrected it more persistently than he did 'A Youthful Journey'. Even towards his life's end he left wavering marginal directions (perhaps to himself): 'Cut all these pages fiercely', for instance, and once enigmatically: 'Keep my eyes open.'

More than 'A Youthful Journey' the diary gives us the author's earliest voice: the guileless pleasures and misgivings of a youth. It betrays his insecurities, even his panics, as well as his delight in grappling with a Greek world of which he was later to become so knowledgeable and so fond. In our choice of the diary's corrected versions – there were sometimes at least four – we have tried to preserve its raw freshness, while cleansing it of some repetition. Rarely, when his corrections in old age seem less sure than earlier ones, we have kept the original.

In the end, of course, we have had to confront the difficult question: would Paddy have wanted these two records published? While he was alive, the answer might have been No. But there were signs, in his last months, that he was relinquishing their editing to half-imagined others. There were pieces he wanted cut, he said, and some impressions he wanted modified (and these of course we have done). A contract for the book, signed with Murrays in 1992, was among his papers. By the time of his death, he had expended so much labour and thought on the texts that their relegation to an archive seemed sad and wrong. *The Broken Road* may not precisely be the 'third volume' that so tormented him, but it contains, at least, the shape and scent of the promised book, and here his journey must rest.

Colin Thubron and Artemis Cooper
Spring 2013

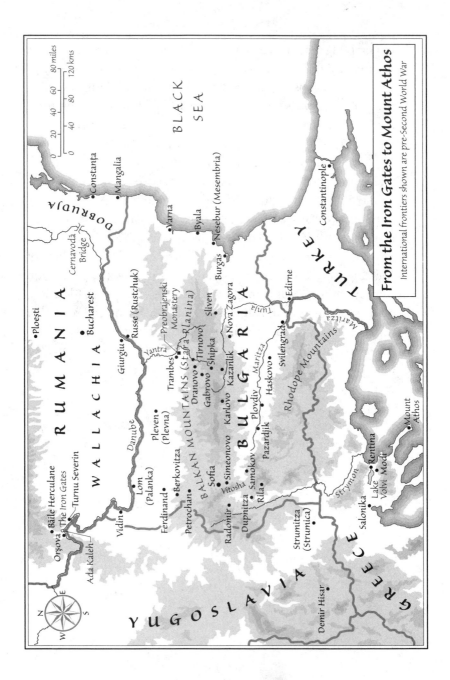

From the Iron Gates to Mount Athos

International frontiers shown are pre-Second World War

I

From the Iron Gates

At Orşova, there was the Danube again. It was nearly a mile broad now, but immediately west it swirled and boiled through the narrow mountain defile of the Kazan – the Cauldron – which is only one hundred and sixty-two yards across. Since I had turned my back on it at Budapest, this insatiable river had gorged itself with the Sava, the Drava, the Tisza, the Maros, and the Morava and a score of lesser known tributaries. A little way downstream from Orşova, in the middle of the river, the small island of Ada Kaleh divided the current. Plumed with poplars and mulberries, the line of the wooden roofs was suddenly broken by a shallow dome and a minaret, and in the lanes strolled curious figures in Turkish dress; for the island still remained ethnically Turkish – the only fragment in Central Europe, outside Turkey's modern frontiers, of that huge empire which was halted and driven back at the gates of Vienna. The steep low mountains that form the opposite bank were Yugoslavia.

Early next morning I found a letter from Budapest waiting in the poste restante* – I had been writing letters and firing them off in volleys dropped in hopeless-looking post boxes, ever since saying goodbye at the railway station at Deva – and I boarded

---

* PLF was hoping to receive a letter from Xenia Czernovits ('Angela'), a Hungarian woman whose relationship with him is recorded affectionately in *Between the Woods and the Water.*

the Danube steamer in a state of excitement. We set off under a flicker of darting swifts. Soon the mountains soared on either side in precipices, and rushed towards each other to form the winding canyon of the Iron Gates. The river suddenly swelled and boiled in protest. Our siren echoed booming down the great causeway. In a few miles the mountains subsided and the Danube fanned out to its normal width. On the Rumanian bank, after the large town of Turnu Severin – the Tower of Severus, where the emperor overcame the Quadi and the Marcomanni – the flat plain of Oltenia, often edged with reeds, and mournful and malarial-looking swamps, slid featurelessly away. The Serbian mountains wavering along the right bank were the beginnings of the Great Balkan range. The river meandered along the Serbian headlands in wide loops. Suddenly, the mountains had ceased to be Yugoslavia and became Bulgaria. Now and then we threaded our way through enormous tree-trunk rafts and overtook dark processions of barges a mile long. I had realized at Orşova, with a moment of shock, and then of delight, as my passport was being stamped August 14, that I had been dawdling in Transylvania for well over three months. Rightly, I thought, rereading the morning's letter for the tenth time.

These cogitations were distracted by the walls and towers on the south bank, of the old fortress town of Vidin. Clamorous boys crowded the landing-stage, selling watermelons. I chose one, then, rather crestfallen, had to give it back, as I had only two English pound notes in my pocket and a handful of Rumanian lei. A fellow passenger, a tall girl with fair straight hair, whom I suddenly realized was English, offered me some of her Bulgarian leva, so we slashed the green football open in bloody and black-pipped slices and then shared it.

It was strange, after these months, to be talking to someone English, and rather exciting. She was called Rachel Floyd and she became a treasured companion. She was on her way to stay with the British Consul's wife in Sofia, who was an old Oxford university friend. We exchanged life histories mingled between cool, gory munchings, and when, in the afternoon, we disembarked at Lom Palanka, we arranged that I should look her up when I reached the capital. She set off by train, and I began to mooch about in my first Bulgarian town.

~

All through Central Europe, from the snowy Rhine, through Bavaria and Austria, the old kingdoms of Bohemia and Hungary and even in the forested confines of the principality of Transylvania, the aura of the vanished Holy Roman Empire and of the realm of Charlemagne and the mysteries of western Christendom hung in the air. The Turkish overlordship of the eastern regions had ended long ago and few traces remained. But here, on the southern bank of the Danube, the mountains were haunted by the ghost of a different sovereignty. So recently had the yoke of Turkey been shaken off that Bulgaria seemed less the south-easternmost corner of Europe than the north-westernmost limit of a world that stretched away to the Taurus mountains, the deserts of Arabia and the Asian steppes. It was the Orient, and clues to the recent centuries under the Ottoman Turks lay thick and plentiful on every side; plentiful, too, was the evidence of the rugged Slavo-Byzantine kingdom which the Turkish wave had submerged. These different elements flourished their data everywhere: in the domes and minarets and the smoky tang of kebabs cooking on spits, in the jutting wooden houses and the Byzantine allegiance of the churches, in the black cylindrical hats, the flowing habits, the long hair and the beards of priests, and in the Cyrillic alphabet on the shop fronts which gave a fleeting impression of Russia. The Bulgars themselves, thickset, blunt-featured and solid, suggested a yet remoter past, the wild habitat beyond the Volga from which they had migrated to settle here, centuries ago, in a fierce Asiatic horde. Rough-hewn and tough, shod and swaddled in the same cowhide footgear as the Rumanians, they padded the dusty cobbles like bears. Thick and scratchy homespun clad them, sometimes dark blue but more often an earthy brown, adorned here and there with a stiff flourish of black embroidery: big loose trousers, crossed waistcoats, a short jacket and the waist enveloped in thick scarlet sashes a foot wide in which knives were sometimes stuck. They were hatted with flat Cossack-like kalpacks of brown or black sheepskin.

In the trellised outdoors eating-house in the little square where I settled down to a rather good, very oily stew of mutton, potatoes, tomatoes, paprika pods, courgettes and ladies' fingers, all ladled from giant bronze pans, I noticed that one or two young men at the next table had let their left little fingernails grow, emblematic of their emancipation from the plough and almost as long as those of mandarins. Three white-moustached and moccasined elders puffed in silence over the amber mouthpieces of their hookahs, toying indolently with strings of amber beads, allowing the grains to drop one on the other with a lulling click, as though to scan their leisurely cogitations. A group of officers, in white tunics buttoning under the left ear in the Russian style, with stiff gold epaulettes, black, red-banded, Russian caps with short peaks, and high-spurred soft-legged boots, sat smoking and talking, or strolled under the trees with the hilts of their steel-scabbarded sabres in the crooks of their arms. No women. Dogs wrangled over a sheep's jawbone. A row of skinned sheep's heads gazed piteously from a shelf outside a butcher's shop, livers, lights and decapitated carcasses dripped, and entrails were looped from hooks in a baleful festoon. The wireless played rousing marches interspersed with the intriguing wail of songs in the oriental minor mode. The scent of jasmine was afloat. Mosquitoes zoomed and zinged.

It was a grave moment. I realized that everything had changed.

~

The way lay south through the roll of the Danubian hills and plains. They were tufted with woods. Here and there a green blur of marsh expanded and the road was plumed with Lombardy poplars. Let us stride across this riparian region in seven-league boots and up into the Great Balkan range. This immense sweep – the Stara Planina, as it is called in Bulgaria, the Old Mountain – climbs and coils and leapfrogs clean across northern Bulgaria from Serbia to the Black Sea, a great lion-coloured barrier of lofty, rounded convexities, with seldom a spike or a chasm: open, airy sweeps and rounded swellings mounting higher and higher to vast basin-like valleys and hollows where one could see the white road paying itself out ahead for miles and twisting among copses and hillocks and past the scattered flocks until it disappeared over the ultimate khaki slope. Now and then I would fall in with long caravans of donkeys and mules – their place was taken by camels in the south-east, towards Haskovo – and strings of carts. The lighter of these were drawn by horses – tough little animals and gangling, hollow-flanked jades – and the heavier, laden with timber, by black buffaloes that lurched stumblingly along under heavy yokes, their eyes rolling and their moustache-like and crinkled horns clashing against their neighbours. The wooden saddles of the horses, ridden side-saddle with moccasins dangling, looked as unwieldy as elephants' howdahs. Watermelons were the chief merchandise, and giant basket-loads of tomatoes and cucumbers and all the garden stuff for which the Bulgarians are famous throughout the Balkans. Each village was surrounded by tiers of vegetable beds and every drop of water was husbanded and irrigated through miniature aqueducts of hollow tree trunk. 'Where was I from?' the fur-hatted, horny-handed men would ask. '*Ot kadè? Ot Europa? Da, dà*', from Europe. '*Nemski?*' No, not German: '*Anglitchanin.*' Many seemed vague about England's whereabouts. And what was I? A *voinik*, a soldier? Or a student? A *spion* perhaps? I got my own back for these questions by extorting in return, with the help of interrogatory gestures, a basic vocabulary: bread, *chlab*; water, *voda*; wine, *vino*; horse, *kon*; cat, *kotka*; dog, *kuche*; goat's cheese, *siriné*; cucumber, *krastavitza*; church, *tzerkva*. These exchanges carried us many miles.

I slept out near a barn the first night, and the next two in the small towns of Ferdinand and Berkovitza: two nights plagued by vermin. By the fourth night we had surmounted the final and highest watershed, and joined a Sofia-bound caravan under a plane tree, which sheltered an old Turkish fountain. The spring gushed into its trough from slabs carved with a chipped and calligraphic swirl of Arabic characters which no one could read any more. They commemorated, it was said, a pasha long dead. We were joined at the fires by a party of shepherds, and, as a circular wooden wine-flask was slung from hand to hand, one of these shaggy men played a yard-long wooden pipe – *kaval* – and another a bagpipe – *gaida*. This was a blown-up sheep-skin pelt with a wooden mouthpiece and the chanter was a cow's horn wrapped in skin into which the stops had been burnt with a red hot skewer. Their favourite song celebrated the Hadji Dimitar from Sliven, a guerrilla leader against the Turks in the gorges of the Shipka Balkans. The cross-legged figures with their turned-up footgear, the fifty sheepskin hats, the broad-boned, firelit faces, the sashes, the shifting animals, the occasional clang of a sheep's or a goat's bell and the low glitter of a multitude of stars hinted at regions much further east than Europe, as though our destination might be Samarkand, Khorassan, Tashkent or Karakorum.

~

I got to Sofia the next day and made my way through a world of Gypsy shacks hammered together out of old planks and petrol tins, and then through a market with giant brass scales where all the livestock of western Bulgaria seemed to be gathered in a whinnying and braying hubbub. I passed by the dome, many metal cupolas and the soaring minaret of a fine mosque and under a network of tramlines reached the capital's heart.

Permanent sojourn here might evoke a groan of dismay, but the aspect and atmosphere of the little capital is rather captivating. The light, airy ambience of a plateau town reigns here, and above it all rises the bright pyramid of Mount Vitosha, throwing the sunlight back from its many facets, a feature as noble and as inescapable as Fujiyama. Then came Czar Boris's* palace with the rampant lion of Bulgaria fluttering from the flagpole, and then the Sobranie, where parliament sat, and a huge state theatre, gardens, trees and a small statuary population of Bulgarian heroes; then, presiding over the wide and leafy avenue of Boulevard Czar Ozvoboditel, the city's axis, the equestrian figure of Emperor Alexander II† of Russia, the Czar Liberator himself; and beyond it, the golden dome and the painted stucco pillars of the Cathedral of Alexander Nevsky. Along this, resurrected from their siestas in the cool of the evening, all the inhabitants of the city slowly strolled in that ritual tide which ebbs and flows each dusk through every European town east of Budapest or south of Biscay. In the cafés, over many a thimbleful of Turkish coffee, the intelligentsia

* Boris III, Czar of Bulgaria (1894–1943).
† Czar Alexander II of Russia, whose campaign against the Ottoman Empire liberated Bulgaria in 1877–8.

told their amber beads and discussed the leading article in the *Utro*. Beyond them, the street shot straight as a bullet into a leonine tableland, dotted with hamlets of Shopi, who are said to be the descendants of the Petchenegs, that appalling barbarian horde from beyond the Urals who pillaged and slew for centuries all along the limits of the East Roman Empire and finally came to rest here and mended their ways.

Thanks to Rachel Floyd, my melon-sharing countrywoman from the Danube boat, I was rescued next day from the hutch I had settled in near the market place, by the British Consul and his wife, Boyd and Judith Tollinton, who charitably put me up. These were happy and luxurious days. It seemed strange to be among English people and talking English again, as strange as being in the midst of foreigners after a prolonged stay in England, and as stimulating. How very agreeable it was to hear all about Bulgaria from my kind, competent Rugbeian host, and to get up from breakfast, Earl Grey in hand, to gaze down at the Royal Guard goose-stepping along the Boulevard Czar Ozvoboditel. The unlimited baths, the clean linen, the huge Russian butler, the terrace, the books, the view over the town to the looming flanks of Vitosha, all seemed marvellous. Best of all the *Encyclopaedia Britannica*; I leapt at it like a panther. What miracles such things appear after a primitive life! The Congress of Byzantine Studies was holding its sessions in Sofia that autumn. It was delightful to listen to the erudite and shrewish chat of Professor Whittemore,* that distilled essence of Jamesian Boston superimposed on the mosaics of Haghia Sophia. There too, suave and suede-shod, impeccably and urbanely clad in white tropical

---

* Professor Thomas Whittemore (1871–1950), an American archaeologist and Byzantine scholar who had recently started important work uncovering mosaics in the basilica of Haghia Sophia in Istanbul.

suits and decorously panama-hatted, were Roger Hinks* and
Steven Runciman† – so kind, under his provisos and reservations
and diverting regional prejudices, the one; so pleasantly feline
the other. Most of their books were still unwritten, except, I
think, Runciman's *First Bulgarian Empire.* We were often to meet
many years later. It is odd how lucidly first impressions engrave
themselves in the memory. I only retain the details of a late,
strange evening in a café, however, as through a glass darkly.

∿

I wrenched myself away from the pleasures of this capital for a
few days and struck across the foothills and valleys of the eastern
slopes of Vitosha, and stayed the night at the American School
at Simeonovo: a large clean, airy establishment with a fine library
and, although it was holiday-time, inhabited by a young and
friendly staff who all seemed to be at work on theses. Over the
hills next day, to Dolni Pasarel, reaching it after nightfall, I stayed
with a friendly peasant I met in the *kretchma,* the ramshackle
tavern in the middle of the village where a number of villagers
were drinking *slivo,* a rough plum-brandy that reeks like a whirled
lasso. We staggered to his house and his wife cooked us a mass
of herbs and potatoes and young cucumbers over a fire of thorns,
which he, she and their children and I all ate out of the same
plate, spooning in turn and seated cross-legged on the rug-covered
floor round a low circular table, filling in the gaps with great
slices of excellent dark bread and white goat's cheese. His wife
had long fair plaits with the ends tied together, below the triangle
of her headkerchief. She wore an apron striped in many colours

---

* Roger Hinks (1903–63), an art historian notorious for his later involvement
in an injudicious cleaning of the Elgin Marbles.
† Steven Runciman (1903–2000), the celebrated historian of Byzantium and
the Crusades.

and a red and blue bodice cut low and circular like an old-fashioned dinner jacket waistcoat, and trimmed by many breadths of braid. It ended at her elbows, where, from broad braid bands, pleated lace frills jutted for several inches, all old and worn, but pretty and odd nevertheless. We all five of us reclined on rugs chevroned with purple, yellow, scarlet and green, spread along the ledge that ran round the wall, all fully dressed, and, except for me, still thonged, swaddled and moccasined. Soon, after exchanges of *leka nosht* [good night], snoring and darkness prevailed except for the oil dip flickering in front of a corner ikon of the Blessed Virgin and another of St Simeon. I went out into the yard in the middle of the night and tripped over something soft and enormous; a struck match revealed the accusing eye of a couchant buffalo.

We rose before dawn with the first donkey's bray, sloshed off Turkish coffee with a burning swig of *slivo* and some bread and white cheese. Mirko refused all payment, tilting his head back and clicking his tongue in that odd negative way that runs all through the Balkans and the Levant. I set out with friendly wishes. This generous hospitality to anyone on the road runs all through the Balkans and reaches its highest peak in Greece. Nights like these dotted the rest of my itinerary through Bulgaria. The day was succeeded by an almost identical one the same evening, in the little town of Samokov, after a long trudge along a river valley with the hills growing steeper and a stiff range of mountains looming ahead: the Rilska Planina.

I was in amongst them next day. These were not huge rounded barriers like the Great Balkan range but a sharp and steep sierra zigzagged with shadowy valleys and darkly thatched with fir and pine, and above it, after gruelling hours of climbing, I saw that these were the buttresses of a mass of cordilleras multiplying southwards in chaos. They reached their zenith a league or two to the east of my track, in the tall bare blade of Moussalà and to the west in a lesser peak called, I think, Rupitè, though I have searched maps for it in vain. This massif is the north-western curve of the Rhodope mountains. They swing south-east along the whole southern border, and the watershed forms Bulgaria's frontier with Greece; then it melts away into European Turkey.

Over the nearest watershed, I dropped into a high enclosed region. It was the wolf and the bear world once more, with eagles drifting on still wings from canyon to canyon. Here and there, under the sunless lee of wild horns of rock, a few discoloured patches of snow still lingered. The rest was a burning wilderness of boulders and dried-up torrent beds that must be a tangled spate in winter. Dead trees, bleached white by the sun, looked like the dismembered bones of prehistoric beasts. My footfall sent a long snake flickering to the shelter of a thyme thicket. All afternoon the valley descended from ledge to ledge in a giant staircase. The sound of a miniature landslide would echo and ricochet from rock face to rock face for many seconds, dwindling along the ravine and dying away in the universal hush. The trees changed from conifers to spreading deciduous shade. In basins of rock, one below the other, two circular tarns reflected the clear blue of the sky. Flocks tinkled out of sight, a pathway began to define itself, and the report of a woodman's axe hinted that habitation was near.

$\sim$

A twist in the valley and a leaf-fringed glance through a clearing brought my destination into sight. This was a fortress-like building, almost a small towered city, embedded in fold after fold of beech trees and pine. The southern ramparts sank into the gorge, and the five tall walls and the tiled roofs formed a lopsided pentagon round the deep well of a courtyard, lined within by many ascending tiers of a slender-pillared gallery hoisted on semicircular arches. In the centre of this courtyard, the great metal dome of a church, poised on a slit-windowed cylinder, floated above a bubbling swarm of shallow satellite cupolas, all of them gleaming and softly shadowed under the westerly sun. Sunbeams glittered in the intricacies of the topmost cross and lay the shadow of a yew tree across the wall-girt flagstones. As I descended from my hawkish height, the gold patches of light inside the walls shrank and faded and shadows accumulated in the well of walls. Suddenly a metallic tattoo struck up from the enclosure as though a musical smith were hammering out a rhythmic pattern on his anvil. The tempo gradually waxed to a brisker and still brisker pace and by the time I reached the dark archway of the barbican, the walls were reverberating. The noise stopped abruptly and left the dusk humming. A black-robed monk replaced his summoning hammer on a gong-like sheet of metal hanging from a cloister arch. Other monks, with black veils floating from their stovepipe hats, were entering the church which was already filled by a horde of laymen in all the costumes of northern Macedonia, hailed thither by the clangour from the trees under which they were camping. These rough gongs or semantra – *klapka,* I think, in Bulgarian – are sometimes replaced by long beams of wood; they play the part of bells in most Orthodox monasteries, as now for the feast of Sveti Ivan Rilski.

St John of Rila is only surpassed in venerability by SS Cyril and Methodius, the inventors of the Cyrillic script, and by St Simeon, in Bulgarian hagiography. The great monastery that he founded near his hermitage in these lonely mountains is, in a sense, the most important religious centre in the kingdom. The church, burnt down again and again in the disturbed past of Bulgaria, was rebuilt in the last century. The poor quality of the frescoes which smothered every inch of interior wall space and the brazen proliferation of the ikonostasis was mitigated by the candlelight. The Slav liturgy of vespers boomed out by a score of black-clad and long-haired and long-bearded monks, all leaning or standing in their miserere stalls, sounded marvellous. It continued for hours. Afterwards, charitably singled out as a foreigner, I was given a little cell to myself, although the monastery was so full that villagers were sleeping out with their bundles all over the yard and under the trees. Many more arrived next day and the inside of the church virtually seized up with the pious multitude. There were an archbishop and several bishops and archimandrites besides the abbot and his retinue. They officiated in copes as stiff and brilliant as beetles' wings, and the higher clergy, coiffed with globular gold mitres the size of pumpkins and glistening with gems, leaned on croziers topped with twin coiling snakes. They evolved and chanted in aromatic clouds of smoke diagonally pierced by sun shafts. When all was over, a compact crocodile of votaries shuffled its way round the church to kiss St Ivan's ikon and his thaumaturgic hand, black now as a briar root, inside its jewelled reliquary.

For the rest of the day, the glade outside the monastery was star-scattered with merrymaking pilgrims. At their heart an indefatigable ring of dancers rotated in the *hora* to the tune of a violin, a lute, a zither and a clarinet, ably played by Gypsies. Another Gypsy had brought his bear with him; it danced a joyless hornpipe and clapped its paws and played the tambourine to the beat of its master's drum. A further castanet-like clashing came from an itinerant Albanian striking brass cups together, pouring out helpings of the sweetish, kvass-like *boza** from a spigot in a tasselled brass vessel four feet high, shaped like a mosque, its Taj Mahal dome topped by a little brass bird with wings splayed.

---

* *Boza*: a Bulgarian malted drink made with fermented grains and sugar.

Kebab and stuffed entrails were being grilled in culinary tabernacles as bristling with spitted and skewered meat as a shrike's
larder. *Slivo* and wine were reaching high tide. The lurching
kalpacked villagers offered every newcomer their circular flasks
of carved wood. (Elaborate woodwork plays a great part in the
lives of Balkan mountaineers from the Carpathians to the Pindus
in Greece, where it reaches its wildest pitch of elaboration. The
same phenomenon applies to the Alps: the conjunction of harsh
winters, long evenings, soft wood and sharp knives.) Under the
leaves, a party of bright-aproned women sat round the feet of a
shaggy bagpiper pumping out breathless pibrochs.

On the edge of this vast Balkan wassail I fell in with a party
of students from Plovdiv. Like me they had come over the mountains, and were camping out. The most remarkable of these was
an amusing, very pretty, fair-haired, frowning girl called Nadejda,
who was studying French literature at Sofia University: a nimble
hora dancer and endowed with unquenchable high spirits. She
was staying on at the monastery three days to do some reading,
which was exactly the length of my intended stay. We became
friends at once. Apart from the stern rule of Mount Athos, women
are just as welcome guests as men in most Orthodox monasteries.
Bestowing hospitality seems almost the entire monastic function
and the atmosphere of these cloisters is very different from the
silence and recollection of abbeys in western Christendom. With
its clattering hooves and constant arrivals and departures and the
cheerful expansiveness of the monks, life was more like that of
a castle in the Middle Ages. The planks in the tiers of galleries
and catwalks were so worn and unsteady that too brisk a footfall
would set the whole fabric shaking like a spider's web. The
courtyards are forever a-clatter with mules. The father Abbot, the
Otetz Igoumen, a benign figure with an Olympian white beard
and his locks tied in a bun like a lady out hunting, spent most

of his day receiving ceremonial calls: occasions always ratified, as they are everywhere else south of the Danube, by offering a spoonful of sherbet or rose petal jam or a powdery cube of *rahat loukoum*, a gulp of *slivo*, a cup of Turkish coffee and a glass of water, to help along the formal affabilities of the visit.

The place relapsed into comparative quiet next day. The great company of pilgrims, after dancing and snoring the night through on the grass, reloaded their beasts and carried a thousand hangovers down the valley.

~

Nadejda turned out a splendid companion. Each morning we would take books and drawing things, buy cheese, bread, wine, purple and green figs and grapes (which arrived from the plains in immense baskets) from a canteen outside the walls, and then set off for the woods, passing on the way the slab under which J. D. Bourchier* is buried. (The passion of Bulgarians for this ex-Eton master and *Times* correspondent earned him a position in the country and a memory which is similar, in a lesser degree, to that of Byron in Greece.) We read and talked and finally picnicked on a shady ledge. Most of Nadejda's homework seemed to be the learning by heart of Lamartine's *Le Lac* – 'He stayed in Plovdiv,' she said, to my surprise, 'I'll show you his house one day' – and, rather inappropriately, Théodore de Banville's *Nous n'irons plus aux bois*. I had to hear and correct her again and again. Then she would return to her books, putting on a pair of steel-rimmed spectacles that looked amazing and incongruous on that rather wild face, until she got bored with it and suggested something else like climbing a tree, which she did with great

* James David Bourchier (1850–1920), *The Times'* Balkan correspondent for many years, and an outspoken supporter of Bulgarian national claims.

speed and skill, or, on the last day before she left, bathing in one of the pools in the canyon, or merely lying and talking on the grass. We discovered to our delight that we were within one day of being twins.

These delightful forest days sped fast in this comic and charming company. When the semantron began to clang from the cloisters the evening before she left, we set off down the hill to the monastery. She told me that it commemorated Noah calling the animals into the ark by beating on the lintel with his hammer: 'that's why they are usually made of wood.' I asked her what animals there were. She thought for a second, then bared her teeth and fixed me with scowling brown eyes and said, 'Wolves', and after a pause, 'young ones', and we charged down through the trees howling.

~

I left soon after Nadjeda, following the gorge downhill until it joined the deep valley of the Strouma. This great river, the ancient Strymon, flows into the heart of Macedonia between the Pirin mountains and the ranges of the Yugoslav border. (These mountains roll away westward across Yugoslav Macedonia until they reach the vastnesses of Albania and Montenegro and plunge into the distant Adriatic.) Then the road and the river corkscrew south through the baleful gorge of Rupel and into Greece under the battlements of Siderokastron: Demirhissar in Turkish times, the Iron Castle. All this is a hotly debated region, which all three countries claim should be theirs and they glower at each other from range to range with implacable hatred. This whirlpool of mountains has always been a theatre of strife. During the last decades of the Ottoman Empire until the Balkan wars, deadly warfare was waged here between the Bulgarian Comitadjis – the partisans of the dissident Bulgarian Exarchate, revived from mediaeval times – and the Greek Antartes of the Ecumenical Patriarchate, the nearest equivalent to the papacy in the Orthodox Church. These religious factors were as crucial as race and language in supporting claims to territory and in the ruling of frontiers when the Turkish power in Europe collapsed. It was destroyed for ever by the massed onslaught of the Balkan king-doms in the brief concord of the First Balkan War: concord which turned into savage fighting over the spoils in the Second. The frontiers have changed again and again in all the subsequent conflicts, and each step in these struggles has been marked by horror: ambush, assassination, burnt villages, uprooting and massacres leaving behind them the curses of fear, hatred, irreden-tism and thirst for revenge.

The Balkan races overlap and dovetail in Macedonia with haphazard geography; ethnological rock pools and minorities are scattered in hostile regions far from their parent masses. These ancient hatreds burn as fiercely today as ever they did: one has only to hear the virulence with which the word *Grtzki* is snarled by a Bulgar, or the word *Voulgaros* by a Greek, to grasp their intensity. On the walls of many of the cafés in this region hung coloured prints of Todor Alexandroff, a Bulgarian Macedonian who had attempted, by propaganda and guerrilla warfare, to hack out a semi-independent state of Macedonia with the capital at Petrich (now in Yugoslavia) and himself at its head: a formidable black-bearded man he looks in his picture, scowling under a fur cap, slung with bandoliers and binoculars and grasping a rifle. Like many prominent Bulgarians – Stambouliski,* especially, springs to mind, who was hacked to pieces with yataghans in the main street in Sofia – Alexandroff was assassinated, in 1924. But his secret society, the

---

* Aleksander Stambouliski (1879–1923), Bulgarian prime minister, deposed in 1923. He was tortured and executed by the army.

Vatreshna Makedonska Revolutzionerna Organizatzio – the Internal Macedonian Revolutionary Organization – still, it was darkly whispered, flourished clandestinely. Also prominent on many walls were maps illustrating the *terra irridenta* that Bulgaria claimed from her neighbours: lumps of Yugoslavia, the Dobrudja in Rumania and, preposterously, Greek Macedonia including Salonika.

Leaning over the Strouma bridge and gazing along the river, I had no inkling how strongly, later on, I was to feel on the Greek side in these questions. I would have been still more surprised if I could have foreseen that five months later, I would be pounding across another bridge over the same river, at Orliako, a hundred miles downstream, alongside a squadron of Greek cavalry with drawn sabres, in the Venizelos Revolution. As it was, I dropped a vine leaf in mid-stream and wondered whether it would ever reach the Aegean Sea.

The way back to Sofia lay through the western foothills of the Rilska Planina: rolling dun-coloured country that turned red at sunset with prehistoric wooden ploughs drawn by buffaloes or oxen. In the villages, the houses were looped with festoons of tobacco leaves drying in the sun, the size, colour and shape of kippers. I slept in a rick, the first night, reached the little town of Dupnitza on the next and got to Radomir the following dusk. I was drinking a lonely *slivo* and feeling tired and a bit depressed when a bus stopped opposite with СОФИЯ inscribed across the top, and a roof laden with a host of roped baskets and bundles. Inside, it was a Noah's ark indeed, for, in every inch not occupied by my kerchiefed and kalpacked fellow passengers, were trussed chickens and ducks, a turkey and two full-grown lambs that bleated shrilly from time to time. We rocked and clanked through the darkness. The half a dozen passengers next to me sang quietly all the way: sad fluttering patterns of sound in the minor mode, quite different from the robust strains I had heard so often lately. I listened entranced. I asked for a particular one over and over again – '*Zashto ti se sirdish, liube?*' * the first line ran – and determined to try and master it later.

After this brief absence in the mountains, the lights of Sofia glittered as brightly as those of Paris, London or Vienna, so resplendent and metropolitan did they seem. I must have been an uncouth spectacle with long, unkempt and dust-clogged hair bleached to a shaggy tow and a face burnt to the hue of a walnut sideboard by the sun; rumpled clothes, a rucksack and a carved Hungarian walking-stick; also – I blush, now, to set it down, but honesty compels it – a scarlet and yellow braid belt bought in Transylvania, a steel-hilted dagger and a brown kalpack from the fair in Berkovitza. I had even taken off my heavy nailed boots to try out a pair of those cowhide moccasins they call *tzervuli*, but after a mile I found them – without the swaddling the peasants use – tormenting except on grass. This hybrid pseudo-Balkan guise was made all the more nightmarish now by a spectral envelope of white dust, and, no doubt, by a less palpable but far-flying aura of earth, sweat, onions, garlic and *slivo*.

I put down the large basket of figs I had bought as a present to my hosts – and a tortoise I had found by the roadside – and let myself into the Tollintons' flat as the cathedral of Alexander Nevsky tolled eleven. The soft lamplight, afloat with the civilized murmur of a dinner party, revealed a shirt front in an armchair here and there, the glint of patent leather shoes, women's long dresses, and golden discs of brandy revolving in the bottom of balloon glasses. The coffee pouring from spout to cup in the hands of Ivan, the giant Cossack butler, dried up in mid-trajectory, the

* 'Why are you angry with me, my love?'

golden discs, arrested by this horrible intruding apparition, stopped rotating in their balloon glasses. A moment of consternation on one side, and dismay on the other, froze all. It was quickly thawed by Judith Tollinton's kind voice – 'Oh good, there you are, just in time for the brandy' – and the spell was broken.

2

A Hanging Glass Box

We must swing eastwards from Sofia, and slightly southwards, across the brown central plateau of Bulgaria as swiftly as the stride of a divider's points across a chart; down the wide and gently descending basin of the Maritza, a baking expanse with the skyline bounded by the cool, flowing peaks of the Balkans to the north and the Rhodope mountains to the south. This as far as history records is the great path from Europe to the Levant: the road to Constantinople and the gates of Asia. It is the track of a hundred armies and the itinerary of those wonderful caravans from Ragusa that joggled their way to the Black Sea and Anatolia, just as their huge argosies of merchandise – when only Venice surpassed the little walled republic in the Mediterranean trade – dropped anchor in all the ports of the Euxine, the Mediterranean and the Red Sea. Here, too, the Bulgarian inhabitants were at their most defenceless during the long night of subjection to Turkey. The Ottoman *beglerbeg* or viceroy of the Balkans, ranked as a three-tailed pasha, had his court and his garrison at Sofia, and between here and the capital, the Bulgars were powerless; the faintest stirrings would unloose a whirlwind of janissaries and spahis and later on, and perhaps the worst, bashi-bazouks. They adorned the towns with avenues of gibbets, the burnt villages with pyramids of heads and the roadsides with impaled corpses. I think it is an Arabian proverb which says, 'Where the Ottoman hoof has struck, the grass never grows again'; and it is true that their occupation of the Balkans – in Bulgaria it started before the Wars of the Roses and ended after the Franco-Prussian War – has left desolation behind it. Everything is still impoverished and haphazard, and history in smithereens. The Turks were the last but one of the Oriental barbarians to cast their blight over Eastern Europe.

I was pondering these matters, slogging along through the twilight beside the banked railway, when a humming along the rails and an increasing clatter behind me indicated the approach of a train. The shuddering cylinder grew larger and larger and soon it was rocketing by overhead; all the windows were alight in a serpent of bright quadrilaterals, and along the coach work, as it crashed past, was painted: *Paris – Munich – Vienna – Zagreb – Belgrade – Sofia – Istanbul* and *Compagnie Internationale des Wagons Lits.* The Orient Express! The pink lampshades glowed softly in the dining car, the brass gleamed. The passengers would be lowering their novels and crosswords as the brown-jacketed attendants approached with trays of aperitifs. I waved, but the gloaming was too deep for an answer. I wondered who the passengers were – they had travelled in two days a journey that had taken me over nine months, and in a few hours they would be in Constantinople. The necklace of bright lights dwindled in the distance with its freight of runaway lovers, cabaret girls, Knights of Malta, vamps, acrobats, smugglers, papal nuncios, private detectives, lecturers in the future of the novel, millionaires, arms' manufacturers, irrigation experts and spies, leaving a mournful silence in the thirsty Rumelian plateau.

~

In Pazardjik I put up in an old Turkish khan. Many Balkan towns are equipped with these caravanserais. This one was a quadrangle of wooden galleries, like the cloister of a monastery. The faded

tiles were blurred here and there by storks' nests, now bristling
with one or two young ones, hatched out since April. The enclosed
courtyard was as full of livestock as a farm yard. Families camped
and cooked beside their wagons and among their animals; there
were tethered horses, buffaloes, mules, donkeys, bleating flocks
of sheep and goats and a swarm of dogs. The men brewed coffee
and smoked, the women huddled and squatted together like
conclaves of crows, some with babies slung across their backs in
portable wooden cradles, gossiping or quietly singing, all the time
spinning the raw wool which had been sheared from the backs
of their flocks. They pulled it from forked distaffs stuck in their
silver-buckled belts, twisting it to a thread between finger and
thumb, and winding it on to a weighted spindle that rose and
fell rotating from the twiddling fingers and thumbs of their other
hand. This enclosure, the huddled groups, the animals, the glow
of the scattered charcoal fires and the quavering and melancholy
songs filled the night with an outlandish and nomadic spell.

The road followed the Maritza all next day. This wide deep
river, the largest in the Balkans after the Danube, slants across
Bulgaria from north-west to south-east, then through the eastern
Rhodope into Greece, whence, till it reaches the Aegean, it forms
the Greco-Turkish frontier, and reverts for the final Greek stage
of its journey to the ancient and hallowed name of the Hebrus.
To Bulgarians the great stream symbolized their country, and the
first line of their rousing and bellicose anthem (which I heard
boomed forth by many a flagpole while the Bulgarian tricolour
was raised or lowered, to presented arms and the salutes of sabre-
grasping officers) began *Shumi Maritza* – 'Flow, Maritza'. I slept
under a willow by its banks for an hour at midday and reached
Plovdiv by nightfall, filled with expectation.

~

Nadejda, my all-but twin, joyfully reappeared next morning, and showed me Lamartine's house – a pleasant whitewashed building in the Turkish style with jutting upper storeys – exactly as she had promised. Better still, she asked me to stay in her own, which was just such another. No question here of the old Bulgarian proverb: 'an uninvited guest is worse than a Turk.' Knowing how strict, straitlaced and oriental the Balkan countries are about their daughters and wives, I had been astonished, at Rila, by Nadejda's freedom and independence. Had I known these countries then as well as I came to know them later, I would have been even more surprised at this friendly and unhesitating invitation. I thought it sprang from a natural independence of character, and so it did; but there were other reasons. Her mother and her father – he was, she told me, a well-to-do peasant from Stenimaka – had been killed in an earthquake a few years before along with a brother a year older, to whom she had been very attached.

She lived alone with her maternal grandfather, who was frail and bedridden, a charming old gentleman with a white beard, and, moreover, Greek. He was one of a former flourishing Greek community that had lived here since the town was founded by Philip of Macedonia, 'when the Bulgars', as he soon instructed me, 'were still a tribe of marauding hut-dwellers beyond the Volga!' He had run a chemist's shop for most of his life in the Taxim quarter of Constantinople. He spoke French fluently and he was steeped in the principles of Western liberalism. The names of Voltaire, Rousseau, Anatole France, Zola, Poincaré, Clemenceau and Venizelos were often on his aged lips; and, I was pleased and surprised to hear, Canning, Gladstone and Lloyd George. But the Englishman he mentioned with greatest reverence, an emaciated hand emerging from his patched pyjama-sleeve as I swallowed my ritual spoonful of *slatko* by his bedside, was Byron. I think it was mostly thanks to this lucky coincidence of nationality that

I was welcomed so kindly. This was the first time, but not the last, that I understood and was struck by the tremendous aura, the apotheosis almost, which, among Greeks, enshrines the poet's name. Also, rather momentously for me, as things were going to turn out in the following years, my host was the first Greek I had ever met. I learnt from him the sad tale of the misfortunes of Hellenism under Bulgarian rule: a harrowing account of oppression, persecution and massacre that came as a timely antidote to many similar tales in reverse that I had heard, and was to hear again, from Bulgarians. Many Greeks had left Plovdiv for Greece during the past twenty years, and they were still leaving. He was too old and ill, he said, and his roots were too deep to be torn up now. It was thanks to his political leanings that his granddaughter was studying French as opposed to German, the universal second language among the Bulgarian intelligentsia. Her independence was partly due to his wider and more metropolitan horizon, partly to his infirmity and partly to the fact that, with the help of an old black-coiffed crone, she ran the house on her own. By some freak of exemption, her dashing and carefree ways, a kind of bohemianism, were tolerated and even admired: a true phenomenon in the stifling atmosphere of Balkan provincial life. Half Greek and half Bulgarian, she was a walking battlefield of the strife between the Patriarchate and the Exarchate: a burden which, I must say, she carried lightly.

Though they lived in reduced circumstances, the house, in the back lanes of the Greek quarter of the town, bore many dilapidated traces of past elegance. The whole upper storey jutted on massive beams in that Turkish style which I imagine to have its roots in Byzantine domestic architecture just as the mosques derive from its ecclesiastical form. Away from the street, a gallery with an outside staircase surrounded a little courtyard sheltered by a vine trellis, heavy with clusters of grapes now, basil flourished in fluted jars and a pomegranate tree suspended its little arsenal of russet bombs. Martins' nests clung to the eaves. Indoors, broken plaster arabesques twirled in baroque designs over lintels and windows. All the way round the long room that filled the jutting upper storey ran a low wide divan reached by a shallow step, and the wooden ceiling was adorned by elaborate carved rosettes the size of wagon wheels. The space above the divan was more glass than wall; in the Turkish *haremlik* this casement would be covered with trellis work, through which the inmates could gaze down into the cobbled lanes unobserved – bright squares split up into many panes through which the sun streamed. A secret, calm, airy world, calling to mind the multiple facets of the poop of a galleon. One side looked over the undulating rose-coloured tiles, the radiating gullies of the lanes and over the chimneys, the nests, the bell towers and domes and the steep granite bluffs that elbowed through them, towards the foothills of the Stara Planina; and beyond them lay the great range itself. South beyond the courtyard lay the Maritza and a green-gold plumage of poplars, and, on the other bank, poplars again, and willows and, bright and distinct in the morning light, the faraway line of the Rhodope. Thrace! Two storks were gliding across the trees and, as we watched them sailing down to the banks of the Maritza and closing their wings, they alighted and paced geometrically through the reeds, their bills lowered in pursuit of the frogs whose giveaway croaking reached our ears; the floating veil of mist was no defence against the shrewd roof-dwellers. 'They're late this year,' Nadejda said. 'They'll soon be off.'

~

To wake up in this hanging glass box – for it was here, in one of the corners of the divan, that my bed had been laid – was to surface into felicity. How tempting to lie floating here under the long, level volleys of early light shooting, adrift with motes, from window to window, and to gaze up at the intricate cigar-box lid ceiling, or out through the morning gleam of glass, cocooned in crystal, into the pale and bird-filled sky. But the sound of hoofs on cobbles, the wheels of carts, the cry of pedlars and the clang of scales were too tempting a lure. After a quick wash under the brass tap in the courtyard, I was in the streets.

I explored the town both alone and guided by Nadejda. The commonplace centre was full of modern public buildings; there was a Bulgarian and a Greek cathedral, and some trim, rather pretty gardens. This ordinary middle soon gave way to a rambling and fascinating circumference. The whole town is built between, up the slopes of, and round, three steep granite spurs – the *tepes* – and down their flanks the roofs poured, with houses hazard-ously perched on ledges and the rock projecting in blades and spikes: round and through them rose and fell a ravelled skein of cobbled alleyways. Some had awnings across them to shade the stones; it turned them into winding tented corridors; metal-workers, tobacco-sorters and wool-carders worked cross-legged in their open-fronted shops. These lanes were a cool penumbra crisscrossed by buckled and twisted tiger-stripes of sunlight. The wool-carders, squatting in a sea of fleece, worked with extraor-dinary instruments – huge curving bows rising three yards in the air and strung taut with a single wire, which resembled the harp, in bible illustrations, with which David assuaged the anger of Saul. Blacksmiths, coppersmiths, tinkers, leather-workers, gun-smiths, harness-makers, mule-saddlers – one of them, surprisingly, a Negro – planed away at their great howdahs, or stuffed the bulbous sheepskin quilting of saddles with wool. Green and yellow melons were piled like cannon balls, grapes and figs were arrayed in enormous panniers; red and green paprikas, ladies' fingers, and courgettes rose in heaps. Butchers' shops displayed their usual carnage, the Temple Bar display of gory heads, glassy-eyed trophies with the front teeth projecting like those of English travellers in French cartoons, and the cobbles outside were a network of fly-haunted rivulets of blood. The stalls were threatened by the swaying of the giant mule-slung baskets; now and then the lane was stampeded by a tidal wave of sheep, entire flocks which overflowed baa-ing into the shops and were cast forth again, pursued by shepherds and barking dogs. Chinking his way through the crowd was the same Albanian *bozaji*, bowed under his great brass vessel, that I had seen at Rila. Sometimes the houses nearly joined overhead. Gateways led out of this pandemonium, to quiet courtyards, to interior glimpses of women click-clacking away at their looms, and, under vine trellises, sheepskin hats and wide scarlet sashes and moccasins clustered round the tables of coffee and wine shops.

There was a pinnacle mosque and the bubbling roofline of a hammam, and suddenly, Turks, the first I had seen except for the little Danubian outpost on the islet of Ada Kaleh, by the Iron Gates. They were sashed with red like the Bulgars, but they wore baggy black trousers and slippers and scarlet fezzes, often faded or discoloured by sweat and use to a mulberry hue round which ragged turbans, some of them patterned with stripes or spots and in every colour but green (except in the case of an occasional putative descendant of the Prophet) were loosely bound. They sat cross-legged, with amber beads in their hands, eyelids lowered over the quiet intermittent gurgle of their nargilehs. Although they were dressed almost the same, a group by a drinking trough, watering a team of donkeys, looked slightly different; some of these, in lieu of fezzes, were hatted with grey or white felt skullcaps that came to a point like an Arabian dome in miniature, or a Saracen's helmet stripped of its chain mail. Nadejda told me that they were Pomaks from the valleys of the Rhodope near Haskovo, in the south-east. Sometimes they arrived with little caravans of camels; but not, alas, just then. I would have given much to see them pad through this throng, with their humps and their nodding supercilious masks almost touching the awnings. If I had struck lucky, I might also have seen some Kutzovlachs, of whom a few are scattered in the Macedonian south-west: semi-nomadic Aruman shepherds, speaking a low Latin dialect laced with Slav and akin to Rumanian, of whom I was to see many later on in Greece, especially in Thessaly and the Pindus. The Pomaks are said to be Bulgarians converted to Islam after the Turkish conquest of the country; they are certainly Muslims and they talk Bulgarian. All through the Ottoman Empire, they were ruthless supporters of the Sultans and they helped their overlords put down their fellow countrymen, butchering them by the thousand, with the true zeal of converts. (Some authorities derive them from early barbarian invaders from the north; and some Greek writers – for there are a number of Pomak villages on the Greek slopes of the Rhodope, round Kedros and Echinos – seek their origins in the ancient Thracian race of the Agrianoi.) In the same folds of mountain, on either side of the border, live tiny pockets of Kizilbashi. These 'redheads' are Shi'ite Muslims who follow Hazrat Ali, like their fellow schismatics in Persia from where they probably came, scattered across Asia Minor in pockets of Shia doctrine by Shah Ismail Safavi while the Turks were busy with their Polish and Venetian wars, and straying to Thrace later on; they are anathema to Turks and Pomaks alike, both of them staunch Sunnites. I gazed at these last berserk apostates with awe.

At a turn in the lane, all the names over the shops would become Greek and the air would ring with this language, already haunted by a ghost of familiarity, the modern version of which I was determined to master in due course. Then the shop inscriptions would have Christian names like Sarkis, Haik, Krikor, Dikran or Agop, and surnames all ending in *yan*; and in the cafés would be Armenians reading from pages of their fascinating script, which to inexpert eyes looks so similar to the Amharic writing of the Ethiopians; or they would be grouped, their eyes bright with acumen on either side of their wonderful noses, in the doors of their shops, like confabulating toucans.

In yet another quarter, the first names would become Isaak, Yakob, Avram, Khaim or Nahum, and inside, presiding among serried bolts of material, or measuring off cascades of cotton or satin, would be Sephardic Jews. Quite unlike my hosts in the Banat,* who belonged to the Ashkenazim, the northern branch of Jewry stretching from the heart of Russia to the Atlantic, the Sephardim are the southern branch of this great family. They arrived here, after the destruction of the temple at Jerusalem under Titus, by a long route: they had followed the conquering Moors across North Africa and into Spain. They flourished there for centuries, under the enlightened emirs of Andalusia, as merchants, scientists, physicians, philosophers and poets and reached their zenith in Maimonides. After the reconquest of Granada in 1492 – the year of Columbus – by Ferdinand and Isabella, the Inquisition expelled them again, some of them scattering, like their refugee cousins from Portugal, to those parts of the Netherlands that challenged the might of Spain; or, in the following decades, to the newly discovered Americas; to Pernambuco in Brazil and then to the Caribbean. It is from the Sephardim that Spinoza sprang, and, in England, families with names like Lopez and Montefiore, Mendoza the boxer, and Disraeli. But most of them moved eastward again, back to the

---

* In *Between the Woods and the Water* PLF encountered a family of Ashkenazi Jews in the Banat, a multi-ethnic region largely in western Rumania.

Levant; contingents settled on the Tuscan coast at Leghorn and Grosseto as guests of the Medici; the rest of them found asylum in the Ottoman realms, where they were welcomed by the Sultans. They settled in trading ports like Constantinople, Salonika, Smyrna and Rhodes, landing, it is said, with nothing but the scrolls of the law and the massive keys of their houses in Cordova, Granada or Cadiz, which, though I have never (in spite of asking) seen, they are still said to treasure. They spread to the lesser Balkan towns during the reigns of Bajazet II, Selim the Grim and Suleiman the Magnificent. They still spoke, I had heard, a version of fifteenth-century Andalusian Spanish called Ladino. I listened beside the counter and heard with delight: '*Que'tal, Hozum? Mu' bien! Y yo tambien.*'

There was one group of supreme interest and rareness: the Uniat Catholic community. Not so much because they were a small atoll of allegiance to Rome in an ocean of Orthodoxy but because of the reasons for this singularity. During the early centuries of Christianity, the Dualist heresy sprang up in Asia Minor, a belief which owed much to Gnostic thought and much to the Zoroastrians of Persia, in which Ormuzd and Ahriman, the powers of Light and Darkness, or Good and Evil, are of equal dignity and evenly matched in a never-ending duel for the souls of mankind. The votaries of this belief were simple and often virtuous folk; but their strange dogmas (which, among many other tenets, included neglect of the Virgin Mary, detestation of the Cross, and a search for salvation through the abhorrence of matter and the eventual extinction of the human race) seemed, understandably, revolutionary to formal Christians, and also wicked and blasphemous. They encountered the merciless rigour of Church and State. Manichaeism, as the heresy is generally called, spread, in time, all over southern Christendom, darkly blossoming under a score of different names. A whole population of Manichaeans, locally known as Paulicians, were uprooted from the Euphrates by the Emperor Alexis Comnene in the ninth century, and exiled to the region of Philippopolis, today's Plovdiv. Here, under the style of Bogomils – so called from the name of the local heresiarch – an identical belief was already in full bloom. From Bulgaria it spread westwards; the Muslims of Bosnia and Herzegovina are Islamized Bogomils. Eastern merchants, abetted locally, perhaps, by the troubadours, carried the forbidden doctrines yet further west and its votaries, the Cathars or Albigensians, abounded in the towns and castles of Provence and Languedoc. Simon de Montfort put them down with rigour in the Albigensian Crusade and the survivors were burnt alive after their last stand in the fortress of Montségur, in the foothills of the Pyrenees. The last adherents to survive as a coherent group, still – albeit heretically – within the framework of Christendom, were the original transplanted Paulicians of Philippopolis, who were finally won over to Roman submission by Jesuit missionaries in the seventeenth century. Their church, by the banks of the Maritza, still stands. In spite of its origins in Asia Minor, the heresy in the West has always been identified with Bulgaria. Thus, the mediaeval French styled their own heretics 'bougres'; and it is from the suspected belief that the Manichaean bias against reproduction misled them into sexual, as well as doctrinal, heterodoxy, that the word 'bugger' first came to enrich the English language.

There was much to wonder at. I loitered for hours in this labyrinth, and sat outside a coffee shop under a trellis, ears wide open – in spite of the dog-eared smack of cards resounding from the beamy shadows within and the clash and rattle of dice and backgammon counters – for the many languages and dialects which sounded in these corridors of shade. This total was now increased by the murmur of Romany from two Gypsy women squatting nearby on the cobbles, smoking cigarettes held in slender steel-ringed fingers. Gypsies were numerous on the outskirts of this moving throng, adding the yellow, orange, scarlet, mauve and purple hues of their many-tiered skirts and headkerchiefs to the colours which already abounded there. A monk, in a patched black habit and rimless stovepipe, hobbled past with a melon under each arm; a Gypsy smith opposite hammered a flat petal of steel to the hind hoof of a donkey. I drank in a composite aroma which seemed the substantive essence of the Balkans, compounded of sweat, dust, singeing horn, blood, nargileh-smoke, dung, *slivo*, wine, roasting mutton, spice and coffee, laced with a drop of attar of roses and a drift of incense, and wondered whether Alexander, as a boy, had ever seen this town which his father fortified on the eastern march of his kingdom against the Thracian tribes. It was enlarged by Trajan and Hadrian and Marcus Aurelius. Rather sadly, it was believed to be the place where Orpheus, breaking his vow by looking at her on the way back from Hades, lost Eurydice.

How odd to think that of all the races now assembled here only, possibly, the Greeks would have been present here when it was founded, unless their own theories of the origins of the Pomaks are correct. The Bulgars would have still been far away between the Volga and the Urals, and the Slavs, whose country and language they took over, were still far to the north, between the Vistula and the Dniester, in the Pripet marshes perhaps. The Turks would have been wandering about somewhere on the Mongolian steppes, the Kizilbashi in the Iranian plains or moun-tains, the Sephardim still settled in Judah or Babylon, the Vlachs in the Dacian highlands across the Danube, the Albanians in Illyria or the Acroceraunian mountains, the Armenians under Mount Ararat or by the shores of Lake Van, the ex-Paulician Catholics by the Euphrates, the Gypsies on some burning Dravidian plain near the frontiers of Baluchistan. And that Negro saddler, in what Nubian valley or lion-haunted and leafy kingdom of the upper Nile or in Ethiopia were his ancestors living then? And, for that matter, what shaggy loins, in what Hibernian bog, druidical forest, sunless fjord, Saxon settlement by the Elbe's mouth or the dismal Jutish coast, were ultimately answerable for me?

Time for another *slivo* and a couple of roast paprika-pods. A shadow appeared on the awnings further up the lane, gliding across each rectangle of canvas towards my table, sinking in the sag, rising again at the edge, and moving on to the next with a flicker of dislocation, then gliding onwards. As it crossed the stripe of sunlight between two awnings, it threaded the crimson beak of a stork through the air, a few inches above the gap; then came a long white neck, the swell of snowy breast feathers and the six-foot motionless span of its white wings and the tips of the black flight feathers upturned and separated as fingers in the lift of the air current. The white belly followed, tapering, and then, trailing beyond, the fan of its tail and long parallel legs of crimson lacquer, the toes of each of them closed and streamlined, but the whole shape flattening, when the band of sunlight was crossed, into a two-dimensional shadow once more, enormously displayed across the rectangle of cloth, as distinct and nearly as immobile, so languid was its flight, as an emblematic bird on a sail; then sliding across it and along the nearly still corridor of air between the invisible eaves and the chimneys, dipping along the curl of the lane like a sigh of wonder, and at last, a furlong away slowly pivoting, at a gradual tilt, out of sight. A bird of passage like the rest of us.

∼

There were the *Larousse XIXème Siècle* and the many volumes of *Meyers Konversations-Lexikon* in Nadejda's house, and plenty to look up in both; also numbers of French books from Constantinople, including a tattered translation of the *Odyssey*, from which, lolling on the divan as she did her ironing, I read great fragments out loud to Nadejda in the sunny upper room. I heard her French recitations again, and introduced her to Baudelaire. My French was a bit better than hers, which redressed the balance of her twenty-four hours seniority in age. She pined, she admitted, to look like a girl student at the Sorbonne. She cut her hair in a fringe and wore a white shirt and black pleated skirt and, whenever she got a chance, a beret at a terrific angle, and succeeded in her ambition very well.

The second morning of my stay she pulled out of an old chest quantities of marvellous costumes, both Greek and Bulgarian, some of them well over a hundred years old: blouses with great stiff oblongs of embroidery, multicoloured aprons, skirts of bottle green and plum-coloured velvet, and turquoise silk bodices heavy with braid and gold and silver wire with hanging sleeves, stomachers clinking with Austrian and Turkish gold coins, belts which clasped over the midriff in two enormous plates, shaped and arabesqued like Persian flames, of chased silver; silk headkerchiefs and shallow scarlet fezzes with long black satin tassels, and pretty embroidered slippers of velvet and soft red leather. Some of the clothes were barbaric, others wonderfully elegant and romantic. I persuaded her – not too hard a task – to try them all on. She made a series of magnificent entries, rustling and clinking about like a mannequin, standing with her arms akimbo, twirling round on one toe, subsiding on the divan like an odalisque – a Georgian or Circassian one with that mass of fair hair – in languishing postures.

At the bottom of this treasure chest we discovered a number of chibooks – those obsolete Turkish pipes with cherrywood stems several feet long, small earthenware bowls and amber mouthpieces – and a small arsenal of old weapons; heirlooms, like the clothes:

long chased silver flintlock pistols, powder horns, semicircular scimitars, ivory-hilted yataghans and khanjars with Turkish, Greek and Bulgarian inscriptions damascened or incised along their blades. We drew these from their silver scabbards, and, seeing we each had a yataghan in one hand and a scimitar in the other, suddenly launched ourselves with common accord into a fierce mock fight, clashing the blades together overhead, closing *corps à corps* with grating steel until the hilts were interlocked in front of our snarling faces, breaking loose again, leaping from floor to divan and back, spinning round, groaning and collapsing spread-eagled in feigned death, resurrecting with shouts and a fresh clangour, until Nadejda's grandfather, alarmed by the shouts and stamping and clashing, called quavering from his room to know what on earth was going on.

In the back of my notebook Nadejda filled about three pages with phrases in Bulgarian that might come in useful on my travels, printing them in neat Cyrillic capitals which, unlike the cabbalistic tangle of the common script, I could decipher by now. The list began with 'Sir, I am an Englishman and I am walking on foot from London to Constantinople': '*Gospodine, az sum Anglitchanin i az hodya pesha ot London za Tzarigrad.*' Tzarigrad? Yes, Nadejda said, that's what Constantinople was called in Bulgarian, the City of the Czars, the Byzantine emperors: Caesartown, in fact. *Kolko ban?* How much money? *Mnogo losho*, very bad; *tchudesno*, marvellous; *Cherno Moré*, the Black Sea; 'How much does that melon weigh?' 'My bed's full of insects, you scoundrel!', and so on. I read them slowly out loud and she corrected the pronunciation.* They ended up with some splendidly extravagant compliments. 'You never know when they'll come in handy,' she said: 'Your eyes shine

---

* PLF was always fascinated by languages. He transmits his youthful attempt throughout this journey (occasionally with more enthusiasm than accuracy).

like stars!' 'Your hair and your eyes make me weak at the knees.'
'You are the most beautiful girl in the world' and 'Fly with me!'

⁓

Nadejda was a knowledgeable and spirited guide. We gazed at the
old Thracian objects in the museum: plaques with warriors and
huntsmen on horseback and strangely masked women and a
wonderful silver death mask of a young Thracian prince. The
beautiful and astonishing treasures of beaten gold that have
emerged since the war, and which I have seen only in pictures
– the glittering dishes patterned with a radiation of faces, the ewer
shaped like a woman's head, the deer's head *rhyton*, the amphorae
with handles of prancing centaurs – were still deep underground.

We visited a little cluster of monasteries on a hill north of the
town. Here – for one can't count the rebuilt church and the
modern iconography of Rila – I saw old Byzantine churches (as
opposed to their recent imitations) which cover the whole of the
Orthodox world, for the first time in my life. Enclosed in walls
and surrounded by mellow-slabbed courtyards or cobbles, embowered by trees and masted with cypresses, these walls of grey and
russet or honeycomb-gold brick and, poised on window-slotted
cylinders, these cupolas of faded tiles curving to their low summits
with the loose overlap of pine cone chips when they are just
beginning to expand, or encased in steel or in ribbed and fluted
lead, were the forerunners of hundreds of churches that I was to
explore during the decades that followed. The small domed
concavity within, with the soft golden light falling from high
windows in the drum, so dark at first, after the blue outside; the
semicircular arched doorways through the donjon thickness of
the walls of the pronaos into the narthex; the transepts, the apses,
the massive ikonostasis – all these were the background for a
painted troop of momentous figures: unearthly, etiolated saints

and angels, crowned kings and queens, interlocking swarms of haloes, Last Judgements and martyrdoms, each wide-eyed head between its Greek descriptive legend in intricate and flaking Byzantine calligraphy. These astounding frescoed saints were, had I known it, on that particular afternoon, the sentries, the lonely heralds and harbingers of a vast army, scattered in hundreds of churches, that I have pursued ever since for many years, and with deepening delight, from Bukovina, in northern Rumania near the Polish and Russian borders, to Egypt, and from Sicily to Cappadocia.

I can't remember the details of these fateful paintings. My virginal and uninstructed eye failed to record them – only the delayed-action vibrations they unloosed; or, rather, only one still sticks: St John the Baptist bearing his head in a dish and strangely winged, and perhaps only this one because he adorned the walls of the monastery of Ivan Preobajenski and I asked what the name meant. Nadejda told me: St John the Forerunner, or, in Greek, Ioannes Prodromos. These peculiar and delible frescoes performed their quiet task of introduction and discreetly withdrew. For that matter, were the domes tiled or were they sheeted in steel or lead – or both, as I boldly set down a moment ago? Or is it the intervening years that have tiled and leaded and metalled them so arbitrarily? Doubt springs. It doesn't matter, but it is odd that memory should be so evasive about the faces and the scene of this momentous interview and so crystalline about irrelevances: the green shade of the overhead vine outside, for instance, and, on the slabs beneath, the random stars and diamonds of light; and, a bit later, sitting under a huge plane tree talking about *Les Fleurs du mal.* One is only sometimes warned, when these processes begin, of their crucial importance: that certain poems, paintings, kinds of music, books, or ideas are going to change everything, or that one is going to fall in love or become friends for life; the many lengthening strands, in fact, which, plaited together, compose a lifetime. One should be able to detect the muffled bang of the starter's gun. This journey was punctuated with these inaudible reports: daysprings veiled and epiphanies in plain clothes.

~

In a garden in the modern centre of the town, among the civic flower beds and the avenues and the trim public buildings and the banks, there was a concrete disc of dancing floor and a band prettily embowered in trees strung with coloured lamps where the flower of the Plovdiv intelligentsia assembled at night. I was taken there by Nadejda and a party of students, some of whom I had met at Rila. To the ones I hadn't met, I was introduced, with offhand ease, as 'my twin' – the day's time-lag had been quietly suppressed. The tunes the band played were even more out of date than they had been in Transylvania. There were a few foxtrots, but old-fashioned waltzes from Central Europe were more popular and, above all, tangoes, which I had scarcely ever danced. I attempted them now in a terrible pair of brown tennis shoes bought in Orşova; rather unfeatly at first, then passably, modelling myself on the passionate gravity of the Philippopolitans who crowded the floor. A woman singer dashingly delivered the words in German from the bandstand: '*O Donna KLA-ra,*' she sang, as we slunk scowling along, '*Ich hab Dich TANZen – geSEHN, O Donna KLA – RA – Du – bist – WUNDerschön!*'

After a couple of hours, prompted by the moonlight, our group sneaked away, armed with a bottle of wine, to a boat in the Maritza, and rowed out on to the wide river singing and drinking in turn from the same glass and moored under a clump of trees. This mild mixed party, it seemed, was in the nature of a tremendous escapade for Bulgaria, even though two of the girls were sisters of two of the boys and a third was almost engaged to another, a young officer cadet. We began challenging each other to drink a whole tumblerful of wine at a single draught and at high speed. The girls hung back from the ordeal, and returned the glass after spluttering, niminy-piminy sips; all, I observed with admiration, except Nadejda. She cried, '*za zdrave!*' and threw a tumblerful down her throat at one long gulp and then shuddered like a dog, tossing her fair mane amid applause. When, as always happens on such occasions, it was the stranger's turn to sing one of his native songs, I fell back, as I had learnt to by trial and error, on *There is a Tavern in the Town*, which I strongly recommend for those in a similar predicament. It can be sung *con brio* or *adagio*, depending on the prevailing mood, and it is soon over. Either this or *Those Endearing Young Charms*. I was impatient to return to their own tunes. At last, and with great delight, I heard, and finally learnt the words, of that strange wavering song the women had sung in the bus from Radomir. I got the students to perform it by humming what I could remember of the tune: '*Zashto mi se sirdish, liube?*' ('Why are you angry with me, my love? Why do you shun me? Is it that you have no horse, or that you have forgotten the way?')

> *. . . Sirdish, ne dohojdash?*
> *Dali konya namash, liubé*
> *Ili drum ne znayesh?*

It ends in mid-air in an oddly unfinished fashion. They sang beautifully the slow and complex tune, with many modulations: an entrancing and melancholy sound over this moonlit river. I wonder what has become of them all?

~

We fished all the costumes out of the chest again next morning and I made Nadejda dress up in the most resplendent and romantic of them: a wide crimson velvet skirt and a tight green, heavily embroidered bodice stiff with galloons of gold lace and edged with small gold buttons and with slashed sleeves which hung loose from the elbow like tulip-petals; then came a belt with huge silver clasps, and all the hanging gold coins and chains we could find; and finally a low, flat-tasselled fez trimmed with gold red askew over the thick, straight-combed mass of her fair hair. Then I arranged her in an odalisque pose, a chibouk held aslant in one hand and the other arm flung negligently along the back of the divan. The sun poured in from the many bright panes behind, and beyond them receded the treetops, the storky roofs, the domes and the mountains: a ravishing hybrid vision, half captured Circassian princess, half Byronic heroine: Mademoiselle Aïssé, Haidée or the Maid of Athens. When all was ready, a large and elaborate drawing was begun (I intermittently but doggedly persevered in this mistaken vocation for a few more years, sometimes achieving, by a slow and painstaking process, something that could just pass muster; more often not). I struck lucky this time – at any rate I'd managed to capture her splendid and deceptive scowl. After an hour it looked as if the result might be presentable – literally, as I wanted to give it to Nadejda, if it turned out all right, for a leaving present, as I was setting off next day. It was all a bit sad. She was an unexpectedly quiet and patient sitter. How marvellous it would be, I thought, as I drew the fez tassel falling on to her green shoulder and spreading there, in a dark silken cascade, to settle in this luminous and enchanting room, reading and writing and talking to Nadejda and hearing her recite *Nous n'irons plus aux bois*. She was so pretty, kind, funny, intelligent and good. With the passage of translated Homer that we had read the day before in mind, I thought: how lovely it would be to stay on here, like Odysseus in the cave of Calypso.

'Wouldn't it be lovely', Nadejda said at that moment, breaking the long silence of her pose with a friendly smile that obliterated any traces of intensity, 'if you could stay on here like Odysseus in the cave of Calypso?'

'That's exactly what I was thinking.'

Actually, my plans had changed radically since yesterday. I had been planning to continue down the Maritza valley, passing the Turkish frontier at Adrianople and then striking across Turkish Thrace to Constantinople. But when talking to Nadejda the night before about the Byzantine frescoes at the Preobajenski monastery, she had said they were nothing compared to those in Tirnovo, far away to the north the other side of the Great Balkan. Moreover, it was the capital of one of the old Bulgarian empires before the Turkish conquest, and as important in Bulgarian history as Rila; more important, even; whereas the Maritza valley was hot and flat all the way to Turkey, full of rice paddies and tobacco, all flies and dust. The students had, when we consulted them, all backed her up. So we spread my maps on the divan and plotted a much more enterprising route: it swooped over the mountains, threaded its way through Tirnovo, then struck east till it reached the Black Sea and moved south along the coast to Tzarigrad. This would add several hundred miles to the journey, but it sounded well worth it, and I hated the idea of missing the Black Sea. After all there was no hurry. The scheme was a stirring and revolutionary deviation.

Boldly flouting convention, we went to the dancing place by ourselves that night and danced till the place shut, and then wandered about the moonlit town from hilltop to hilltop, looking down on the glimmering roofs and empty lanes, sometimes sitting and talking on doorsteps, and got home in the small hours.

I went to say goodbye to Nadejda's grandfather next day. He had insisted that I should do so although it was hardly dawn (I had been to see him often during my three days' stay). He gave me an old leather-bound copy of Fauriel's *Chants populaires de la Grèce* and asked me to greet the Parthenon for him when I reached Athens. He had never been there, '*et maintenant je ne le verrai jamais . . .*'* He uttered this with the sadness of a Muslim speaking of Mecca. Nadejda kept me company as far as a little wood about three miles to the north of the town, walking arm in arm. Here she gave me a parcel of bread, halva, cheese, boiled eggs, apple, a circular wooden flask full of *slivo* and, as a parting present, some six packets of English cigarettes which she must have slipped out and bought in secret. The bearded bluejacket's head on the packet was hidden under band upon band of import-duty stamps; she could no more afford them than I could. I was deeply moved. We were both overcome by emotion; we parted only after many long and only half twin-like hugs. Slowly and very reluctantly we turned away at last to our opposite directions, feeling suddenly forlorn, and looking round to wave: hoping that, from a distance at any rate, these flourished arms looked more cheerful than their owners felt.

∼

Goodbyes like these were the only sad aspect of this journey. The whole itinerary was a chain of minor valedictions, more or less painful ones, seldom indifferent, only occasionally a relief. There was something intrinsically melancholy, a sudden sharp intimation, like a warning tap on the shoulder, of the fleetingness of everything, in bidding goodbye to people who had been kind, as nearly everyone was, and knowing that, in all likelihood, I

---

* 'And now I'll never see it.'

would never see them again. But when, through some natural affinity, fostered by the demolition of the wonted barriers that their preordained transitoriness imposed, these encounters plunged deeper and spread their quick roots of friendship, affection, passion, love – even if it were unavowed, the electrical flicker of its possibility – these farewells became shattering deracinations; as they had been in Transylvania and as they were now.

Voici l'herbe qu'on fauche – in the words that I had been listening to often recently – *et les lauriers qu'on coupe.**

* See, the grass is cut down and the laurels are felled.

3

Over the Great Balkan

Now for a burst of speed that drove me due north, across a hot
plain pronged at random with swing-wells, each with a sprinkled
population of men and women breaking up their baked fields.
They had wooden ploughs and adzes, scraping, planting and
irrigating in allotments and tobacco fields: a thirsty and, somehow,
distressing scene of Georgic diligence. In the distance there were
occasional patches of eerie green. Were they swamps, a mirage,
or the rice fields I had heard about? Hard work in hot plains fills
one with confused sentiments of malaise: joy that one isn't hard
at it oneself, guilt about this joy. Visually plains are only tolerable
if they are absolutely barren, like deserts, tundras, or steppes, just
fit for grazing; though it is hard to deny splendour to an ocean
of wheat. But these visions of pettifogging and grinding prosperity
strike the observer with sorrow, and hamstring its practitioners.
They are never much good at anything else.

But the redeeming and beautiful line of the mountains sailed
across the northern horizon. I pounded towards it, heading for
the notch that marked the pass between the Sredna Gora on the
west and the Karadja Dagh on the east. Finally, to hoist myself
faster out of the plain, I followed a track that led up the side of
the Sredna Gora, and, after finishing most of Nadejda's supplies,
slept in an abandoned shepherd's lean-to of branches. It was
higher and colder than I thought. I woke up to watch the dawn,

as I lay luxuriously smoking one of the precious cigarettes. To the north spread a deep green valley about a dozen miles wide, and on the other side of it soared the tall golden brown range of the Great Balkan. A new world! After a drink and a wash at an icy spring trickling into a broken trough hollowed from a tree trunk, bright with green weed and surrounded by an almost fossilized humus of droppings, I struck downhill munching the last of Nadejda's apples. The cloud shadows sliding along the flanks of the Stara Planina were buckled by the scarps and the ravines. I reached the other side by late morning and crossed a river, reduced by the drought to a winding thread of pebbles which carried me to the town of Karlovo.

It was built up a gentle staircase of rock above the river in layers of wooden roofs and coloured walls – white, green, ochre and red with an overflow of treetops and a crown of pinnacles, and beyond it, the wooded slope of the mountain. Cobbled lanes climbed into it among willow-shaded brooks, and houses enclosed in tree-filled courtyards with tall wooden gates. The lanes turned into staircases sagging in the middle from long use. They were lined with climbing tiers of shops where saddlers, smiths, tinkers and carpenters were at work, and primitive hatters with blocked sheepskin kalpacks lined up in the sun on truncated wooden columns. Next came white groves of moccasins, overlapping in pyramids and hanging in garlands: Turkish slippers, loose and easily shed for devotions, or for lying on divans; then after that, crimson shelves of fezzes.

These sloping lanes converged on a raft-like square with a large mosque on one side standing among its minarets. Turks in turban and fez were everywhere, and trousered women with their heads and torsos obscured in black *ferejes* that left only their eyes visible: top-heavy figures balancing baskets and pots on their heads or bearing yokes across their shoulders from which hung swaying bronze water-cauldrons.

It was the first time I had seen a gathering of more than half a dozen of this astonishing race. The evidence of their vanished empire had been steadily thickening for the last few hundred miles and I gazed at them with wonder. They were the westernmost remnants, the last descendants of those shamanist tribes of Central Asia, kinsmen of the all-destroying Mongols, who had surged westwards, turned Muslim, founded the Sultanate of Rum and then conquered the Roman Empire of the East, and finally, by capturing Constantinople, inflicted the greatest disaster on Europe since the sack of Rome by the Goths a thousand years earlier. Their empire spread deep into Asia and Africa and covered three quarters of the Mediterranean shore. It stretched to the Pillars of Hercules and reached north to Poland and Russia and westward to Vienna; one extraordinary sortie had even plunged as far west as Ratisbon, only a day's march from Munich. When we remember that the Moors of Spain were only halted at Tours, on the Loire, it seems, at moments, something of a fluke that St Peter's and Notre Dame and Westminster Abbey are not today three celebrated mosques, kindred fanes to Haghia Sophia in Constantinople.

The capture of the city fell on a Tuesday and that day of the week is still deemed a day of ill-omen by the descendants of their Orthodox subjects: an inauspicious one on which to start a journey or launch an enterprise. Could the unluckiness of green throughout Europe (but not in Asia, where it symbolizes descent from the Prophet) spring from the colour of the Turks' conquering banners? I have often wondered. If one blesses the names of Charles Martel and Sobiesky for rescuing western Christendom from Islam, one must execrate the memory of the Fourth Crusade, and the greed and Christian sectarian bias that sacked Constantinople, destroyed the Byzantine Empire and called down the doom of Christendom's eastern half. It is as vain to blame the Turks for spreading westwards over the wreckage as it would be to arraign the laws of hydrostatics for flood damage.

Their armies advanced across Europe. It must have been a daunting sight: Anatolian infantry, wild Asian troops of horse, Bedouin cavalry, mounted archers from eastern deserts, contingents of Albanians, Tartars and Tcherkesses, Negroes from Africa and, under their strange emblems and their fan-plumed helmets, the Janissaries. These last were mostly Christians abducted as children, converted into fanatic Muslims and drilled into merciless warriors: a corps whose martial music, furnished by beating the sides of their giant bronze soup-cauldrons, blended strangely with long horns and kettledrums. Then came half-mad dervishes, endless strings of camels and gigantic dragon-mouthed cannon, and, rocking overhead, the banners of the pashas – the number of horse-tails fitting their different degrees – and, everywhere, under spiked brass half-moons, the baleful green flags. At their head, in early centuries, would be the Sultan himself, a ruthless or magnanimous paladin. Later on, when the names of Bajazet the Thunderbolt, Mohammed the Conqueror, Suleiman the Magnificent and Selim the Grim were retreating into myth, the standard of the Grand Vizier, the Seraskier or a three-tailed pasha led the host, while the Sultan himself, who, until his accession, perhaps had lived all his life in a cage,* would be far away in the kiosks and arbours of the Grand Seraglio: checkmating plots, spending his days with his wives and concubines and minions, cultivating tulips, writing quatrains in Turkish and Persian and Arabic, or – passions so absorbing that by default of attention to anything else they nearly ruined the empire – amassing

---

* From the early seventeenth century, for some two hundred years, brothers of the Ottoman sultans were confined in palace quarters known as the *kafes*, or 'cage', to ensure their loyalty. If a sultan died childless, his brother might emerge to the sultanate from this confinement, often unfit to rule.

ambergris or sables. The Sultan was not only the Emperor but the Caliph as well. When his distant followers stormed a Christian fortress, they were engaged in a holy war. If a warrior fell in battle and his giant white turban – one of those vast pleated globes depicted by Bellini and Pisanello – rolled away, an unshorn tassel of hair would uncoil from his razored scalp, giving purchase for the twining forefinger of a celestial hand, which would twirl him aloft and set him down among the cool streams and the doe-eyed girls in paradise.

Many of their descendants in the square had a wild and uncouth look. They were all, like their Bulgarian neighbours, herdsmen and cultivators and they were clad in patched and pleated trousers, faded turbans and discoloured fezzes. Their general air – rather contradictorily – was one of inbred tiredness. Sitting cross-legged in the sunny loggia that ran along one wall of the mosque, they conversed quietly together, sipped their thimbles of minute coffee or bubbled away at their nargilehs or busied themselves at ritual ablutions. When a newcomer joined them and touched his heart, his lips and his forehead, the soft generous murmurs of answering salaams were accompanied by the same triple flutter of hands, ending with the palm laid across the bosom and an inclination of the head: an unperfunctory-seeming greeting of infinite grace and repose. I received this flattering salute when I asked the hodja – an old man with watery eyes of the palest blue, a white spade-beard and a gentle smile, a beautifully laundered turban bound flat round his fez – if I could look inside the mosque. We padded unshod into the carpeted and whitewashed penumbra. There, under the dome's hollow, was the niche of the mihrab pointing towards Mecca and the flight of steps leading to the little platform of the mimbar, where at the appropriate times he would read aloud from the Koran. There was nothing else. After pointing these out, he left me to myself. Soon, after a slow sequence of ritual bows and tilting forward from his knees to touch the carpet with his brow, he recovered in a single rocking motion, and remained seated cross-legged and absorbed in prayer. From time to time he raised his hands, palms uppermost, on either side of his body for a few seconds, as though he were offering a light and invisible gift; then folded them again in his lap where the pleats of his voluminous trousers fanned out from the scarlet edge of his sash. I left him there, and with his permission climbed the minaret.

From the little walled parapet, hot as a flat iron and blinding after the shadowy mosque, I could gaze across the wooden roofs and the treetops of the town. Beyond them uncoiled the valleys and the long swelling cordilleras of the Sredna Gora and the Karadja Dagh. When I stepped down again from the dark helix into the mosque, the hodja was still sitting there, gazing into the air with his upturned palms still lifted. I tiptoed outside.

After a siesta under some mulberry trees, I walked to a deep cold cataract tumbling down the rocks' face – the source of the willow-shaded streams that thread their cool veins through the little town – and arrived back, just as I hoped, a few moments before sunset. For there, halved at the waist by the parapet with his hands raised level on either side of his face, fittingly outlined across the reddening sky, the hodja was standing in mid-air; and soon the slow, wailing, high-pitched Arabian syllables of the first affirmation of the muezzin's call wavered across the evening air and fell silent. After a long pause, they were repeated. Another hush followed; and then the second and longer clause sailed slowly into the sky and stopped.

The long intervals of silence were like the spreading of rings across a pool; the last vibrations must die away and the surface of the sky be still again before the next phrase, of which each word is a pebble dropped into the void, can launch its new sequence of circles. The muezzin was shifting along his little walled platform to another point of the compass and the next sentence; when it reached the ear, his wail had sunk a little to a different key. He completed his circle and the final summing-up slowly spelled itself forth until a longer pause lengthened into ultimate silence. The last hoop of prayer had expanded to infinity. The famous words faded from the air and from these infidel mountains. The parapet – which swelled three quarters of the way up the pale shaft of the minaret, then tapered to a lance-tip topped by an upturned crescent – was empty; the invisible muezzin was already halfway down his dark spiral. The sun had dipped below the last blue stage-wings of the Stara Planina and the Sredna Gora, and under the mulberry trees the flit and swoop of the swallows filled my ears with a noise like the swish of scissors round one's head in a barber's shop.

~

I was woken next day by the same high-pitched intoning of prayer, the light this time striking the minaret on the opposite flank. How odd, I thought, as I set off, that the relics of the Turks in Europe, to which, after all, they brought nothing but calamity, should be distinguished by so much charm and grace: the architecture of houses, the carved wooden ceilings, the baroque plaster work, the wells and fountains, the pillared loggias and above all, these globes and these elegantly ascending pinnacles that ennoble the skyline of the meanest hamlet. The latter, in big towns, sometimes crowd as plentifully as an asparagus bed; and what about those colonies of shallow cupolas swelling from the roofs of hammams and round the cloisters of tekkes and madressehs? Their architects understood the use of shade and space and trees and the manipulation of water for purposes of ease and repose and pleasure to the eye. It is impossible too to think without delight of those slender, almost semicircular bridges with which the Seljuks and the Ottomans have spanned unnumbered rivers and torrent beds from the Balkans to the Taurus mountains. They float from flank to flank of ravines – away from the plane trees and oleanders and the darting wagtails – as airily as rainbows.

Against all this one must set the fact that the Turks were the only people in Bulgaria, apart from the collaborating *Tchorbaji* landowners, who had the right or the means, in these subject territories, to build anything more aspiring than a hovel; also that these formulae were adapted from the Byzantine style that they discovered in their newly conquered empire. Byzantine architects and masons, indeed, designed a number of the great mosques; but nevertheless, a separate Turkish style does exist in its own right. The suavity and the ceremony that dignifies their greetings, even among these ragged and dusty survivors, may, like the buildings and gardens and fountains, owe much to their early neighbours; for, when they first arrived from the steppes and slowed down and took root in Asia Minor, these neighbours were, apart from faraway China, the most civilized nations in the world: the Greeks, the Persians and the Arabs. All this is so; but one must rejoice that the Turks had the wisdom to follow these models and later, when they were not ordering the bastinado, the bowstring and the gallows (or, as late as 1876, the Bulgarian atrocities that horrified Gladstone and – no doubt to the Turks' sincere astonishment – the whole world) they were laying out gardens and fountains, decreeing pleasure domes and plotting the fall of a shadow. The Ottoman Empire has joined the eastern Roman Empire which it destroyed; but a posthumous and perhaps deceptive glow of charm and elegance pervades its mementoes. How apt are these shady gardens for drinking coffee and for meditation, for listening to stringed instruments or the tales of the Forty Vizirs and the loves of Leila and Majnoon!

One of these mementoes lay just outside the town: a cypress-shaded Turkish cemetery with a forest of turbaned monoliths, and among them, tearing with the point of his sickle at the weeds which had been hardy enough to outlive the summer, the hodja himself. He straightened up with his fluttering salute and a wrinkled smile and we stood happily tongue-tied among the stones. Some of the marble pillars were only a foot high and topped by a sculptured fez, some of them nearly as tall as a man, all of them swelling as they ascended. The lower and older ones, chipped, split, tilted askew and leaning at all angles, were crowned with extravagant carved headgear. (The fez, imposed by Mahmoud II in the 1820s and abolished by Atatürk inside the frontiers of Turkey in the 1920s, had exactly a century's official life.) They expanded like giant pumpkins and vegetable marrows, intricately pleated round a cone, and sometimes a helmet's point pricked through the bulbous folds; others were coil upon stone coil of twisted linen; yet others, jutting fluted cylinders adorned with broken aigrettes. What pashas and agas and beys, what swaggering bimbashis, what miralais with mandarin whiskers, could have worn these portentous headpieces? I would have known if I had understood Turkish, for their moss-covered biographies, in Arabic script and enclosed in tapering baroque cartouches, were incised on the stelae below. The hodja haltingly read out a few of them: Osman, Selim, Mehmet, Abdul-Aziz, Djem, Mustapha, Omar, Ferid . . . Each inscription ended with the same two melodious words, at which, each time he uttered them, the hodja's voice reverently fell. There is something haunting, almost Hawaian, about the airy vowels. I only learnt years later, what they mean: it is 'murmur a *fàtiha*'. The *fàtiha* is the first *sura* of the Koran: 'Glory be to Allah, the lord of all the worlds.' It is almost as frequent a prayer as the alliterative syllables from the same *sura* without which little, in Islam, begins or ends: '*Bismillah ar rahman ar raheem*: 'in the name of Allah, the Most Compassionate, the Most Merciful, whose pity is without bounds'.

~

Below, the Tunja river meandered eastwards at the bottom of a wide valley. The path I followed on the flank of the Great Balkan range, high above the main road and the river, heaved its way along from dry torrent-bed to buttress, down into the next torrent-bed and out again, in a series of scallops. The side of the Balkans sloped upwards on my left, occasionally showing perpendicular cliffs, then subsided again. Shepherds leaned on their crooks grazing their tinkling flocks across the thorny slant of the middle distance. I waited to see whether they were wearing sheepskin kalpacks or the turban and fez – for both wore the same broad scarlet sashes discernible from afar – and then shouted '*Dobro utro*' or '*Salaam aleikum!*' accordingly. It is the duty of strangers to greet first. After a few seconds, back would come their answering hail. Some of the hamlets far below were clustered round the alert perpendicular of a minaret. After one of these affable long-distance exchanges with a Turk pasturing his flock about a furlong up the slope, my interlocutor began shouting something. Thinking that he was asking, in the usual way, where I was going, I shouted back: '*za* Tzarigrad' 'and then 'Istanbul'. He waved the information aside and continued to shout, pointing westwards up the mountainside with his crook. Something unusual was happening there.

An indistinct blur darkened the air above a notch in the skyline: a wide blur that seemed almost solid in the centre. It thinned out round the edges in a fringe of numberless moving specks as though the wind were blowing across a vast heap of dust or soot or feathers just out of sight. The shoulder of mountain passed, this moving mass, continually renewed from beyond the skyline, dipped out of silhouette on our side of the range and began to expand and to declare itself as more comparable to feathers than to dust or to soot; it became predominantly whiter. The vanguard spread wider still as it sank lower and grew larger, rocking and fluctuating and heading for exactly the stretch of mountainside where we were standing so raptly at gaze. It was a slow airborne horde, enormous and awe-inspiring, composed of myriads of birds, their leaders becoming distinguishable now as they sailed towards us on almost motionless wings, and at last, as they outlined themselves once more against the sky, identifiable. Storks! Soon a ragged party of skirmishers was floating immediately above, straight as the keels of canoes from the tips of their bills to the ends of their legs that streamed behind each one of them like a wake, balanced between the almost motionless span of their great wings, the sunlight falling golden between the comparative transparency of their feathers and the dark bobbin-shaped outline of their craned throats. Only their outstretched feathers flickered. The broad black edge of their wings stretched from the tips to where they joined the body in a dark senatorial stripe. The leaders were soon beyond us. A few solitary birds followed, and then all at once we were under a high shifting roof of wings, a flotilla that was thickening into an armada, until our ears were full of the sound of rustling and rushing with a flutter now and then when a bird changed position in a slow wingbeat or two, and of the strange massed creaking, as of many delicate hinges, of a myriad slender joints. They benighted the air. A ragged shadow dappled the mountainside all round us. A number of birds flew below the main stream of their companions, cruising along in their shade, others alone or in small parties were flung out on either side like system-less outriders. One of the low fliers subsided to the mountainside through the fluctuating penumbra under an inward slanting V of wings, and suddenly earthbound, took one or two awkward steps on its bent scarlet stilts, its wings still outstretched like a tightrope-walker's pole. After shaking its beaked head once or twice, it levered itself into the air and rose again with slow and effortless beats to the sliding pavilion of feathers overhead. Looking back, the specks were still showering over the skyline as plentifully as ever, then sinking a little way down the mountainside like a steady waterfall and out again almost at once and over the valley in a sinuous and unbroken curve. The leaders, and soon the first units of the main horde, had now sunk just below the level of our line of sight: we could see the sunlight on the backs and wings of their followers as their line lengthened. Their irregular drawn-out mass, rocking and tilting and disturbed by living eddies and with a whirlpool flutter and ruffle round the outskirts, moved beyond the great empty gulf of air between the 6,000-foot watershed of the Shipka Balkan, which they had just crossed, and the lesser heights of the Karadja Dagh. Soon their leaders were dwindling to specks, then all of them began to cohere in a dark blur, high above their long irregular shadow, which followed them a mile below their flight like the shadows of a navy on the sea bed. Gradually the supply began to dwindle; the rope of birds grew thinner, the loose-knit parties smaller, until at last there was nothing but a straggling rearguard gliding eastwards. Several minutes later, when the last of them had winged away over the wide valley of the Tunja, an ultimate stork passed overhead beating a slow and solitary path: Make haste! one felt like crying. They had soon become a long slow swerve effortlessly navigating the invisible currents of the sky, growing dimmer and dimmer until at last they vanished from our straining eyes, leagues away down the Balkan corridor.

The Turkish shepherd shrugged his shoulders and raised his arms and then let them drop in an ample outward sweep that seemed to say, 'Well, there we are. They've gone', but shouted nothing, as though, like me, he felt too overcome for speech. Perhaps, like me, he was saddened in the thought that these beautiful and auspicious birds, the companions of the spring and the summer, were abandoning Europe.

I wondered where they were coming from. Judging by the direction, it would be Transylvania and Hungary, perhaps from Poland. They settle in summer as far north as the Baltic. The storks of Eastern Europe, western Russia and the Ukraine usually congregate more to the north and the east of the line these had been following. The Dobrudja is their meeting place. Then they follow the Black Sea coast to Constantinople, across the Bosphorus and along the shores of the Levant to Egypt, keeping in sight of land all the way. (Unlike the cranes: these, undaunted by the open sea, fly across the Greek archipelago and Crete and the empty expanse of the Libyan Sea until they strike the desert.) When the storks reach Egypt, some of them head south-east to the Arabian oases, but most of them continue southward, heading for the Equator and often beyond. A minority of them spread westwards as far as Lake Chad and the Cameroons: some have been found, on their return to Europe, with arrowheads embedded in them of a kind only made by the tribes of those regions. Here they must encounter the eastern-spreading fringe of their West Europe relations – from Alsace-Lorraine and Spain and Portugal – who cross into Africa at Gibraltar and fly southwards across Morocco and the Sahara. As all the storks of Europe cross by one of these two narrows – the Bosphorus and the Pillars of Hercules – the two bird communities might be conveniently classified as the Byzantine and the Herculean.

I don't know the exact date of the passing I had just witnessed, but it must have been well on in September. Nothing had indicated a change of season: no hint that the autumn equinox was not far off. Everything in that charred landscape still spoke of summer; everything, that is, except a slight truce from the wringing heat of solstice and a scarcely perceptible advance of sunset. Everyone had been remarking on the phenomenally long sojourn of the storks this year. The birds too must have been deluded by the amazing summer into thinking that warm days would never cease. What subconscious intimations of the shift of the earth's axis had told them that it was time to go? A drop in temperature, moisture in the air, an assembly of vapours, the warning formation of a distant cumulus, or a faint breeze from an ominous quarter? A syndrome of hints: Worthies away! The scene begins to cloud!

~

It was a great surprise, in the town of Kazanlik, after a long day's trudge, to be led by a boy in a café, with an insistence that was not to be withstood and as though it had been prearranged, to the house of a compatriot. Really, an Englishman, I asked the boy? *Da, da Gospodin! Anglitchanin!* And he was quite right, for there, under the trees in his garden, at the head of a table, with spectacles and thick white hair, sat my unmistakeable countryman, Mr Barnaby Crane. I displayed becoming confusion about bursting in on him at a meal. 'Don't be soft, lad,' Mr Crane said jovially. 'Sit down and have some supper'; so I did as I was told. Mr Crane, who was from the North Country, had settled and married in Bulgaria countless years before and sunk deep roots. So deep, indeed, that I noticed several times during the evening that his discourse, scanned by the leisurely click of the green tasselled string of amber beads in his right hand, was halted by the search for a word which would have come more readily to his lips in Bulgarian. His memories of England, dormant for many years and silted over by the decades of his Balkan sojourn, were becoming dim and effaced. Mild homesickness pervaded the Laurentian scenes of his youth: horse-buses in Manchester bristling with billycock hats, Sunday rambles by bicycle against a skyline of Satanic mills. He had come to Bulgaria in connection with the beginnings of the textile industry and was now, as he deserved to be, a loved and respected figure in Kazanlik. I felt, when we said goodbye, that he would never see Lancashire again. The Stara Planina and Karadja Dagh had stolen his heart away.

~

The entire valley is covered with rose bushes, hundreds of thousands of them, all despoiled now by the long summer and the fingers of rose-harvesters; for Kazanlik is one of the chief places in the world for attar of roses, that powerful distillation of rose oil which was so highly prized in the courts and harems of the Orient, especially in India and Persia. The deep crimson, yellow-centred Damascus rose, famous for the sweetness and pungency of its scent, is the favourite flower for attar, and armies of men and women toil in the valley gathering the petals, culling them soon after dawn, before the high sun can drain them of the dew and the perfume which the night hours have been storing up. Then in Kazanlik, these showers of petals are poured into enormous vats, the oil is collected and the grey slush of petals, stripped of colour and scent, is thrown away. The precious remainder, then, like Calvados in autumn in Normandy, is distilled through a battery of alembics and so concentrated in the essence which finally emerges that it takes over three thousand pounds of rose petals to produce a single pound of attar. The valuable elixir is then bottled in tiny gilt and cut-glass phials, a mere thread of attar to each, and sold, understandably, for enormous prices. The smell is captious, overpowering and a little cloying. The perfumes of Arabia that, in spite of their power, failed to chase the reek of Duncan's blood from the hands of Lady Macbeth, were probably exactly this. At the height of the rose harvest, everything in

Kazanlik smells of it. The valley is aswoon, and the petals, bursting out of their sacks on the carts and wagons in which they are piled, scatter the dusty roads with crimson like the lurching retreat to his cavern of a mortally wounded ogre.

Ahead to the north lay the Shipka Balkan, and I was soon climbing through woods of walnut and oak and beech, empty except for an occasional swineherd and a swarm of razor-thin pigs: dark hairy creatures rootling for the beech nuts and acorns which crackled underfoot. The trees died out and the bald and ragged side of the mountain soared steeply, scaled by the road which led to the pass in a succession of long loops that I bisected with scrambling short cuts, reaching, in the afternoon, a wooded ledge of the mountains, where, before my unbelieving eyes, stood a lesser version of the Cathedral of St Basil in Red Square: a cluster of tall and tapering onion domes covered with a glittering and fish-like reticulation of green and gold scales. On these twirling pinnacles gleamed a Russian cross with its three crossbars (the shortest and highest symbolizing the INRI label, and the lowest, placed diagonally against the shaft, the footrest). The monastic buildings gathered about this strange fane were dotted with solitary figures or little groups in those attitudes of rather sad listlessness that accompany penurious and unwanted leisure. Most of them were middle-aged or old; many walked with sticks; their features differed from the Bulgarian cast, and the snatches of Slav conversation contained a greater range of modulation and flexibility than is detectable in the vernacular. Their patched and threadbare clothes were worn with an attempt at self-respecting trimness. The only clerical figure among these lay monastics was a tall benevolent Rasputin with his habit caught in by a wide buckled belt and his fair bobbed hair hatted with a tall velvet cone adorned over the brow by a triple cross.

They were veterans and invalids, about two hundred of them.

They had subsisted here, on a pittance from their ex-enemies, ever since the disintegration of the Imperial Russian armies after the Bolshevik Revolution. One of them, an ex-artillery lieutenant who had served in Kolchak's* counter-revolutionary army, conducted me round the buildings. The church and monastery were built after the Russian victory over the Turks in the Russo-Turkish War of 1877–8. My guide, who spoke perfect French with a captivating Russian accent, explained the campaign over a map as though he had fought in it himself. He described the advance of the Russian armies across the Danube, drew with a stick the dispositions of Generals Skobeloff, Gourko, Prince Mirsky, and the Czarevitch – later Alexander III – and of Suleiman, Osman and Vessil Pashas. He recounted the siege and fall of Plevna, and, above all, after a murderous stalemate of many months, the terrible slaughter in the midwinter snows on the Shipka pass immediately above us. The words of Skobeloff's despatch at the end of the action, '*Na Shipke vseo spokoino*' – 'All quiet over Shipka' – became famous, and the phrase, to Russians and Bulgars alike – for Bulgarian volunteer battalions had played a brave part in the action – came to epitomize the whole war, which, at the Treaty of San Stefano after the Russian armies advanced to the walls of Constantinople, secured the liberation of Bulgaria from the Turks.

After looking at the rather new and ugly interior of the church, and at ikons from Russia studded with brilliants, we joined a group of veterans sitting round a samovar in a long grey room decorated with pictures of Czar Nicholas II, of Kolchak and Denikin, and of Moscow and St Petersburg, the Nevsky Prospekt under snow, the battles of Plevna and Shipka and the Crossing of the Beresina.

---

* Admiral Kolchak (1874–1920), supreme leader of the White Russian forces from 1918 until his execution by the Bolsheviks in 1920.

The conversation, in varying kinds of French for my benefit, revolved around their old regiments and past wars and especially those desperate White Russian campaigns in which they had nearly all taken part. The overt assumption of their drift was that the present phase was a transient one and the Soviet regime a temporary madness rife with the germs of its own dissolution. Another turn of the wheel would place Grand Duke Cyril* on the throne and set the double eagle fluttering once more over Peterhof and Tzarskoe Selo and the Winter Palace and translate them all, by magic, to honourable retirement in their homes in Kiev, Tamboff, Odessa and Ekaterinoslav. Deep sighs punctuated this talk, and sudden giveaway silences. Autumnal sadness filled the long room.

~

I met nobody else on the remainder of the road to the top except a few carts. Sturdy horses drew them and the shafts on either side of them were bridged by curious curved swingletrees which arched over the horses' withers in wooden semicircles. A treacherous nail in my right boot soon began to inflict pain; by the time I reached the pass, which is really not a pass at all as there is scarcely a dip in the line of the watershed, this had become so tormenting that I sat down under the huge lion that commemorates the battle and did my best with stones and a jackknife to locate and flatten this excruciating spike; one of my toes was raw and bleeding. This was unsuccessful, however, as when I tried my boot on again, the invisible nail felt not only longer and sharper, but, when I attempted to walk on it, red hot.

The famous battle had raged all round this windy saddle. Somewhere nearby a skilled geographer would have been able to

---

* Grand Duke Cyril Vladimirovich (1876–1938), grandson of Czar Alexander II, and controversial claimant to the Russian throne from 1924 until his death.

put his forefinger on some sharp stone on the precise edge of the watershed and know that, should a raindrop strike it and divide in half, the northern half-drop would in time flow into the Danube and eventually into the Black Sea, while its fellow, heading south downhill, would reach the Tunja and then the Maritza and at last drift through the wide Hebrus's mouth and become part of the Aegean and the Mediterranean seas.

The approach of dusk was beginning to blur the detail of the hollow worlds that glimmered with steadily waning light on either side of the pass. The descending night and the plight of my foot prompted a twinge of concern. I hobbled on through the twilight with my ears pricked for the welcome rumble of a cart. At last, an empty cart with two peasants on the bench bore down. It was driving in the right direction. The driver reined back in answer to my supplicating wave, and I asked if he was heading for Gabrovo. He was. I explained that I had a bad foot and demonstrated it by limping stagily for a few paces: could he give me a lift? The kalpacked rustic looked me up and down and then said: '*Kolko ban?*' Astonished, I asked him what he meant, though I understood perfectly well: 'how much money?' He repeated the question, grinning and rubbing the thumb and forefinger of an extended hand together, as though fumbling a dream banknote. Thinking he was joking, I said, '*Edin million*', and joyfully prepared to climb in. But I was stopped by the hand that held the whip and the question was repeated. I had plainly misinterpreted the grin. He proposed to give me a lift to Gabrovo for the equivalent of ten shillings. As I had only one pound left, I urged poverty, lameness and strangeness in these parts. The colloquy was curtailed by a negative click of the tongue and backward tilt of the head, and with a crack of his whip off he clattered into the night. Before I had recovered from astonishment at conduct so unprecedented on any of the roads of Europe, my ear was struck by the noise of another cart approaching. All was not lost! But a few minutes later the sound of wheels was dying away again after an almost identical exchange with another surly wagoner. (This passion to make money out of chance trivialities, like giving a pedestrian a lift in an empty cart, is a phenomenon I met several times in Bulgaria, but nowhere else in Europe, before or afterwards. One hears of cases in Italy. Such conduct in Greece, especially if it involved a stranger, let alone a lame and benighted one, would call down life-long shame.)

There was no question of spending the night in the pass, as a fast and biting wind was sweeping across it. There was neither shelter nor cover. It was as bleak as a desert. After walking a couple of miles I espied with joy a wayside house in the rising moonshine. My approach unleashed a frenzy of barking from a white sheepdog. As I reached the front door, the line of light went out under the shutters. I knocked on the door and the shutter, explaining myself in Bulgarian as lame as my foot. 'I am an English traveller, my foot is bad. There is a big cold wind (*gulemo studeno*). May I come in please?' I could hear whispers indoors where there had been talk before; then there was silence, except for the barking and snarling of this slavering hell-hound only a few precarious feet away. The repetition of my dismal litany gradually lost all conviction. At last when all hope had drained away, I lurched on northwards and downhill, swearing, comminating and shouting aloud, blinded with tears of fury and frustration. None of Nadejda's phrases seemed adequate to the occasion. This cursing and gesticulating figure might well have struck terror. But bewilderment was my chief emotion. What passion of xenophobia, predatoriness or timidity lurked in this horrible mountain range? Did they think I was a bandit or a murderer masquerading as a wandering foreign student and talking pidgin Bulgarian to corroborate his disguise? Or a djinn, an afreet, a demon, a werewolf or a vampire, ravening

in the same odd livery, or some other of the many wicked super-
natural denizens that infest the Balkan darkness?

After an hour's tormenting crawl through the windy moonlight,
I spied a gleam of light in a wide hollow to the left of the road.
The wind dropped as my track, sinking below the trajectory of
its flight, dipped into a quiet dell full of beech trees. At the end,
on the edge of the spinney, tall dark pyres smouldered and an
aromatic tang of woodsmoke hung on the air. Light radiated
from the doorway of a hut. It was cleverly woven of branches, a
leafy cave, and inside it, three satanic figures, their rags showing
a dusty black by the light of an oil dip, were sitting cross-legged
on a carpet of leaves and playing cards with an upturned sieve
for a table. They were charcoal burners. How different was the
welcome here! All three leapt up, led me to a place in their midst,
helped me off with my blood-filled boot, washed the damaged
foot with *slivovitz* and wrapped it in a clean handkerchief, then
plied me with *slivo* for internal use and then with bread and
cheese. Finally, after commiserating over my reverses, they made
me a leaf-bed of freshly cut branches and bade me goodnight as
they rolled over to sleep. One of them blew out the light and
went out into the moonbeams to see to the stoking and the
damping down, among the white-gashed sapling stumps of the
ravished wood, of their three great smouldering cones.

One of these Samaritans located the nail in my boot next
morning and cunningly hammered it flat by using an adze blade
as a combination of last and anvil. Axe blows rang through the
glade, interrupted every so often by the report of a falling tree
trunk. Billhooks lopped off the branches, and the dismembered
limbs were packed into place on the dark cones and heaped over
with ashes; sinister fumaroles of smoke leaked through the charcoal like a brittle volcano's surface about to erupt at a score of
places. Clambering up the sides of these smoking pyres and

poking at them with forks and staves, my black benefactors bore the aspect of stokers in hell. We waved goodbye and I climbed out of the glade up to the road and, after a long day of unwinding downhill, reached Gabrovo.

~

A long day of unwinding downhill. This is easily written and rightly succinct; because, unlike the southern flank of the Great Balkan range and the climb from Kazanlik, of which each detail remains clear, I can remember nothing whatever about it.

This brings up the whole question of piecing together things which have happened a number of years ago – twenty-nine in fact – and I ought to have tackled the whole question earlier on.

Bad luck dogged my notes and my sketches all through this journey. The first lot of diaries and papers was stolen in Munich. I started a fresh lot immediately, in German stiff-covered notebooks and drawing pads, and kept them up, at least the notebooks, until the end of the journey that these pages cover, and later on, in Greece. The sketches – rightly, as they were never much good – became scarcer and died out. The notebooks I had with me five years later, when the outbreak of war overtook me in High Moldavia, in the north of Rumania.

For the previous four years, this had been my base in Eastern Europe, and I had spent half my time there and half in the Greek islands, varied by one rather dull year's return to England, and by sojourns of varying length in Paris, the Île de France and Provence, and by the slow return train journeys across Europe (made slower still by halts to visit old friends in Vienna, Hungary and Transylvania). Obviously, I had little grasp of what the war entailed and still less prophetic flair, for when I set off for England in September 1939 to join the army, I left all my books and papers in this house in Moldavia. I had planned to return there when the war was over. But when the war ended, this house, like most of the places in this narrative, was out of bounds beyond the Iron Curtain. It had been smitten by fire and earthquake and its inhabitants scattered, imprisoned and driven from their homes – but, alas, not over the frontiers of Rumania into the free world.

The only tangible data that remain from my actual journey are two tattered maps and a thin pencil-line marking my itinerary, punctuated by a cross-bar for every overnight sojourn. These are largely, but not entirely, unnecessary, as during this walk I pored so often over the various stages of the journey and repeated the place-names that spanned it so often that I can reel them off, even today, almost without a break. The only other contemporary document to survive is the passport trustingly issued in Munich to replace the one which had been stolen. It fixes the date of each frontier crossing. This sparse calendar is augmented by the memory of my whereabouts on important days like Christmas, Easter, famous local saints' days publicly celebrated, and private anniversaries like family birthdays; still further by remembering where I was when I heard the news of some striking political event: the verdict of the Reichstag fire trial,* the June purge,† the February Revolution‡ in Vienna, the murder of Dollfuss.§ (It was a record year for assassinations.) In a

---

* The Reichstag Fire Trial (21 September–23 December 1933). The fire that broke out in the Berlin Reichstag on 27 February 1933 was blamed on both the Bolsheviks and the Nazis. To Hitler's fury, the High Court convicted only a single suspect, the (possibly insane) Marinus van der Lubbe.

† The June Purge (30 June–2 July 1934), the so-called 'Night of the Long Knives', in which Hitler eliminated the SR Brownshirts, as well as more liberal opponents.

‡ The so-called February Uprising in Austria (12–15 February 1934) saw factional fighting between socialist and conservative militia, at its fiercest in Vienna.

§ Engelbert Dollfuss (1892–1934), dictatorial Chancellor of Austria from 1932 until his assassination by Nazis on 25 July 1934. PLF had glimpsed him in procession in Vienna earlier in the year: a tiny man in a morning coat, 'hurrying to keep up'.

year when something new was happening to me nearly every day, either geographically, psychologically and often both, these sparse data help to narrow the field yet closer. Undated events can usually be located, by deduction, to within a week of the day when they must have occurred, sometimes even less.

All these dispersed fragments cohere in a jigsaw which is far from complete; but, by driving my memory back, by coercing and focussing it on one particular gap, I find that the missing pieces often slide to the surface and dovetail. Perhaps the fact that I have already recorded this particular tract of the past in a note-book, even though the records are lost, has helped to fix much of it several strata deep. Tones of voice, moods, lighting, details of landscape or costume, streets, castles, mountain ranges, warts, eyelashes, gold teeth, scars, smells, the arrangement of a room, a line of a song, the taste of food or drink tried for the first time, the name of the book left open on a bench, a paper headline or, quite often, some irrelevant object on sale in a shop window that I neither admired nor coveted, a bowler-hatted or trilby-shaded face under a lamp-post or in a bar that I never met or conversed with or wanted to, but merely observed – how distinct from the galaxy of Baudelairian passing strangers I longed to know, like the figure in *A une passante*! – come running or lounging or sidling out of the cobwebby dark that has been harbouring them for close on three decades. But there are some gaps that no feat of concentration can fill: the missing piece is lost for good.

There are plenty of these gaps. Gabrovo is one. I remember that it is a textile manufacturing town on a small scale – did somebody call it 'the Bulgarian Manchester?' – but I can't remember (though there must have been several there) a single factory chimney; or indeed, anything about it at all, except – and this is why it is odd: how did I get there, and who led me? – that I was leaning at dusk over a half-door, rather like that of a stable,

and the top half was open. It was in a back street sloping down
to a tree-reflecting river, with the mountains, which I had just
crossed, piling up behind. Here I leaned, talking to the occupant
of the room. She lay in bed, in the further corner of the room,
under a patchwork quilt, propped up on several pillows in a
long-sleeved white cotton nightgown with a wide collar, her long
fingers stroking a tabby cat that dozed on her lap. She was an
English woman married to a Bulgarian, and, like Mr Barnaby
Crane, from the North, but this time from Yorkshire, as her most
soft voice soon made clear. She was recovering from some infectious disease: hence my relegation to the threshold. Was it measles?
Or scarlet fever? I can't remember, any more than I can remember
who brought me there. She was called Betty and was in her early
twenties; her cheeks were hollow from illness and her eyes were
the palest blue, her fair hair was long and straight. She was as
pale as a water sprite or an etiolated Rossetti heroine. How very
peculiar it seemed, in the depths of the Balkans, to be listening
to these charming, faint Yorkshire syllables through the twilight.
We talked for hours, and exchanged brief autobiographies. She
was a farmer's daughter from a remote farm in the Dales, so far
from everywhere that in bad weather they were sometimes snowed
up and out of communication with the outside world for a week
or a fortnight on end. She seemed eager for talk. 'You get a bit
lonely like, only talking Bulgarian for months on end, and I
haven't learnt it properly yet.' Her father sounded a splendid
chap: everyone was fond of him for miles around: a great one
for racing whippets, expeditions on foot to Wensleydale and
Swaledale and Fountains Abbey with other children. I have
forgotten how she met her husband (who was away for a few
days in Sofia). I think he had been studying the textile industry
in the nearest town. Her father was opposed to the marriage at
first, but he gave in in the end; and here they were. She liked

the Bulgarians; though, she said, they were a funny race: terribly superstitious. An animal terror of illness of any kind haunted them, not only infectious ones.

She had fallen ill twice since settling in Gabrovo, and had felt an outcast both times: shunned, feared and sent to Coventry. 'They're a daft lot.' Her laugh, coming faint and tired through the half-light, was very attractive, and her conversation, especially about the rainy and misty world she came from, sent sudden waves of homesickness rolling through the darkening room. One by one the details of this interior faded from view: the bookcase with *Black Beauty, Pears Encyclopaedia, Jock of the Bushveld, Chatterbox, Precious Bane, Angel Pavement* and Rupert Brooke's collected verse; the upright piano, the sewing machine, the framed print of York Minster, the patchwork quilt and the sleeping tabby cat, until all that remained was the pallor of her nightgown and face and hair and the sound of our voices. It was quite dark when somebody came to lead me back to the lights of Gabrovo. I could just discern the valedictory flutter of a white-sleeved arm raised as she waved goodbye. I returned to the town under the wheeling bats and oblivion closes the scene.

⁓

The same forgetfulness covers the next day's journey and the little town of Dranovo; a blurred pencilled cross on the tattered map, drawn there nearly three decades ago, indicates that I must have spent a night there. The view suddenly clears again in the late afternoon of what must have been the next day as I rounded a turn under a steep cliff. Between this sharp drop in the roll of the mountains and a tall monolithic pinnacle of rock on the other side of a road, and enclosing the view like something seen through a giant keyhole, the town of Tirnovo a couple of miles ahead was wedged. It rose from a canyon like an emanation, a sharp flight of houses hovering in ascending waves along the lip of a precipice which swung airily away and then back again in three quarters of a circle. The rock face, as the town gained height, fell beneath it into a chasm of organ-fluted rock, all stressed and heavy with shadow, to the sinuous bend of the river Yantra. The tiled roofs of this winged insurrection of houses were plumed by belfries and trees, and the highest rocks at the farthest point of this all-but amphitheatre, after the town had died away, were scattered with churches. The airy town jutted with oriental balconies craning on diagonal beams above the gulf, and hundreds of windowpanes threw back the evening sun in tiers of square flaming sequins, as though fires were raging within.

I understood Nadejda's enthusiasm at once. My own grew with every advancing step and overflowed into excitement when I found myself climbing the long, narrow staircase of a main street winding endlessly upwards. Vines, heavy with grapes, coiled over the doorways and under the jut of the wide eaves and leaned out across the flags and the cobbles on trellises. The lanes that branched off to the right on the valley side, where the almost Tudor-looking upper storeys of timber and plaster thrust forward as though striving to merge balconies with the opposite houses, ended like rocky diving-boards in the sky. Moccasins, scarlet sashes and sheepskin hats crowded the steps and intermingled with flocks, donkeys and mules, climbing and descending the steep thoroughfare like the traffic of Jacob's ladder. An enormous priest with a spiralling beard was in difficulties with his horse; he clutched his umbrella and the reins, and the slithering and rearing of his mount on the slippery stones had jolted his cylinder hat awry and shaken his bun loose down his back in a long flapperish coil, nearly capsizing the tray of earthenware yaourt jars balanced on the head of a passing dairyman.

At one point all this coming and going of humans and livestock was effectively dammed by a long wagon slanting across the street outside a wine shop. This cart was a sort of rough wooden trough on wheels and inside it two men, naked to the thighs, were treading and stamping in a tangled slush of grapes. Others were constantly tipping in fresh loads and catching the streams of juice that gushed from a tap in tin cans which they carried indoors and poured into the waiting barrels and jars. A little further on, men in blood-stained aprons were busy with knives and cleavers on the carcase of a pig whose death throes, not long before, must have deafened the neighbourhood. A rather sinister little boy, squatting among the scarlet cobbles and the cats and the flies, had been given the intestines as a task or a toy. With cheeks expanded, he was inflating one: each puff blew up another sinuous length of gut until the whole thing was buoyantly uncoiled like the serpent in the band of an old-fashioned village choir. From the side lanes nearly horizontal stripes of mealy evening sunlight slashed across all this hubbub. There are moments (and this was one) when hill towns in the Balkans seem as remote as Tibet.

A cloud slightly dimmed all these details. I had only the equivalent in leva of a few shillings in my pocket, and my boots, though no longer the instruments of torture they had been in the Shipka pass, were coming to bits. I had written from Plovdiv giving Tirnovo as the next address for money to be sent from England, several pounds this time, as I had not sent an address since Sofia. I used to try and let these weekly pounds mount up as long as possible, in order to get them all in one dollop, rather than hang about each time in some town chosen at random on the map in the hopes that it would coincide with my vaguely forecast itinerary. Better by far to wait till the registered envelope on the ledge of the poste restante yielded three or four of those brown pound notes – this had seemed, before setting out, the most sensible way of transferring these small sums, and so it proved. (Not once during this entire journey, did any ever go astray.) The thin calligraphic and richly crinkling white tissue of a fiver was a larger sum that had to be changed all at once and evaporated all the quicker, so it was better to spin out each note as far as it would go before turning another into guilders, marks, schillings, pengos, leis or levas – but not in the banks of Rumania or Bulgaria; for the black market rate, which any grocer or baker or street corner money changer would supply, was almost double the official one. It was a charitable bank clerk who, seeing me gullibly on the brink of a huge financial blunder, first whispered this secret to me across the counter. For somebody travelling as modestly as I was – I enjoyed smoking but could (how improbable it now seems) do without it painlessly, and drink (equally enjoyed and equally dispensable and equally incredibly so today) – life cost almost nothing. It was getting too late to sleep out of doors much longer – no more rolling up under a tree or a bridge – but the humble quarters I haunted were anything but dear, and how often I seemed to end up under some friendly roof scot free! The pound, before the war, was worth three times its value nowadays, perhaps more. Add to this the amazing cheapness of life in the Balkans then – a normal traveller could live comfortably on three or four shillings a day and one could eat a monster meal of many courses for sixpence – and it will be seen that my plight, living at a cost not far removed from that of a mediaeval palmer, was not nearly as much to be pitied as it sounds. Getting by on a pound a week had been something of a pinch in Western and Central Europe, even at my low level; but here, a strange and very relative sort of plenty showered over me, a queer cornucopia.

But it was on the point, at this very moment, of drying up. Only about two shillings remained, and so recent had been my

letter asking for more, that the delay of Bulgarian postage threatened a lean wait. But it was not only this looming shortage and
the state of my boots that weighed on me tonight. I kept thinking
of Plovdiv and the kindness and fun of Nadejda. There had been
something a bit sad about Mr Crane's expatriate contentment.
The churlishness of the inhabitants and the wagoners of the
Shipka pass, trivial enough, had left a taint of gloom behind and
something rueful and lowering had infected the soft-voiced charm
of the White Russians in the monastery. The twilight talk with
the ailing Yorkshire woman in Gabrovo was weighted with
unavowed distress. The defection of the storks, more than
anything, spelled a season's end. The days were still bright and
summery but there was a thread of autumnal pallor in their gold.
The sum of all these minor considerations united into a general
depression and robbed my step, as I climbed that romantic
thoroughfare, of some of its wonted lightness.

I bought half a loaf of warm bread at a baker's and went into
a grocer's shop to buy a slice of that delicious white goat's cheese
they call *siriné*, and another of the yellow kind called *kashkaval*.
(I suppose it is the same as the Italian *caciocavallo* – 'horseback
cheese', though whether the Bulgar word is a slavicization of the
Italian, or the other way about, I don't know. Instinct says the
former, but it is often wrong.) My plan was to carry this hoard
off to some quiet corner, slice up a couple of onions in my
rucksack with my huge dagger, sprinkle them with red pepper
from a twist of peppercorn, and then sleep somewhere in the
lee of one of the spurs outside the town, establishing a sort of
rocky lair until my ship came home. The lights of the town were
beginning to twinkle in every window, the sun had set, and the
prospect of this St Jerome-like hermitage loomed rather bleakly,
especially compared to the gleaming interior of the grocer's: the
barrels of anchovies, the hanging flitches, the lamplight refracting

a battery of bottles, the dried figs impaled on skewers of bamboo, the kegs and crates and jars and the pyramids of wares from Germany and Austria, the scarlet bacon slicer with its flashing disc of blade, the huge cheeses and the cubistic mounds of halva. It glowed like Aladdin's cave.

But the shop was empty. A boy of about my own age who had been sitting reading a book on the doorstep got up and followed me in. Where was I from? Whither bound? Cheerful alacrity and a friendly glance accompanied these questions. When we got bogged down linguistically, which happened as soon as my shallow hoard of Bulgarian gave out, we shifted to German, which he spoke well, with a queer Slav accent. We were soon perched on the edge of barrels, clinking *slivo* glasses and exchanging autobiographies. Gatcho was the grocer's son, and he was looking after the shop while his father was at some ex-officers' anniversary celebration, a reunion of old comrades from the Balkan wars. Gatcho, rather prosaically, was on holiday in his home town from the Höhere Handelsschule in Varna; he had gone there after finishing his studies at the Tirnovo gymnasium, to prepare himself for a job in a thriving export-import business in Sofia owned by his great-uncle. This meant, perhaps, travel, seeing somewhere, anywhere, outside Bulgaria: Budapest, Vienna, Munich, Paris perhaps. Did I know these towns? Cologne, Düsseldorf, Rotterdam? It was my moment, and I waded in. Within an hour, my kit was dumped in his brother's room (who was away doing his military service in Berkovitza, *der arme Kerl*)* and half an hour later I was sitting in a lamp-lit room behind the shop with Gatcho and his two little sisters, attacking a delicious stew cooked by Gatcho's bulky and cheerful mother and learning about Bulgarian poetry, Hristo Boteff, the national bard,

* The poor fellow.

and Ivan Vasoff ('The Bulgarian Wordsworth'). Everything had changed. No more thoughts of the cold hill's side.

I had struck lucky by going into the grocer's shop. There was a bed, and, as often as not, a meal with Gatcho's family. Also, one of his uncles was the best cobbler in Tirnovo. Gatcho carried off my battered and disintegrating boots and next day they were delivered back, scot free, looking brand new, the heels armed with miniature horseshoes, the soles a-glitter with businesslike studs that struck sparks from the worn cobbles and flagstones of Tirnovo. But they were better saved for the highways and mountains: gym shoes were the wear for these vertiginous lanes. Gatcho's brother's little room with an ikon to St Nicholas in the corner was a godsend. I lay there on the bed reading for hours every day, or squatting or lying prone – there was just room for it – on the minute balcony, propped on my elbows, and laboriously bringing my journal up to date.

Those battered stiff-covered notebooks an inch thick in which I scribbled away so industriously – how I wish I had them at this very moment, to equip these sentences of memory with the sharp edge of immediate recording. But fragments remain nevertheless: the recession of the surrounding mountains and the twists of the river below and, closer by, the swoop of walls piling up one side, the sharp subsidence of housetops on the other, falling away below with the abruptness of the storeys of a house of cards. The tiles of many of them were bushy with empty nests waiting, like summer villas on modish coasts, for the spring return of their tenants. (Had they settled by now, I remember thinking, or were they still labouring southwards with the Equator already behind them, peering down at the forests and the great lazy rivers, swerving to avoid a hut-sprinkled clearing that recalled the whirr of arrows, pushing on till a disposition of roofs, the remembered geometry of woods and habitations and streams, and the final corroboration, on closer scrutiny, of last winter's nests, told them that they were home? How long had the birds been shuttling like this between the two? How many stork-generations? The town had been inhabited a long time. It had been the imperial capital of the second Bulgarian empire in the twelfth century, but a town had thriven there much earlier. What about that horseman carved in relief on the rock face outside the town, dating probably from Alexandrian times? There must have been dwellings for them to perch on then; only twelve hundred eggs ago and more in the direct line. In its European stage alone, a dozen religions had ousted each other, a score of empires had soared and crumbled and a hundred wars been waged under the itinerary of these unheeding migrants. A formidable tenure! Gatcho's indoctrination about the history of his town had not been falling on deaf ears.)

Gatcho turned out to be a kind and a timely friend. He was a moody person, cheerful, excited and extrovert one moment, silent and brooding the next to a degree that rather intimidated his family; but not, fortunately, with me. There was a relaxed and holiday feeling about Tirnovo. I was woken up on the first morning by the trundling of empty barrels downhill with a noise like thunder. Peering from the balcony, I was just in time to see one break loose from its trundle and bounce from step to step like a runaway animal, frightening donkeys, capsizing fruit stalls and only just dodged in time by the citizens, and making a din that sounded like the fall of Jericho.

This further reminder of the vintage season was followed up by a bicycle trip to a farm a few miles away belonging to yet another relation of Gatcho's, for the wine pressing. The place was an old Turkish *tchiflik*, the dwelling of some vanished bey, surrounded by fields and vineyards and shaded by tremendous plane trees and a cool line of water-betokening poplars. Tufts of down from the withered thistles drifted in the air and skimmed across the surface of the stream. About fifty people were assembled here, and in the centre three men, like the ones I had seen the night before, unmoccasined, unthonged and unswaddled, were treading bare-legged and spattered round a tremendous shallow tub. Everyone took his turn, and the feeling of the grapes exploding and squelching underfoot – a feeling which I experienced again, whenever I got a chance, several times in Greece and Crete – was amazing. The stuff seethed round our ankles and almost up to the knees. It was a festive gathering. The new grape-must was started and gallons of the old were swallowed from demijohns. Kebabs smoked on their long skewers, and the treaders with hands on each other's shoulders thumped the dust, soggy now with dropped grapes and spilt wine, in an unsteady and purple-shanked dance to the tune of a violin and a curious oval, thick-necked stringed instrument roughly hewn out of a single piece of wood, like a Neolithic fiddle, held beneath the chin or propped upright before the player's body, and scraped by a short semicircular bow. (They called it a *tzigulka* or a *gadulka*; it was kin to the Montenegrin *gûzla*, as I later learnt, and a poor relation of the Cretan *lyra*.) Finally everyone settled on red and yellow rugs spread underneath a giant plane tree whose lower limbs were a-dangle, where they swung close to the ground, with the wooden flasks and knapsacks of the guests, for more eating and drinking and singing. Everything smelt of crushed grapes and was sticky to touch; flies, wasps and menacing brown and orange hornets abounded, but even this zooming tangle failed to blight the hilarity of the gathering or to ruffle the heavy slumbers that followed, as, one by one, we slanted wilting from our cross-legged session and snored where we lay.

When I awoke among the coiling roots, I couldn't make out where I was. All had changed. Long shadows were streaming down the glade. Men, shod and hosed once more, but with their gait and their manoeuvring hindered by a giveaway clumsiness, were exhorting beasts in the middle distance and loading them with wineskins like the damp and bloated phantoms of goats, squelching and bald, for they were inside-out, with the lashed stumps of their legs distended in rigid gestures. There were many moths. Gatcho was shaking my shoulder. If we didn't get back to Tirnovo, we would be late for a students' party. We found our bikes and wobbled back to the town through the dusty and twilit vineyards.

This particular season, once more, seemed to be crowded with holidays and parties and religious feasts, which kept us up late and beset the mornings with headaches. Gatcho demonstrated a way of finding out if the next day was going to be a feast day, by a method about as reliable as predicting a stranger's arrival by tea leaves. He found my sheepskin kalpack among the heaped-up chattels on my bed; some dormant sense of ridicule had prevented me from wearing it for the last week or two, possibly some teasing comment of Nadejda's. He pounced on it with glee, crying, 'Let's see whether tomorrow is a *prazdnik* – a feast – then lifted it above his head and flung it on the floor, which it struck with a dull thud. His brows knitted with vexation. He repeated it several times. If the hat hit the boards fair and square, he explained, it would give a loud report like the explosion of a paper bag. 'There we are,' he said. 'All's well. *Prazdnik* tomorrow.' And so it was.

In the small hours of one of these celebrations, we found ourselves with half a dozen of the blades of Tirnovo in a hut on the outskirts of the town, smoking hashish. The dried and powdered leaves were packed into the tube of a cigarette paper from which deft fingers had laboriously prodded the tobacco. Lit, and then solemnly passed from hand to hand until the clouds of smoke enveloped us with a sweetish vegetable reek, it brought on a faint dizziness and a gregarious onslaught of helpless laughter. The slightest word or gesture was enough to send us off into fresh paroxysms until we fought for breath and our cheeks were wet with tears. Bulgaria, it appeared, was one of the richest natural hashish gardens in the world. *Cannabis indica* thrives in embarrassing abundance. Its cultivation, which is scarcely necessary, and its smoking, my companions explained between puffs, were strictly forbidden: '*Mnogo zabraneno.* Ha! Ha! Ha!' But the ban seemed about as effective as legislation against cow parsley or nettles. Regular smokers were few. It only came into play as an occasional lark. I longed for the opportunity to say 'the party went with a bhang!' The lack of opportunity to say so, however, didn't stop me saying it, and dissolving in transports of hilarity at my own wit.

This sojourn in Tirnovo, already enjoyable enough, took a still better turn with the arrival of the money. There, at the poste restante counter after a couple of days, was the anxiously awaited registered letter in its blue-crossed canvas oblong and – how far away it seemed in space and time and mood! – its Holland Park postmark; and inside, better still, the exciting accumulation of pound notes, still new and crisp. The repayment of some of Gatcho's hospitality, a clear route to the Black Sea, a new shirt, a couple of pairs of socks, another notebook, papers, pencils, a rubber, cigarettes, tobacco, and a cake of soap to replace the thin wafer I had been husbanding, a new toothbrush, meals, wine, *slivo* – luxury in fact. I walked back to Gatcho's father's grocery on air.

Thanks to all the festivities, three days had passed and the churches which were the pretext for this wide northern sweep in my itinerary were still unseen. Stocking up with cheese, salami and sardines from the rich paternal counter, we set off in the late morning. The ridge on which the town was built continued climbing until the houses thinned out and dropped away, and swept in a curve to the hill where all the churches I had descried from the road before reaching Tirnovo were gathered. The remains of battlemented walls girt this almost inviolable rock and a Turkish bridge connected it to the ridge. From the windy raft of the hilltop, the rock face fell steeply into the valley, in some places as straight as a curtain. At one point on the rim of this precipice captives and malefactors used to be hurled, and from here one could see the round solitary tower in which Baldwin of Flanders, one of the four Frankish emperors of Constantinople during that strange Western rule that followed the capture of Byzantium at the Fourth Crusade, taken prisoner by the Bulgarian czar, had languished for many years and died.

The czars of the second Bulgarian empire, the Asens (possibly of Vlach origin), whose stone mementoes covered this rocky hill, were a fierce and drastic dynasty. Imitators and rivals of Byzantium, these Peters and Ivans and Androniks and Kaloyans are as hard to imagine or to bring to life – so scarce are the records and so formal the chronicles that commemorate their treacheries, magnanimities, massacres and conquests – as the frescoed figures that smothered the walls of all the churches and monasteries, many half ruinous now, with which they so prodigally scattered the surrounding heights. Only one of these monasteries was still inhabited, and this one by a little community of nuns. One of them, a pale pretty girl in a black habit and a black pillbox hat covered with a black kerchief knotted under the chin, timidly offered us coffee and a spoonful of jam in a whitewashed guest room.

We wandered from church to church. In some of them, every available inch of wall was a painted bible scene or a martyrdom. We saw pale kings and princes too, and pale warriors, splendidly dressed in the robes and the armour of those dim courts and scarcely conjecturable wars. Yet the deeds of one of these shadowy twelfth-century czars, Peter Asen II, who spread the frontiers of the Bulgarian state westwards from the shores of the Black Sea clean across the Balkan peninsula to the Adriatic and in the south as far as the Aegean, have left a legacy of unease in Bulgaria, a dream of vanished empire, which has haunted the minds of Bulgarians ever since. This irredentism is, with the Orthodox Church, the only thing to survive from ancient Bulgaria throughout the all-destroying catalepsy of Turkish occupation. This blow, scattering the crowns and sceptres, the czars and princesses and the furred and brocaded boyars, fell on Tirnovo in 1393, sixty years before the capture of Byzantium extinguished the Christian empires and kingdoms of eastern Europe for several centuries. Bulgaria was the first to be subdued by the Turks and almost the last to be liberated.

How the Bulgars hated the Byzantines, just as their descendants abominate the modern Greeks today – and how abundantly the hatred is returned! With what relish, in the Church of the Forty Martyrs, Gatcho translated the inscriptions commemorating the victory of Ivan Asen over the Byzantine host and the capture of Theodore Comnene! The hatred is epitomized on either side by the act of one Byzantine emperor, Basil the Bulgar-slayer, who totally blinded a captured Bulgarian army of ten thousand men, leaving a single eye to each hundredth soldier so that the rest might grope their way home to the czar: a spectacle so atrocious that the czar, when the pathetic procession arrived, died of grief and shock. This dark mediaeval deed is still a source of sombre pride to fierce rustic enemies of Bulgaria in Greece and, to judge by history, the Bulgars have been attempting to redress the balance ever since. For one reason or another, the Bulgars have always detested all their neighbours. They have their hate to keep them warm.

For hours we loitered in the vaulted and painted interiors, gazing at the resplendent walls and craning our necks to peer into the pictorial vaults and cupolas and domes. In one of them Gatcho pointed out a column inserted there by its Asen founder, adorned by an inscription of the Khan Omurtag, an early ruler of Bulgaria in the ninth century. It came from a time before Czar Boris adopted Christianity and made it the religion of the state: a venerable relic of the years when the Bulgars, an Asiatic horde of pagan, shamanistic, fur-hatted mongoloid horsemen from beyond the Volga, first irrupted into the country, conquered and ruled it and, after bestowing their name upon it, were swallowed up by the milder Slavs who had settled there two or three centuries earlier. The rough sounds of their Asiatic tongue, probably akin to the Ugro-Finnish-Turanian branch of the Ural-Altaic, were drowned by the softer Slavonic syllables of the surrounding population and finally lost. The Bulgarian race had emerged with the Czar Krum of the first Bulgarian empire, still of the harsh conquering stock, and his shaggy hierarchy of landowning boyars. Half a century later Czar Boris became a Christian, and the great ruler Simeon I extended and consolidated the empire, and the never-ending strife with Byzantium began.

The Bulgarian conversion was to leave a lasting stamp on eastern Christendom and the whole Slav world except Poland, Bohemia, Moravia, Slovenia and Croatia, which received the Christian message via the Catholic West with Latin as the liturgical tongue. But the Christianity that SS Cyril and Methodius brought to Bulgaria – and their adaptation of Greek letters to accommodate muffled Slav vowels (and the *j* and the *sh* and the *sht* sounds, unknown to the Greeks) – gave birth to the Cyrillic script which became the alphabet of Bulgaria, Serbia, Russia, and, until it was reformed in the last century, even of Latin (though Orthodox) Rumania. Thus Old Slavonic, a strictly liturgical language closer to Bulgarian than to any other branch of the Slav language group, became the religious lingua franca of all Slav Orthodox (until nationalism replaced it piecemeal with local vernaculars), just as Latin became the universal liturgical language of western Christendom.

Examples of this beautiful lettering, in blurred and disintegrating calligraphy, accompanied the pictures of the kings and saints on the surrounding pillars and walls in complex epigraphs, and was inscribed on their giveaway scrolls, fulfilling the role of caption balloons in comic strips by setting forth their key utterances in the hands of stylites and martyrs. As we disentangled them, and as Gatcho unfolded their significances in his urgent German, the prophets and paladins and anchorites and holy athletes and headsmen stared back at us through ten thousand unblinking eyes. Odd to think of this battered casket a few years before Crécy. Then it was new and the interior still spun with a web of scaffolding, ladders and sunbeams, in which the spiderlike monks were suspended under the half-blank arcs and hemispheres, pounding cinnabar for a burning fiery furnace or the destruction of Sodom and mixing whites of egg for the yet more spidery hands of their celestial sitters, all raised in benediction or warning or rebuke. Fresh from the quarry, the flagstones underneath them would have been littered with eggshells as if a multitude of chickens had just hatched out before legging it.

The dim light of this vaulted world of interlocking haloes grew dimmer still. Far too dim, in fact, for that hour of the afternoon. The sky outlined in the archway at the end of our last church had turned a peculiar colour. We saw, as we emerged, that it was covered by an electric blue-green lid from horizon to horizon. Shadows were dulled and the air was heavy and windless, but along the canyon below – and it looked almost level with our high vantage point in the amphitheatre of hills – a threatening and solid line of clouds was trooping towards us on its own private breeze like a procession of purple boxing gloves, swelling, as they approached, to the size of bagpipes, wineskins, cattle, a herd of elephants, a school of whales until the sky was filled overhead as though by the huge, sagging roof of a dark and many-poled marquee on the point of collapse.

Below us, along the twisting course of the Yantra, the motionless trees began to twirl like shaken mops. Raging puffs of dust swelled to the height of elm trees, tiny figures far below scuttled for shelter and suddenly, with a roar, the wind smote us as though it would send us spinning backwards into the frescoes and tear to bits the ancient church in whose porch we were sheltering. With a hiss the dusty, ruin-cumbered hill all round was instantaneously leopard-spotted with giant black raindrops, a rash which in another second cohered in a universal moving glitter, then into a hundred dancing puddles and sudden rushing khaki rivers. In a few moments the raindrops turned to hail: the pellets as big as blackcurrants and gooseberries which bounded and ricocheted among the rocks and rattled on the Slavo-Byzantine tiles overhead with a din like machine-gun fire. Then they vanished and a steady curtain of perpendicular rain spirited us into a submarine region. '*Regen*,' Gatcho had uttered in an awed voice, when the first drops had fallen, and '*Hagel!*' with the hail; truthfully enough; and, as the first lightning flash forked through the watery air with a simultaneous splitting crash of thunder which boomed and volleyed along the gorges and grumbled echoing in the church behind us, '*Donner und blitzen!*'

I suppose it must have rained once or twice that summer and autumn, but I can't remember it. My impression remains one of endless dry weather and burning sunlight, almost of drought; certainly nothing to compare with this apocalyptic storm. Deafened by those salvoes of thunderclaps, we sat under the twelfth-century archway of the church porch peering into the grey downpour, listening to the swish of its descent, the gurgling of the runnels everywhere, and the clash of pebbles. Each flash of lightning brought us a shuddering vision of the town, the valleys and the mountains in a strangely focussed close-up that defied distance and dimension. We felt isolated and marooned among the ruins of this hilltop, as though the rest of the world were drowned; or rather, we decided, finishing our picnic, passing the wine bottle to and fro and lighting our cigarettes as we peered into the untimely twilight of falling water, as though we were deep sea divers exploring a submerged cathedral or a cave of coral on a pinnacle of the ocean's floor – or did the domes and cupolas compose a diving bell? – while fleets above our head were smashing each other to bits at point-blank range: Lepanto, Trafalgar, Navarino, Jutland. We imagined, the slow blur sliding past us into the chasm, a flagship foundering heavy with cannon and treasure and drowned men – some of them, if the battle were early enough, still chained to their benches among a geometric chaos of oars – her spiral journey plumed with twining gyres of silver bubbles and froth.

Or suppose this hill were Mount Ararat, as in the many frescoed floods on narthex walls, and the rest of the world were lost in this second flood, and only this sacred summit, with its two denizens spared – the waterline halting at the battlement's foot? Yes, but what about the repopulation afterwards? After a pause for this baleful thought to take root, we turned to each other simultaneously and said with an identical note of accusation, '*Schade, dass du nicht ein Mädel bist.*'* The fact that neither of us was a girl condemned the race to extinction. What about mermaids, Gatcho suggested, uncorking a second bottle with a pop; suppose a beautiful shoal should slither ashore with their harps and settle all round us in a watery harem? Ah, but how to

---

* 'What a shame you're not a girl.'

tackle them, lay siege to those scaly and inviolate loins? Surely there were some with double tails, like divided skirts? Were they viviparous or oviparous? And what would the offspring be? Human to the knee? Then laminations to the calf and, with our granddaughters, to the ankle. But given long life and unfaltering vigour – surely this would not be denied us – there was hope. Perhaps some great-granddaughter would approach our twin death-beds on cautious fin-tips and proudly display to our old eyes the longed-for toenails on their squealing burdens, a boy for Gatcho and a girl for me, or vice versa: and we would breathe our last in the knowledge that we had set mankind on its feet again: a beautiful amphibian brood of subnereids and crypto-tritons with nothing to betray an aquatic streak except, perhaps, a giveaway but not unbecoming greenish light in their blond locks: skilled cliff-scalers, anglers and harpists, living – as no ark had rescued the world's animals or its tree-dwelling birds – on a healthy diet of gulls' eggs and their own distant kinsfolk of the deep.

With as little warning as its outbreak, the storm stopped. The lash of the falling water was hushed, and the veil lifted. The clouds, threadbare and empty now, fell to pieces and fluttered away in tatters across a laundered and peaceful sky of turquoise. All was changed, the sharp faceted mountain ranges had taken a long stride forwards, the roofs and walls of the town below flashed the slanting sunlight back, the windowpanes kindled, and diaphanous belfries rose. Washed clean by the long downpour, hundreds of temporary brooks swished downhill to join the swollen Yantra. The summer's monochrome had gone under a winding garland of steam. These curling vapours turned the clumps of trees, for a quickly dwindling moment, into Mesozoic spinneys. Dun-coloured slants of ploughland were deep chocolate now, the vineyards a stormy green, the rocks and loose stones that the rains had scattered were multicoloured nuggets and polyhedra and pyramids of gleaming mineral. The bushes and flowers and herbs had shaken off a long trance: a confusion of scents, stifled since spring by the dry months, roved the air. The trees were made of metal, the glittering leaves were wired to them with silver, and across the canyon, like a Hispano-mauresque archway in a circle which was all but complete, hung a rainbow of sufficient solidity and brilliance to make the boldest and least circumspect of painters flinch.

Perhaps it was an illusion that the stripping of the rain had altered the resonance of these ravines and sharpened their echo. The revival of each sound – a bell round the neck of a goat or hung in a tower, a bleat, a bray or the voice of a herdsman ricocheting up from the chasm – sent up a clearer note. As we returned, a prismatic property in the air, like a million suspended needlepoints of water, cast a deceptive spell of transparency on this post-diluvian landscape, peopling the gleaming slopes with diamond donkeys and goats chipped out of crystal. The lane to the perspicuous town was a circling turmoil of glass dogs, drunk on mixed smells.

~

As in Plovdiv, the social hub of Tirnovo was an open-air restaurant-bar and dance-floor combined, a circle of cement surrounded by tables and tired acacias on a jut of the cliff on which the town was built, so that from the railing at the edge one could peer down at the lower world through swooping layers of kestrels and swifts and pigeons. But, unlike the more metropolitan Plovdiv, there were seldom any girls. A few shopkeepers and countrymen who had come into market were here, but mainly the dashing young men of the town, the older students of the gymnasium and groups of young officers in their white Russian shirts, red-banded caps and spurs, nursing their tasselled and twirly-hilted sabres, as they sat over their minute coffees or their *slivo*, listening to trim military tangoes and foxtrots. I used to write my diary here in the late afternoon, or to read, sometimes haltingly piecing out the text of Vasil Levsky or Ivan Vasoff* while Gatcho slowly read their poems aloud, or expounding to him my very immature ideas on English literature. The only authors he had heard of were the same ones who seemed to have gained a unique foothold throughout Central Europe, in German translation or Tauchnitz: Dickens, Wilde and H. G. Wells, then, after a gap, Galsworthy, Somerset Maugham, Charles Morgan and, rather surprisingly, Rosamond Lehmann. Their bugbear, because of *Arms and the Man*, was Bernard Shaw.

Suddenly, one evening, the mild hum of talk was interrupted by a shot from the entrance. We saw the nearest tables rise and cluster excitedly round a paper-seller who was bearing his wares ecstatically. The band stopped and everybody joined the group. A student I knew was reading out loud from the columns under the giant headlines in tones of breathless glee. Intent, beaming faces surrounded him, and now and then one or other of his listeners interrupted him with a cheer or an incredulous admiring laugh until hushed by the rest so that the reading might continue. Mouths were agog, eyes opened wider and the glow expanded unmistakeably as the eager cataract of syllables flowed on. What had happened? I could only pick up a word here and there: Serbski Kral, attentat, Marseilles, Frantzuski, Trianon, Malko Entente, Makedonski again and again. When the page was finished, a great cheer went up and everybody was talking and laughing and stamping, hugging and kissing their neighbours and thumping each other between the shoulder blades. At last I managed to ask

---

* Vasil Levsky (1837–73) and Ivan Vasoff (1850–1921) were celebrated Bulgarian revolutionaries against Ottoman rule.

Gatcho what had happened. His face shining with delight and grinning widely, he said, '*Man hat den serbischen König getötet! Heute! In Frankreich! Und es war ein Bulgare, der hat ihn umgebracht!*' 'They've killed the Serbian King! Today, in France! And it was a Bulgar that did him in!'

In disjointed fragments when I could extract him from the hubbub, I learnt that King Alexander of Yugoslavia* had arrived in Marseilles that morning on a state visit to France. Louis Barthou, the Foreign Minister and thus, ex officio, his partner in the Little Entente† and the Treaties of Trianon and Neuilly, which had reduced the frontiers of Bulgaria after the war, had received him. During the ceremonial procession from the quay an assassin had sprung from the crowd toward the open car and emptied his revolver into the two passengers, killing them both. And as though this were not good news enough, the assassin was a Bulgarian, a Macedonian; it is true that he was killed by the police on the spot, but what a deed! (There was a rumour in the papers later that the assassin was not a Bulgarian at all, but a member of the Ustasha, the westward-looking and Catholic separatist group in Croatia, bitterly opposed to the inclusion of their province in the new and more backward Balkan kingdom of Yugoslavia – a rumour which reduced the Bulgarians to fury; after all, one of them told me with indignation, the assassin had *svoboda ili smert* tattooed on his arm – Liberty or Death, the old motto of the Macedonian Revolutionary Committee. His name was Vlado

* King Alexander I of Yugoslavia was shot by a Bulgarian revolutionary named Vlado Chernozemski, who was instantly cut down by a policeman's sabre, then beaten to death by the crowd. Barthou died of wounds, a few hours later.
† The Little Entente, created in 1921–2, saw an alliance between Czechoslovakia, Rumania and the future Yugoslavia, backed by France, as a check to potential Hungarian or German aggression. The Treaty of Neuilly (1919) had drastically reduced the borders of Bulgaria, in favour of Greece, Serbia and Rumania.

Chernozemski and he came from Strumitza – Croatian indeed!) Gatcho's disjointed account was silenced by the singing of *Shumi Maritza*, the fierce national anthem of Bulgaria. They bawled out the chorus till the veins stood out on their brows: '*Marsh! Marsh! S'generala nash! V boi da letim, vrag da pobedim – dim – dim – dim. Marsh*'* – and so *da capo*.

The tables round the concrete disc were filled with outbreaks of cheering laughter, excited talk and shouts for more *slivo*. Was this the sort of atmosphere that reigned in Belgrade, I wondered, when the pro-Karageorgevitch party assassinated Alexander Obrenovitch[†] and Queen Draga and threw their bodies out of the palace window; or, for that matter, when Princip shot Archduke Franz Ferdinand and the Duchess Hohenberg in Sarajevo? The tinkle of a thrown *slivo* glass on the dance-floor evoked a cheer. Soon they were whizzing and smashing all over it. Tumblers and wineglasses followed until a full carafe sailing through the air and exploding in the centre with a crash and a dark star of spilt wine brought everyone to their feet and sent them jostling on to the floor, their forearms flying round each other's shoulders until a giant *hora*, with which the musicians tried to keep pace, was whirling them round in a ring. Even the officers' corner was deserted, a tangle of abandoned sabres; their spurred boots were crossing and stamping with the rest, grinding the fragments of glass to smaller fragments as the dance revolved. The tables were empty except for an old priest smiling benignly in the serene spiralling nest of his beard and beating time with his umbrella, and for me, discordantly skulking long-faced at the

---

* 'March! March with our general! Fly to war and crush the foe!'
† King Alexander I Obrenovitch of Serbia and his unpopular queen were assassinated by an army faction in 1903. He was replaced as king by Prince Peter, head of the royal house of Karageorgevitch, which had a long-standing feud with the Obrenovitch dynasty.

bar. Somebody had written on the wall in bold capitals, the stick of chalk grasped in the middle to make the letters larger, 'The Serbian King is dead!'

Later I saw Gatcho lurching between the tables arm in arm with half a dozen other students; they were whisking off the tablecloths with a cascade of whatever glass or cutlery had survived and tying them round their heads like turbans, singing a song that held all the youth of Bulgaria, that year, in its grip. '*Piem! Peem! Pushim!*' they bawled, '*Damadjani sushim! Da jiveyet tarikatite!*' 'Let's drink and sing and smoke till the demijohn is empty! That's the way the lads do it!' The manager, concerned at the breakage, was hustling towards them, but a still graver diversion made him change course. One of a party of peasants had found a fully-laid table by the balcony. Grasping it by two legs, he had lifted it above his head. The manager dashed forward, but he was too late. With a shout and to massed clapping and cheers, the peasant hurled it over the edge, where it turned over and over in a falling nebula of knives, forks, spoons, jugs, glasses, cruets, sliced sausage and anchovy and rolls till it hit the rock face a long way below and bounded disintegrating into the ravine.

~

A few days later I was heading north across the rolling autumnal hills between Tirnovo and the Danube, not due east to the Black Sea as I had planned. Roughly working out my eastward route on the map with Gatcho in Tirnovo, I had seen the tempting line of the Danube to the north, and, beyond it, the irresistibly beckoning triple cartographic circle of Bucharest. Again, this loop was hundreds of miles off my itinerary and, quite literally, diametrically opposed to my goal of Constantinople; but why not? Gatcho was against it: he was going back to Varna in a week or so; why not come too and stay in his rooms there, and then push off south to Turkey? But I could do this, I argued, after I had left Bucharest, and had walked south again across the Dobrudja. The real reason was his hatred of Bulgaria's northern neighbours. The Rumanians were a terrible lot, he said: liars, robbers, thieves, villains, immoral. I said they couldn't be as bad as all that. 'They stole the Dobrudja,' he said with a contorted frown. 'All the land between the Danube delta and the Black Sea. It's pure Bulgarian.' I said that I wanted only to see what they were like, on their own ground, not as I had seen them, through Hungarian eyes, in Transylvania. 'They stole that too!' he cried. I wasn't a political observer, I went on; races, language, what people were like, that was what I was after: churches, songs, books, what they wore and ate and looked like, what the hell! Surely he, who was interested in foreign literature and the republic of the arts and wanted to see the outside world too – just like me – could understand that? Monasteries, temples, paintings, I went on, mountain ranges, art, history. 'This is history!' he interjected hotly, and scored an important point.

We sat in silence. I had to gain lost ground. 'Suppose the King of Rumania was murdered,' I asked, 'would you have cheered and danced as you did last night about King Alexander of Yugoslavia?' Gatcho laughed. 'Of course I would. And I'd have rung the church bells too.' Things were building up my way. 'And', I said, with the insidious quietness of somebody laying a trap, 'the King of Greece?' Gatcho laughed snortingly. 'There isn't one. Not at the moment. You ought to know that. But of course I would.' The trap had fallen apart. 'I know why you are asking all these questions. England is France's ally. You're on the side of France, on the side of the Little Entente.' I protested hotly that I loved France, that we all needed her if we weren't all to be barbarians, but that I didn't care a damn about France's policy in the Balkans, or England's either; surely one isn't necessarily committed to one's country's policy? 'Oh yes, one is,' Gatcho replied. 'It's all right for you in England, with your huge Empire. You've never been invaded or conquered. Thanks to being an island.' 'Yes we have!' 'Oh? When?' I gave the date rather lamely. 'Nine centuries ago! There you are!' 'Well,' I said, 'you hate all your neighbours, Greece, Rumania and Yugoslavia anyway. What about Turkey?' They were the worst of the lot, he said, the ones who ruined Bulgaria in the first place. Nearly six centuries of occupation. Indeed, this enormous span, stretching from Chaucer to Dickens and embracing almost half of the country's history since it emerged as a nation, was a sombre thought. 'But we've beaten them once, in the First Balkan War.' 'With the help of the Rumanians, the Serbs and the Greeks,' I put in; he brushed these ex-alliances aside, 'and we could beat them again. Why, we nearly took Constantinople!' After a pause for brooding I asked him if there was any foreign country that he did like. After another long pause, he said, 'Russland.'

I wasn't as surprised as I might have been at Gatcho's exemption of Russia from his general aversion, in spite of his dislike of Communism, which was intense. There was no hope of solution to Bulgaria's irredentist problems there. Indeed, although he had no sympathy for the present regime in Germany, he would sometimes wonder in a speculative tone whether, in terms of what he called realpolitik, Bulgaria should look Germany-wards for rectification. (This is, of course, exactly what Bulgaria did a few years later; and for a short-lived year or two, as Germany's ally, Bulgaria was suddenly swollen by huge slices sawn off her neighbours.) But, quite apart from political leanings, there existed throughout mystical Bulgaria a deep-seated, instinctive, almost fondness for the idea of Russia. As the champions of Slav Orthodoxy in the past, she had been a counterweight to the hated Greek ecclesiastical supremacy at Constantinople under the

Turks. It was the Russia of Alexander II that delivered them from their long slavery and, as it were, created modern Bulgaria; and Bulgarian and Russian, of all the Slav languages, were the two which were closest kin. The present Soviet Union's bitter hostility to the Russia of the Czars which had showered down all these benefits was, in some curious fashion, no bar to this deep-rooted sympathy. Except among communists, where the ambiguity would not arise, political aversion and racial attraction coexisted in the teeth of all ordinary logic; the great Slav lodestone made Bulgaria react and deviate from the true north in the same way that allowance must be made on a compass for the magnetic. It was a case of *le coeur a ses raisons*. This instinctive bias, however, was no bar to Bulgaria siding in the First World War, impelled by short-sighted opportunism, against her old benefactors, and with calamitous results for the country. (The same reasons again placed them on the wrong side in World War II, and the results were worse still; though the final disaster would perhaps have come – as it did, alas, to the other Eastern European countries – regardless of which camp they were in.) Bulgarians have a perverse genius for fighting on the wrong side. If they had been guided more by their hearts and less by their political heads, which usually seem to have lacked principle and astuteness in equal degrees, their history might have been a happier one.

I said nothing of all this – all, that is, that could be said at that date – because a rather strained silence had fallen, like angels flying overhead. Gatcho was leaning in the café with his hands in his pockets, a frown on his stubborn handsome face, his eyes fixed on the table and his black hair falling on his forehead. The same glance-avoiding awkwardness had haunted the rest of the day. But it thawed in the evening. I asked him if it had been prompted by anything I had done or said. No, he answered, nothing at all. It was merely one of the black moods under which

I had seen his family writhing. He apologized with real distress. Later as we were discussing Gatcho's companions and contemporaries who had been our messmates for the last days, 'What do you think of Vasil?' he asked, mentioning the last of them all. 'I don't like him much,' I admitted. 'Nor do I,' Gatcho said. 'And he doesn't like you either.' 'Why?' 'He thinks you're a spy.'

My first reaction to this was a loud and incredulous laugh. Gatcho joined in. 'He must have got the idea from seeing you always poring over the map,' he said, pointing to the tattered Freytag's *Reisekarte* open on the table in front of us. 'But surely I don't look like a spy,' I protested. 'Ah!' Gatcho answered, 'they never do.' I wondered if Vasil's idea had started the same suspicion in Gatcho, and began to think that I had noticed a hint of withdrawal in our companions during the last day or two, a trace of coldness. 'Of course I don't,' he said with vehemence, 'nor do any of the others.' Then after a pause and most unhelpfully, he added, 'Anyway, why shouldn't you be?' Seeing that I was beginning to work myself into a state of outrage, distress and puzzled disclaimer, he put his hand on my shoulder and shouted for some more wine. It was my turn to fence myself round with injured sulkiness and to return to the theme with fresh, though dwindling exasperation, which I really felt, between songs, for the rest of the evening.

It was the first of many times, since an incident on the Czechoslovak border, that I had struck the hazard that every now and then, and more especially in time of trouble, plagues travellers in the Balkans, not excluding Greece. The anger it arouses in the accused is all the more hopeless by its impotence. Fortunately, the charge seems to evaporate with the same frivolous ease that it arises, blowing away like an idle speculation. It takes some time to perfect the weary sigh and the pitying smile which is the correct completion of the gambit. But at first, even after its retraction, it always leaves a disagreeable trace behind, like the itch after the removal of a sting. Gatcho was truly upset because I was so obviously so. When I set off next day, he made me promise again and again to stay with him in Varna on the way south.

4

To the Danube

The region I was crossing bore an illusion of no change, but insidious forces had been at work. All trace of summer haze had been driven from the sky, and the glare was tempered to a thin lemon-coloured clarity, with frailer shadows. The distant ranges to the south were chiselled and veined with valleys and the spread of the Balkans, stretching northward and then veering east of my track, was distinct to the smallest rock. On some of these uplands, red patches of flames and trailing smoke showed where shepherds were setting fire to the undergrowth to strip the ground for next year's grazing. The sky was seldom without a cloud: cauliflowers sailing overhead, towing their shadows twisted and bent by the ravines, like ships' anchors, across the whale-shaped undulations, or hovering in the high mountain passes as lightly as ostrich feathers, or slanting along the horizons in pampas plumes. The setting sun turned each of these into the tail of a giant retriever. Whenever the slopes slanted nearly horizontally to the eye, the rain had fledged them with a green froth of tender herb. Young blades sprouted in the dark earth, which was scattered with cyclamen and autumn crocus. But the leaves were still green and undiminished in the branches; only a faint tinge of gold in the vines gave the season away (where they had been sprinkled with copper sulphate, entire hillsides were now the colour of verdigris): these and the walnut trees that were beginning to show their steely grey limbs, and the poplars by the stream beds, which were to shed their green-gold leaves from their roots upward till they were tall spectres with a last bright puff at the tip like a candle's flame.

Many of the vines were still loaded with unplucked grapes. When I swooped down into a valley and the pale ribbons of smoke announced – before the chimneys and tiles and thatch had come into view – that I was approaching a village, I ate these grapes in quantities, with wonderful apples and pears. Women were filling their aprons with quinces for *slatko*, which they offered their guests in little spoonfuls. There were plenty of crab apple trees and wild pears, small, hard and with just enough sharpness to leave a faint prickle on the gums. Quantities of walnuts had appeared in the villages and I ate them with honey out of a spoon and filled my pockets, shelling and crunching them as I went. On the outskirts of one of the villages, I came across a peculiar bee garden where the hives were tall cones of mud, like the huts of certain tribes in the Cameroons. Sometimes on the thorn bushes and on the ground of these hamlet approaches there were bright blankets spread out to dry, covering an acre or so with stripes and zigzags in amazing colours. The calm scenery was dotted sparsely by figures, lopping, pruning, gathering, burning, yoking buffaloes, driving donkeys, or calling to their flocks and their dogs.

The second equinox of my journey was over and this new northward leap across country which I had never planned to see, after the first purifying rains, seemed a long, limpid and peaceful reprieve among the far-tinkling flocks. Quietness dropped from the sky. The swallows had not yet left; they gyrated and now flew low in the villages; but in the hills, crossing and recrossing the path or standing on the dark furrows, magpies abounded. These, and the crows and the rooks, with an occasional owl, were the birds I most often saw or heard for the rest of the journey. Often, sitting or lying under a tree, I was startled out of my torpor by a whirring clatter and a huge grasshopper with bright eyes and twirling feelers would land on my knee. Night fell earlier now – these changes, although they are a continual creeping process, suddenly dawn on one and become, for a time, fixtures, like turning round in Grandmother's Steps – but the stages of late afternoon and sunset and twilight were spun out into a longer and more elaborate ceremony thanks to the new presence of the clouds: gold, zinc, scarlet and crimson over the westward roll of the Great Balkan towards Plevna – leagues of gold wire, shoals and lagoons, berserk flights of cherubim, burning fleets and the slow-motion destruction of Sodom.

To avoid the tedium of the main northward road, I followed tracks in the foothills to the east of it, or struck across open country. On the second evening, I found myself climbing and descending under just such a sunset along a narrow track on the slant of the mountain with a friendly black dog. It was no good telling him to go home. This happened several times on this journey; short of company, they sometimes attached themselves for hours. An amazing sunset faded and a grey twilight deepened, and just before it became completely dark, a turn in this hill track confronted us with an enormous full moon. It loomed in a shock of white out of the steep hillside and if I had been on four legs, I would probably have let out a long howl of surprise like the black dog at my side. He galloped forward and then stopped, barking in his tracks as though to drive it away. But in a few minutes, as the path sank into a hollow, the moon sank with the hills. The dog grew quieter, only to burst out afresh when a dip in the landscape once more laid the moon bare. He rushed forward, followed by his enormous black shadow, frightening it below the skyline, as the answering slope blotted the moon out again, and then bolted back to me with wagging tail, gazing up for approval. During half an hour the moon rose and set a dozen times in this sharply altering landscape, each time with the same effect on the dog. When the moon was free in the upper sky at last, it took some time for my companion's frenzied barks to sink to a disapproving growl. By this time the path led down into a wide wooded ravine through which curled a shining stream. We followed its windings through a glimmering leafy world. A mile or two along the stream's course we came on a clearing surrounded by linden trees, and on one side of it, a small derelict mosque surrounded by blackberry bushes. I picked and swallowed here for half an hour accompanied by intermittent moonward wails.

The mosque must have been half ruined for many years. The dome and the walls were almost intact but most of the plaster had fallen away and the minaret was broken diagonally near its base, exposing to the moon the twist of the stairs round their central pillar like the volutes of a smashed ammonite's fossil. It seemed a strange place for a mosque, so far away from any village. Perhaps it was a tomb or the hermitage of a solitary dervish a couple of centuries ago. Once more there was a tantalizing marble slab embedded on the wall, inscribed with many lines of Arabian characters. A rusty horseshoe, wisps of hay on the moonlit floor, an old tin plate, a pile of faggots and the black smoke-marks on the walls suggested that the place sometimes sheltered mounted travellers for the night. It was a perfect lair for a band of haiduks, those Robin Hood-like bandits who played such a part in Bulgarian life under the Turks. I explored the small clearing. Half a dozen moss-grown monoliths, each topped with a turban and one broken in half with its pleated capital prone in the grass, were nearly swallowed up in bracken and weed and the brambles of the blackberries. A large flat stone jutted into the gleaming stream.

This wonderful place seemed to be miles from a village, so I slept there. I built a large fire inside with the welcome faggots and a few-half burnt logs that I discovered tucked away in the remains of the mihrab, and shared a Hungarian sausage and half a loaf with the dog – who, passant, sejant then couchant, settled by the fire as though he had never lived anywhere else – and then finished up with some pears and walnuts; setting out, afterwards, for the big stone by the stream to smoke. On the way there, we almost trod on an owl which must have been standing in the grass. It sailed into the trees without a sound. By the brook I put off going to sleep from cigarette to cigarette as the moon followed its journey through the sparse clouds. The place was holy and enchanted. This spell was only faintly disturbed by the black dog, mercifully inured by now to the phenomenon overhead, whizzing into the undergrowth with hackles like a clothes brush at the faintest rustle of nocturnal stirring, always returning panting, empty-jawed, and with tongue hanging out through the semblance of a smile, to fling himself down on the bank with a lunatic upward gaze of appeal for advice or approbation which pats on his pacified scruff seemed only partly to satisfy. The curl of his tail remained a dark symbol of interrogation. After sitting under these silver leaves and listening to the water running by for most of the moon's journey, we returned to the mosque. Lying beside the crackling faggots with my head on the familiar billet of my rucksack and the dog stretched crusaderishly at my feet, soon deep in a sleep that no phantom quarry disturbed, I felt another access of one of the great and recurring delights of these travels: the awareness that nobody in the world knew where I was, and in this case not even I with any certainty. My hand outstretched over the bright thorns sent a giant shadow-hand clean across the flickering firelight in the hollow of the dome, ringed with concentric circles like the grooves on an oil-jar to the summit just above. The owl hooted from a tree nearby.

The dog had vanished when I woke. It was just as well since, if he had accompanied me any further, he might have lost his way back: but I was sorry. At that very moment he was probably bounding home. Outside the mosque a brilliant dawn was spreading down the valley, sweeping away the morning dew like the hounds of Hippolyta. A flock grazed across the meadow the other side of the stream, and the tufted ruin caught the morning light in a bright positive print of the dark and silvery negative of a few hours ago. Spreading long shadows on the damp grass, the almost level sunbeams revealed something that the deceptive glimmer of the night had hidden: a confetti of mushrooms, all round the mosque and in the field beyond, huddling in groups. I filled a big red bandanna with them before setting off.

～

A difficulty crops up here. The distance on my map from Tirnovo to Rustchuk could easily be covered on foot in under a week. There are, in fact, only five pencil crosses on this journey indicating where I slept. Perhaps I forgot to enter some. Yet according to two of the bare dozen only exactly ascertainable dates on this journey – the assassination of King Alexander and a customs stamp on the Bulgarian frontier – the journey took thirteen days. There is nothing unusual here; there was no hurry, and in Transylvania I had taken a great deal longer sometimes to travel far less. But in Transylvania there had been every reason for dawdling – exciting company, libraries, horses, friends and sentimental involvements, and every room with its furniture and books and the view out of the windows, and every face and every name, including those of neighbours and servants, horses and dogs, I can remember as if I had seen them three minutes ago. But not here. Why was I so slow? Perhaps something tremendous occurred to hold me up, which will burst on me in an illuminating thunderclap the moment these pages are irrevocably out of my hands.

But for the moment, concentrate as I may, all is dim, except a few lucid alcoves of memory scooped out of these nebulous kilometres. But in the case of these surviving cartouches of memory, such as those of the last few pages where each detail, like a torch held up to a bas-relief in a cave, suddenly juts, I can still taste the blackberries and recapture the owl's note and the texture of that black dog's coat. Indeed considering how often since, and at the expense of a thousand others, I have thought of those eventless hours, prompted by an affinity of wood or out of the blue in the middle of a dinner or waiting for a train, the space allotted them here is a great feat of compression.

Perhaps one of the reasons for the vagueness of the following days lies in the contours of the country. Unlike the sharp southern descent, all Bulgaria north of the Balkan watershed descends in a succession of waving ledges that tilt gradually down to the Danube's bed in plateau after plateau, each wide step of the shallow staircase becoming tamer until the lowest merges imperceptibly with the diligent lowlands; and with each downward tread the line of the watershed falls further south: no diamond peaks at hand to incite the mind, hills and recollection growing blunter pace by pace, and both merging at last in the *tabula rasa* of the plain.

The moonlit ruin might have had some crucial significance in a fairy tale and so might the next surviving apparition, the last of the wonderful Ottoman bridges on this journey, flying over the water – probably over the same flow that turned the mill-wheel, further downstream – in a steep semicircular loop of cobwebbed grey masonry. The mood of folktales pervades the blur of these days. The imminence of a village was often announced by meeting a crippled and toothless crone picking up firewood and bent in two under a vast burden of sticks, identical with folk-tale figures who, had I been the third feckless son and shouldering her burden, might have granted me three wishes and made my fortune. But our exchange was confined to *'dobro vetcher, gospoja'*,* on my side, or *'dobro den'* on theirs.

Another moment: an ikon of St Irene behind glass in the recess of a wayside store ikon-stand, and a bird hovering and fluttering before pecking with loud taps as though bent on breaking and entering. It may, I think now though I wouldn't have known then, have been a wheatear, for each upward beat showed a brilliant white flash of tail and body which the downstroke of its more sober-coloured wings obscured. The old candle-end inside must have looked like a bit of bread or a slug. It was ten minutes before this pecking and fluttering siege was raised and the besieger sheared off empty-beaked. The next lantern slide to drop into its slot is a village dairy, where I was finishing a small earthenware dish of my favourite food in Bulgaria: yaourt. (It seems in retrospect that I almost lived on this stuff, sprinkling sugar on the dimpled crust and then spooning away. I had yet to learn how to squeeze lemon on top until the sugar is soaked, in the manner of some cunning Athenians. I was further still from the delicious Cretan method: pouring in a circular helping of honey from a rotating spoon-tip and then scattering the chryselephantine whorls with fragments of peeled walnut. It is indescribably good.) Bulgarians are held to be the best yaourt-makers in the Balkan peninsula; in fact, their skill as dairymen is second only to their mastery of market gardening. Oddly, though, the word 'yaourt' is never used in Bulgaria; they call it *kissolo mleko*, 'sour milk'.

A party of six settled at the next table, all countrymen in homespun, rawhide footgear and sashes, but two in broad-brimmed hats of plaited osier, the others in cloth caps. They seemed of a finer grain than the ordinary Bulgarian peasant and quiet-voiced, eyes wide with different but friendly openness,

---

* 'Good evening, ma'am.'

untroubled smiles and good-humoured wrinkles round their eyes and the corners of their mouths. An indefinable presiding charm emanated from them. Anyone would have felt calm and happy in their neighbourhood. Appropriately, as I divined – more from their giveaway gear than the unfamiliar words of their eaves-dropped discourse – they were a party of itinerant beekeepers travelling up and down the region and tidying up the hives for the winter. I wondered how they dealt with those curious cones of mud I had seen; they looked proof against apiarists. A fallout of the manna of their calling, as gentle as pollen, touched me with grace – a change in this fiery kingdom with its 'talk of peace that always turned to slaughter' (in the words of the poet Kapetanakis); to think of them, armed with nothing more harmful than a smoke-gun, going about their Georgic business; dealing with nothing but bees, and wax for sculptors and cobblers and candles, and honey for everyone; mobled in muslin, calm-browed comb-setters and swarm-handlers of the scattered thorps.

~

I usually got up at dawn or soon afterwards on this journey, except when I struck lucky by staying with someone, or in circumstances of unusual comfort; but not always. Occasionally I would lie in bed on squalid pallets reading till noon, and once all day until dinner time. Not that there was anything to complain of in my quarters in the little town of Boritza, where I had taken a room for the night in a sort of loft above a wheelwright's. Looking through a trapdoor and down a ladder almost beside my bed, I could see the bald patch on the crown of the wheel-wright's head as, ankle deep in shavings and surrounded by a disorder of herbs, spokes, felloes and swingletrees, he hammered and planed or sawed his way through planks with a square and biblical-looking saw in which the blade was strung with thongs between a square wooden frame, or chipped and sliced at a block with a hammer-backed adze or thumped with a mallet. All his tools had a look of Nazarene antiquity. The sunbeams falling across this scattered gear danced with sawdust and the smell of the freshly sawn wood floated up the steps, a scent only bettered by a baker's shop when they are shovelling the loaves out of the oven. Hoofs and wheels clattered and creaked over the cobbles under my window, and beyond them, a chorus of frogs.

But these impressions only penetrated intermittently: I was halfway through *The Brothers Karamazov*, which I had started the evening before and read all through the night: my first introduction to Dostoevsky, in a French yellow-back translation by Le Comte Prozor. Helplessly spellbound, I postponed getting up from half-hour to half-hour, in spite of the bright autumn morning outside. But at about eleven o'clock, the light lost its brilliance on the page. Clouds had collected and soon the sky dissolved. A steady downpour started. This lets me off, I thought with delight, settling down more comfortably to the doings of Alyosha, and only descending the staircase at two, rather shamefaced to seem so idle a lodger. I sat on in an eating-house all the afternoon, brushing away the lazy autumn flies that loitered across the print, only dimly aware of the steady patter of the rain, interrupted every now and then by the friendly bewilderment of the owner, who sat swishing the flies from his brow at the other window. 'You read a lot,' he would observe hourly – '*mnogo* [much].' '*Da*,' I answered faultlessly. The only other people there between meals were two frowning policemen who sat for an hour at the next table in silence with their rifles between their knees, fixing me with unsettling scrutiny. My heart sank. At last one got up, saluted, and asked me politely if I could spare two of those English cigarettes I had been smoking, for him and his pal. I bestowed several on them with relief. (I had recklessly bought two packets of Player's Navy Cut in Tirnovo.) I had thought the police might have been tipped off by someone in Tirnovo to dog my footsteps, having heard Vasil's suspicions about my being a *spion* at umpteenth hand. The book carried me all through supper until closing time and by candlelight until half-past three in the morning, when I finished it at last, exhausted and excited.

Dostoevsky ever since, and even the mention of his name, evokes a momentary impression of rain and fresh-sawn wood.

~

The following days were raining off and on the whole time, soaking the lowlands and an ever-thickening crop of villages. I stuck to the main road, watching occasional cars pass, and, more temptingly, buses, with PYCCE plastered across the front – Russe, the Bulgarian name for Rustchuk. There was little else but carts, all with their semicircular yokes, and, inevitably, Gypsies, the many-flounced dresses of the women flapping round their ankles with the wet and their long hair glued to their cheeks. All were barefoot, with several babies in the backs of the wagons, stark naked among the pots and the half-woven baskets and the tent poles. At one point I found myself trudging through the middle of some large-scale army manoeuvres: platoons labouring through the downpour under enormous packs of matted cowhide with their bedding strapped round them. Horse-drawn cannons creaked past along the straight, flat road, and at one moment a troop of cavalry wheeled, trotted and then galloped across the road and away over the plain, scabbards dancing up and down against the flanks of strong and shaggy horses. They were rather impressive, reminiscent of those full-page drawings of the Balkan Wars in bound volumes of the *Illustrated London News*. The soldiers were now in winter uniform. I, too, had changed into my long-folded breeches and puttees – and even into my overcoat – out of commission for months except as a covering at night.

On one of these drizzly stretches, I fell in with a fellow wayfarer heading north like me, a young barber from Pazardjik called Ivancho, threadbare and urban and with a face like a hare's. Where was I from? *Anglitchanin? Tchudesno!* – 'Wonderful!' This revelation was followed by a burst of talk that needed no answer. It was uttered at such speed that I could scarcely understand a word – at the same time eager, confidential and ear-piercing, and without the faintest trace of punctuation, accompanied by many gestures and with a fixed smile and those hare's eyes projecting and rolling, as though loose in their sockets. It continued for mile after mile till my head began to swim and ache. I tried to detach myself and draw on inner resources, merely muttering *Da* or *Nè* when a pause occurred. But these were not always the right answers and my companion would begin again, catching me by the elbow and prodding me with his forefinger with redoubled urgency and a crab-like veer of his fast and tripping gait that always edged me across the road and nearly into the field, till I darted round the other side and into the middle again, only to be seized once more and harangued off the road on the other side with the same smiling urgency and with eyes peering mesmerically so that it seemed impossible to deflect them. Sometimes he was walking backwards in front, almost dancing along the road in reverse, the unstaunchable flow gushing unbroken from his smiling and gabbling lips. Once I turned round in a circle and he danced briskly round in a wider circle still talking faster and faster. I tried to counter-attack by resolutely bawling *Stormy Weather*, but it was too slow. He dived in between the bars, so I shifted to the *Lincolnshire Poacher, Lillibulero, On a Friday Morn when we set Sail,* and Maurice Chevalier's *Valentine,* over and over again. Whenever he tried to hammer in a wedge of speech or when I paused for breath, I made more noise marching ahead with exaggerated resolution, faster and faster, glaring straight ahead. When

I fell silent after a terrific crescendo to see if I had won, there was an outbreak of claps and high-pitched laughter and the tide of speech swept on. I was routed. After another hour, I stopped in my tracks, flourished my hands to the sky, shouting 'Please! Please, Ivancho! *Molya! Molya!*' At one moment I believe I actually seized and shook him by the shoulders, but laughter and a million syllables was the only response. I stumbled on like a sleepwalker or a condemned man with sunk head and closed eyes, but the piercing spate broke over me unhindered. My head was splitting and I sighed for the tomb and the silence of eternity. People had often teased me for gasbag tendencies, especially when a bit drunk. If only they could see this retribution!

There was only one hope. Ivancho belonged to some kind of pan-Bulgarian barbers' guild – he had showed me a dog-eared card with a snapshot glued to it – and in two nearby villages that we had passed before I realized how it worked, he had entered a barber's shop, displayed his card and emerged with a handful of leva. In the next village we came to, I took discreetly to my heels and ran full tilt along the road. Looking back, I saw him emerge, catch sight of my diminishing figure, and set off in pursuit. But I had a good start and the distance widened. I pounded on like a stag with a lightening heart and finally, when the road stretched bare behind me, slowed down, free at last. But a few minutes later a northward-bound car slowed down and Ivancho, with a forefinger wagging in playful admonition, leapt from the running-board.

There was nothing for it. All the evening, and all through dinner, the torment continued till at last I lurched to bed, but not to sleep for any time. Fortunately, though, owing to lack of room, different roofs were sheltering us. After a few nightmare-ridden hours, I got up in the dark, paid, and slipped out before breakfast, and away. But I had not gone a furlong before a waiting shadow detached itself from a tree. A cheerful voice, refreshed by sleep, wished me good morning, and a friendly hand fluttered to my shoulder. Day broke slowly.

Stunned and battered, I saw my chance early in the afternoon. We were sheltering from the rain, drinking Russian tea an inch deep in sugar in the *kretchma* of a large village. How pungently the memory of those *kretchmas* sticks: the cubicle of wooden railing in the corner, where the bottles were lined on shelves, tin tables, rickety chairs, perhaps a hobbled ram in a corner and half a dozen live fowls trussed together by their feet, stertorous hawking and trajectories of spit, a Slavonic hubbub, the padding of swaddled feet across the puddles, wagoners drinking whip in hand and the smell of *slivo*, coffee, sweet tea, rank tobacco, damp homespun, sweat, charcoal, dogs, stable and cowshed. I rather liked them! There was always so much going on. A battered bus was drawn up outside, and the driver-conductor was drinking with some cronies at another table. I left the table with the excuse of the lavatory, and, outside, made a pleading gesture towards the conductor through the glass top of a door. He joined me, and I haltingly explained my case. He had heard and seen the social amenities rattling about my table; perhaps he could tell from my eyes that he was talking to a soul in hell.

Back in the main room I made the treacherous suggestion to Ivancho that we should take the bus to Rustchuk and get out of the rain: I would pay for the journey. Would he please buy the tickets, I said, handing over the money, as my Bulgarian was so bad? He assented eagerly and volubly. There was a hitch at the bus door: he insisted I should get in first. We struggled and the driver shouted impatiently. I managed to shove him in and the driver pulled the lever that slammed the door, and moved off. I could see Ivancho gesticulating and shouting but all in vain. He shot me a harrowing glance from his hare-eyes, I waved, and the rain swallowed them up. In a few minutes, I took a side-path through a field of damp sunflowers. Taking no chances, I followed a wide loop far from the dangers of the main road. The guilt implanted by Ivancho's reproachful glance almost managed to mar the ensuing feelings of relief and liberation, but not quite. Not even the bitter wind from the east, as steady as an express train, could do that.

One of the rare attacks of gloom and doubt that now and then tempered the zest and excitement of these travels, smote that night. Though some of it was caused by remorse about my slightly discreditable escape from the racking eternity of Ivancho's company, the falling depression had been hammered home by the unbroken downpour, lashed into a spiteful anti-human fury by the unrelenting north-east wind that felt as though it was blowing without let or hindrance, as it probably was, direct from Siberia. (After all, now that the barrier of the Balkans lay away to the south, there was no windbreak this side of the Urals to thwart its onrush.) The angry rain-bearing blast had cursed every step of my plod down the glutinous byways till long after dark.

And what about being suspected of being a spy? This general dejection prompted me to turn and rend the Bulgarians in general and *in vacuo*. All their obvious qualities, their courage and scrupulous honesty, their frugality, their doggedness and diligence and the passion for literacy (I had been told again and again that Bulgaria, of all the Balkan countries, was the one with the lowest percentage of illiteracy) – all this was forgotten or discounted, and with it, their hospitality and their odd and beautiful songs and their gift for music and, in many cases, a certain attractive, rather melancholy seriousness. Gatcho, whom I really liked, and Nadejda, whom I adored (anyway, she was half Greek, I would have argued), were set on one side as exceptions, and with them, on lower thrones, the many Bulgarians I had liked or who had been amusing or kind, or both. Stripped of all this, how heavy, boorish and sometimes bloodthirsty they seemed (though I didn't, in my romantic idea of the Balkans, mind this last characteristic, which is common to all Bulgaria's neighbours, as much as I should, and their political role as Europe's villains had a certain dark glamour). I made no allowances for the stunting and stifling damage of barbarous occupation for half a millennium, gave no pat on the back for the compensating break with mediaeval feudalism – reproach rather, for lack of its relics and traditions; similarly, no pity for their exclusion from the Renaissance and the eighteenth century, nor congratulations because there had been no Bastille to besiege or Industrial Revolution to undergo. Instead I reproached them for their unilluminated literalness: a bread without yeast, a jokerless pack. Perhaps unjustly, this last accusation is the only one that still seems to me, out of all this railing in the dark, to have some substance.

The theatre of these ill-tempered and gloomy thoughts only exacerbated them, thanks to my masochistic passion for ungracious living – a passion which is still not quite extinct. Back on the main road, I had made a dive through the soaking darkness, like an outlaw claiming sanctuary, towards the first lighted window on the edge of the first village. (It might have been signposted Dolni Pasarel – I remember this name, and its neighbour Gorni Pasarel, the Upper and the Lower Village, but which one was it? I daren't risk it.) I had sloshed through a yard full of pigsties and offered, perhaps, out of wetness and fatigue, rather rudely, to pay for a night's lodging. It was accepted with a touch of ill-grace, probably because no payment was needed or asked for; and here I was in the most primitive village house I had so far seen. Through the rain all the houses had looked curiously squat, as though they were sinking into the ground under shocks of bedraggled, thatch-like, ill-kempt fringes. They were socketed in the earth for about a third of their height, so that on entering one went down several steps into a single, semi-troglodytic and windowless room, with a damp earthen floor and a ledge all round. The walls were of wattle, whitewashed outside but with the uncovered mortar and straw and wicker bare and bulging within. The low ceiling was of bamboo laid across heavy beams, cocooned in cobwebs and black and oily with decades of soot. No chimney was visible: standing, one's head disappeared in a pendant layer of smoke from which one stooped again red-eyed and coughing: a limitation which imposed a more bear-like gait than usual on the room's seven denizens. (For the hundredth time, in rustic dwellings in Eastern Europe, the thought of the lack of privacy arose. Nobody is ever alone, whether engendering, giving birth or dying; dark nocturnal tussles and Neolithic midwifery and death rattles and dirges are all, at the very least, within earshot.) We had swallowed a fasting supper of boiled spinach, cheese like concrete, and water, in semi-silence, a silence probably cast – a fresh cause for later guilt – by my scowling mood, and then retired.

Lying on the ledge in this shadowy room, with the wind and rain outside competing with the stertorous polyphony indoors – a chorus which was startlingly varied every so often by a change of key or by one of the seven sleepers abruptly falling silent – I could just discern, by the ikon's glimmer and the diminishing glow of the logs, in front of which my boots and coat and festooned puttees were steaming, a few, detached landmarks on the ledge and the floor: a jutting whisker, a gaping mouth, the upturned cowhide canoe-tip of a moccasin at the end of a rawhide, cross-gartered and outflung leg. There can have been little change since Omurtag's day. It was the world of Gurth and Wamba, a Saxon swineherd's hut just after curfew. It can't have been later than ten, and here I was fumbling for the track of a flea, or possibly two, under my damp shirt, and as far from sleep as I was from any familiar geographical or psychological landmark. (I have only said so little about vermin in this narrative because

Balkan travellers enlarge on them so exhaustively. They wrecked many nights.) But the trouble wasn't this, or even the related thought of all these weeks without a bath, apart from an occasional slosh in ponds and streams; or the weather, or the petty vexations of the road, or the fug and the claustrophobia.

Nor again, was it the dissimilarity of my habitat from Chenonceaux or Chatsworth, or the anguish which at certain seasons among the ruins of Luxor, in the Atlas passes or on the very slopes of the Parthenon, suddenly halts more sophisticated travellers than I was, catches them by the throat and mists their eyes with a faraway look: the thought of missing the young peas, new potatoes in early summer, and raspberries and cream, or – at this time of the year – partridges, before all their brief spans are over; or, less compellingly, because their seven-month lease is not so sharp a reminder of the fleetingness of time, oysters.

My dejection was not as specific as this, but, in one way, it was akin, and it was incurred by two things. One of these is easy to explain. It is this: ever since I could remember, my boredom threshold had been so high that it scarcely existed at all. With the exception of a minute handful of physical and mental types, surroundings and landscapes and atmospheres and orders of conversation, I was unboreable, like an unsinkable battleship. I seemed to be unequipped with the saving instrument that enabled everyone else to segregate from random circumstances whatever would stimulate, entertain and reward them intellectually, concentrate on these and discard the rest. My trouble was that practically everything, not only the most disparate, contradictory and mutually exclusive things and people, but many others that everyone else found repellent, painful, unrewarding and above all tedious, filled me with the same wild fascination. I think it was the confusion brought about by all these indiscriminate and concurrent and totally undisciplined enthusiasms that had landed me in the soup so often. They would boil over; the sack followed. (Like many young I also suffered intermittently from the conviction, which puzzling reverses fail for a long time to dispel, that had they time and inclination they could confute philosophers, command armies, rule countries, compose operas, paint and sculpt better than Michelangelo, beat the record up Everest, write a sonnet sequence in a fortnight that would make experts reassess Shakespeare, and then, after discovering the cure for cancer and winning the Grand National steeplechase, break out into metres and thoughts that would fix the mould of poetry for several generations.)

This calamity-ridden anti-boredom was extremely active before I started this journey. The moment the Channel was crossed, it had broken into a gallop and unbelievably without mishap: so far, at any rate. It would be impossible to exaggerate the passionate excitement and delight that infected every second. My mouth was as unexactingly agape as the seal's to the flung bloater. There was hardly anything detectable by the five senses which was not sharpened and transformed, and which, strangely and miraculously, did not increase in intensity of enjoyment with familiarity and repetition. In spite of countless rustic sojourns, this half-subterranean abode, instead of seeming as it did tonight, a den of squalor and doom, could have been as thick in marvels as Aladdin's cave. I might, judging by my response to phenomena for most of these thousands of miles, have been a serious drug addict. This euphoria is bound, thanks to the time lag, to be one of the things that elude this narrative. But it intensified tastes, transformed smells, studded faces and landscapes with illusory lights and facets, gave extra resonances to sounds, complicated surfaces, shapes, textures and consistencies, and stepped up the voltage to a degree that must sometimes have given the impression of a screw loose.

The corollary of this was a nightmarish gloom of an equally exaggerated pitch, usually arriving without warning, but fortunately not often, and for the last months, more seldom still. The blow had fallen tonight. I lay and scratched in the dark, loathing my surroundings. What a godforsaken place. Even if I spoke the language properly, instead of a voluble smattering, what would there be to talk about with the noisily hibernating rustics swathed all over this stifling hell-hole? Crops? Wars? Pig-raising? Vegetable marrows? Werewolves? Vampires? Surely I'd heard enough about them during the last few months? Brittle alternative fantasies, and very conventional ones, began to glow and proliferate in the shadows, each with the wavering shape, the shimmering colours and the lifespan of a soap bubble: Oxford or Cambridge now harbouring so many schoolfellows and friends, where an effortless virtuosity in Greek, Latin, history and literature went hand in hand with a marvellous time on the lines of *Sinister Street*. Heidelberg for a term or two, surrounded by stained glass windows, lidded mugs, conifers and scarred Junkers with names like distant cannon fire? Perhaps, but more beckoningly than these, the Sorbonne, talking half the night with dashing and brilliant companions all about how to bring out books of verse, and beautiful girl students at café tables under trees or in studios modelled on illustrations? A hunting scene would wobble briefly towards the ceiling and pop inaudibly.

I noticed that I had transformed such scenes into a curious hybrid. The protagonist of these fleeting and absurd success stories was a sort of super-me ten years older or more, with the worldly poise of a Moss Bros advertisement (a young commodore on leave?) but also with a European and cosmopolitan polish: lolling at ease under tiers of gilt-backed books softly lit from below, just out of a bath, deep in an armchair by a fire, lifting a heavy cut-glass tumbler of whisky and soda. He would appear again – it was half-past ten in this dark cottage now – at the end of dinner in a thin film of cigar smoke, amazing old and young with acumen and omniscience and wit in a constellation of candle flames and brandy glasses – balloons within balloons – pausing on the way down a staircase into a candelabra-forested ballroom beside a cool and shadowy beauty, while, from below, volleys of longing glances sailed towards her along a hundred radii, bouncing off like arrows from a buckler into the bright air. With lowered lids, silent, expert and aloof, they began to float rather than to dance; the longing glances wound themselves like numberless threads on the slow revolving spindle of the two dancers, until at last they gyrated anti-clockwise towards the French windows, and the unwound threads dropped loose again as they glided out of sight among the trees. By this time the semi-stranger had become so insufferably suave that he had lost all identity with his part-owner and inventor; to such an extent that I was left behind, part of the jealous press of faces against the panes. I had noticed, anyway, with some surprise as they vanished, that he was a foot taller than me, with black hair, a narrow moustache and a mole on his left temple. I revenged myself by annihilating him.

There was much thought of these unmet women. At moments like now of revulsion against Balkan rawness, the dominant abstract figure would, by reaction – like the abolished alter ego before he got out of hand – tend towards urbanity and sophistication, her clothes slightly rustling when in motion. All were beautiful and all romantic; at one end was a rather wild girl, interested at the very least in literature or painting or one of the arts, knowing about as much – not a very hard task – or, ideally, slightly less than me. At the other end was someone of the same order who knew a great deal more; much calmer and more worldly-wise, probably several years older, the one in the ascendant at the moment, but with enough in common with the other to be the same person separated by a number of years; both had a similar laugh.

As the night advanced these or similar thoughts replaced the initial gloom, and the excitement of this wholly imaginary relationship with somebody whose face I never saw, was too great: too great and too anxious; for it was no longer any good smiling dismissively in the dark and trying to go to sleep; the accumulation of data had lifted the situation clean out of hypothesis and installed it somewhere very close to reality. (And as it turned out, not wrongly, as six months later, long after the end of this book, it miraculously happened.)

The inevitable dismantlement was swift and painless. As dawn approached, the frontiers of Western Europe, which had merged in a confusion of homesickness and so tortuously prompted the familiar thoughts of the last hours, and marked them with their geographic setting, were back in their places, the capitals disentangled, the provincial cities with their bridges and embankments shining in the water. There, most of them still unknown, they waited at the other side of the night. The distance seemed enormous. Would this Scythian wind, which was still slashing the wattle walls with rain, cross the intervening plains and ranges, and with a thousand scattered creaks, set all the weathercocks of the West on the move?

Earlier on, these westward thoughts had raised another, a more general and far more disturbing problem, one which only assailed me at moments of depression and low resistance: what on earth was I up to? An embarrassing question, and one which I will try to answer between here and the last page. But now all had changed. Depression had vanished; the interior of the hut, pitch dark except for the twinkling light suspended in the corner, was harmonious and severe; or was that a line of watery daybreak surrounding the door? There was a faint stir among the sleepers and it would soon be time to get back to the road to Rustchuk.

〜

It seemed, when I got there next evening, rather an exciting town, with its bright shops and electric lights, the multitude of cafés, the fiacres with their ribbed hoods raised, even a taxi or two, and, at the bottom of lamp-lit streets, the Danube with its landing stages, warehouses, cranes and anchored craft, including three gunboats which were the hard core of the Bulgarian navy.

All this, to my unjaded eyes, supplied the little riverine port with an almost metropolitan aura. I have heard from other travellers that it is considered an ugly, charmless place. Nothing pre-Turkish and very little before the nineteenth century. But not to me. Parts of it had a dilapidated Victorian feeling; better still, thanks to the great river on which it was built, a slight, but distinct and rather seductive alloy of Mitteleuropa tempered its Balkan consistency. There was even a bookshop and newsagents with foreign newspapers, mostly German and Austrian: *Neue Freie Presse, Frankfurter Zeitung, Hannoverscher Anzeiger, Berliner Tageblatt,* then the *Pesti Hirlap* – no good to me, alas – *Le Matin,* and, yes, *The Times* and *The Continental* and the *Daily Mail.* I wondered who these real and putative readers could be. Better still, a pile of unbought back numbers. I bought an armful of these, and, after an immense Viennese coffee, read through the whole fortnight-old drama of the assassination of King Alexander and Barthou. Nobody seemed to challenge Bulgarian claims. Gatcho would be pleased. Then, as the puddle of rainwater grew larger round my boots under the table, I sat back coughing happily over one of those nearly black Austrian cigars, savouring the lights, the dryness and the water, and the pleasant mixture of bustle and leisure. I felt like a seasoned traveller in the Balkans, Central Europe or Russia from the stories and novels of Saki. I gazed out at the bright street outside, liquescent and broken up like a pointilliste painting by the light-refracting raindrops that splashed and wriggled down the windowpanes, savouring the expanse of heavy marble-topped tables (that wonderful surface for covert drawing with a pencil, or, better still, a fountain pen) and, near the door, the flimsy architecture of ribboned chocolate boxes, so often and inexplicably surmounted by a celluloid baby or a powdered marchioness in satin panniers – for this was a *Evropaiski* establishment, reluctant to serve Turkish coffee and ready to faint should anyone suggest a nargileh. I had taken to these at once, and spent hours gurgling in their toils, mumbling quatrains of the *Rubaiyat of Omar Khayyam* (I had it nearly all by heart from a pocket edition sent by my mother) in humbler latticed cafés. But this one, alongside the elaborate tiers of western cakes and the puffed, shiny and cream-filled, poppy-seed and caraway-sprinkled crescents and Struwwelpeterish pretzels, was not so European as to exclude an array of oriental sweetmeats, notably *kadaif*, like a dish of sweet shredded wheat, and, far better, baklava. I had several times peered into warm vaults in the small hours to see pastry-cooks cross-legged in a ring on large, flour-dusted wooden platforms, stretching almost transparent membranes of pastry several yards in circumference, before folding them, layer on layer, each interval anointed with honey or syrup and chopped almonds and walnuts, into flat pans the size of Trojan shields and then, after a deft circular trimming with long knives, sliding them with long poles into dragon-breathed ovens. They emerge in crumbly brown discs, to be sliced up with trowels into delicious dripping shapes with the consistency, but not the taste, of millefeuilles. These triumphs of taste and sensory delight spread all through the Balkans and Levant, and though they are known as Turkish, they are probably, like so much that the Ottomans inherited from their forerunners, Byzantine in origin. I feel that they were known to logothetes and sebastocrators long before a pasha ever buried his teeth in them. They are invariably sliced up by intersecting strokes into a lozengy pattern; in fact, they have given their name, in demotic Greek among rustic joiners, to all forms of trelliswork. A Balkan businessman, slipping away from his office for a moment in the late morning, is far more likely to be heading for a quick baklava than a drink.

Idly I inspected the circular electric light plugs that were sprinkled at random over the café walls, or gathered here and there in huddling constellations, and the number of prongs and loose ends of flex projecting from the plaster like whiskers: proud emblems of victory, all through the Balkan peninsula, over the bad old days of oil and wax. (The abandoned riot and borborygmus of exposed piping, and the unhealed scars of its entries and exits, through the rooms of every plumbed house, even if it had been rusting there since the reign of Czar Ferdinand, tell similar tidings of modernity.) Here, too, overhead, hung the opaque white globular lampshades – in the smarter cafés they were clouded alabaster bowls hanging from three metal chains – darkly blurred at the bottom by a decade's worth of dead flies. I had spent unnumbered happy hours reading and writing in these havens during the last few months and was well versed in their details and degrees. I looked for another invariable adjunct: an enlarged Victorian photograph of the founder, and there it was, with high unaccustomed collar and lacquered moustaches with a Kaiserish twist, also the hanging portraits of Queen Joanna and – sad, primly moustached and sympathetic in a white uniform with his hands resting on his sword hilt – Czar Boris.* (It always came as a surprise when knowing Bulgarians reminded me that their royal house – Saxe-Coburg-Gotha – is, in the male line, the same as ours. Czar Boris was immensely popular, and rightly so by all accounts.)

Two card games were in full swing, and each card in its turn

---

* Czar Boris III married Joanna, daughter of Victor Emmanuel III of Italy, and succeeded to the Bulgarian throne in 1918. He died in 1943, perhaps poisoned by Hitler for his reluctance to enter the war in support of the Axis.

was flung like a gauntlet: dominoes were shuffled and dice rattled, the cards smacked from spike to spike, and waiters summoned by brisk salvoes of masterful claps. It was clearly the hub of Rustchuk café life, the resort of merchants and the smarter retailers, of doctors, lawyers and chemists and officers. There was a table full of young naval officers with hanging, gold-mounted dirks and there was a *vladika* with a silver-topped pontifical staff and a gold pectoral ornament, his raven habit a-billow, delivering a homily to – I learnt – the mayor and the town clerk; his white beard gushed from his ears, his nostrils, his cheeks and almost out of his eyes, which fulminated under a mobile and hoary brow. As he underlined the flow of his rhetoric with a huge and eloquent forefinger, I could almost see the words that rolled from his mouth, in line upon line of Cyrillic script illuminated on the vellum of a missal's page. I was filled with admiration, as I had been in contemplation of the high clergy in Sofia and Rila, by the enormous height of this prelate. Later on, in Greece, I formed the idea that Orthodox bishops might be promoted by height; metropolitans are all tall, archbishops taller still and patriarchs, enormous. A friend deeply versed in these matters thinks the height comes later, in spiritual stature: preferment pulls them out like telescopes. Their long hair and all those voluminous beards seem to represent strength, as with Samson, turning them into hairy athletes of God; the opposite of the monastic humility that the shorn jowls and the stubbly scalps of the West portend. It must be on this principle that even the clergy of the Catholic Mirdites of northern Albania all grow beards. For these beards in the Greek Orthodox world suggest majority and divine majesty like the cloud that enveloped Zeus on Tenedos.

Many of the newspapers in their stiff racks were German and their readers conversed together in Austrian accents. The Armenian readers argued in Armenian, and the Sephardim ravelled their way in Ladino Spanish. All, as dealers or local agents, were connected in some way, I imagine, with the Danube trade. A sort of trance overcame me in these places. It seemed impossible to wrench myself from the lulling influences of this slowly developing continuum, the tentative permutations and exfoliations, the conjectural biographies and the hidden rapports implicit in the almost eventless flux. It had once or twice taken as long as half a day – worse than Horace's river-gazing yokel leaning over a bridge – but I had to find a hotel. The wrench was made.

~

'You look like a drowned rat!'

Already pretty wet, I had rashly set out coatless in a lull in the rain and had been caught in a cloudburst. The words were uttered with friendly concern, in German, and a few moments later, the time to fetch a towel, my head was being briskly rubbed, to an accompaniment of commiseration, with half-scolding clicks of the tongue.

I had determined to stay the night somewhere that was a bit grander than my usual squalid style, and have a bath at last, the first place I alighted on. The Czar Ferdinand? Christo Boteff? The Bulgaria? The Balkan? I found a small hotel, not far from the river, but the name has vanished. A nice-looking woman in a clean starched apron was sewing in a wicker chair in a small office room with a postcard of Archduke Otto on the wall. She switched her enquiries into German. Where had I come from? It had been raining all day. What I needed was a hot bath. She would light one at once. 'Just look at you!'

This was a rare event; the furore which demands for a bath usually aroused, were more than it was worth. This was marvellous. I had left my rucksack at the café while I hunted for a hotel, and she said the hot water would be piping hot by the time I got back with it. I set off jubilantly through the soaking streets. I soon had to wipe the smile off my face. The rucksack had gone. I had left it by a hatstand near the door. Nobody had seen it disappear, though it had attracted notice when I first splashed in with it. All enquiries were in vain, and finally the proprietor insisted on coming to the police station with me; details were given, my address recorded, general pessimism expressed, and I went back to the hotel in a gloomy frame of mind.

It was the worst thing that could have happened. I had my passport and money, the loss of the clothes would be a nuisance, the sketchbook, in which the entries had been growing scarcer, was more easily written off than it would have been a few months earlier. But it was the ten months of notes that mattered. Why on earth hadn't I posted them back to England? They weighed little enough. Why hadn't I handed the rucksack over to the clerk in the café? Why hadn't I . . . the numerous alternatives were infuriating and distressing. In a way, my whole life had seemed to revolve round these stiff-covered exercise books; keeping them up to date had acquired the charm and mystery of a secret religion, solemnized daily, and sometimes several times a day; and the books themselves had become cult objects containing the detailed log of every day's travel, flowery descriptions, conversations, rough notes and elaborate essays, verses, 'thoughts', addresses, sketches of costumes, buildings, tools, weapons, saddlery, patterns, sketch maps, plans, glossaries, first steps in German, Hungarian, Rumanian and Bulgarian, fragments of Romany and Yiddish, the words of lots of songs, attempts at verse translations from French and Latin, limericks, private puzzles and word games – all the telling but temporarily unemployable data put by for a rainy day (but almost never used), all the scribbled by-products that solitude and leisure and paper and pencil throw up. I used to gloat over these volumes, spread them out on beds, weigh them alternately in my hand and stroke their mottled bindings. The loss of the other rucksack in Munich had seemed irreplaceable at the time, but then only a month's alluvium of notes had had time to silt up. How fiercely at first I had guarded its replacement! This second loss was an amputation.

My reappearance at the hotel must have been even more woebegone than the first. The white-aproned woman at once saw that something was badly wrong. She understood this at once. 'Never mind. You're sure to get it back.' She insisted that I was shivering and, feeling sorry for myself, I willingly fell in with her solicitude. She produced a bottle of Austrian schnapps and made me swallow a couple of glasses, while I moaned with obsessive despair about my lost books. How I would have enjoyed the waiting bath at another time! It was filled from one of those tall Central European cylinders of hammered bronze, and a special fire had to be kindled for each bather. When I padded to my room – towel-swathed, clothes in one hand – I couldn't believe my eyes: there was a bedside lamp! Usually there was only a bare bulb in the middle of the ceiling. But here was a majestic reflected mahogany wardrobe, and a great Biedermeier bed with – never found in my usual humble hotels and khans – gleaming clean sheets, the top one buttoned, Mitteleuropa fashion, on to a bright red eiderdown. On the wall hung oleographs of an Alp at dawn and Lake Maggiore with the Borromeo Islands (stirring childhood memories for me) and a lute-playing love-scene from *Orlando Furioso*. Laid out across the eiderdown was an old-fashioned white nightshirt. I donned it, and slipped in. The soles of my feet met the surface of a giant earthenware hot water bottle. It was unbelievable! All passion spent, I lay back, stripped of possessions, in a floating condition of melancholy peace. There was a touch of the relief and impotence that might overcome an outlaw in the prison infirmary apprehended after a long chase over the moors. But only a touch; the rest belonged to the *Arabian Nights*.

I was roused from it by the pressure of a tray: 'Sit up, drink it while it's hot.' She was off again. There was some delicious soup, a jug of wine and a hot roll wrapped in a napkin, butter, pepper, salt. In five minutes this wonderful woman was back with some eggs scrambled in butter and a pear. She sat down and folded her hands in her lap. 'I went to the police while you were in your bath,' she said, 'and told them you were a famous English author, in spite of your youth; *weltberühmt* like John Galsworthy, only younger. They'll try their best.'

My benefactress (she was called Rosa) was the head maid in the hotel, in fact at present the only one, and really the manageress too. The place had seen better days, the owners took no interest in it; she did her best. It was often empty, as it was at the moment (except for me) so she'd been able to put me in the best room. Otherwise, it was rather a sad, echoing place. These bare passages! No carpets! All the repairs that needed doing! '*Ayi, mayi!*' she sighed, pulling her sewing in her lap. 'If only they'd let me do it up! You'd see!'

Rosa was from Rustchuk, but had gone as a maid with the family of a tobacco representative to Vienna at the age of seventeen and stayed on when they returned, doing various jobs in service in Austrian families, ending as lady's maid for a number of years to the wife of a Viennese banker. She had married an Austrian who drank heavily and eventually died, not before – I gathered by implication rather than statement – he had spent nearly everything. She had returned to Bulgaria only a year ago, when her employer had also died in America, where she had been planning to join her. She had travelled all over Central Europe with her mistress, and had even been to Milan and Paris. The easy manners, the style, the efficiency, the unfussy neatness were all explained. She was about forty, rather plump, with her hair in a neat round coil at the back of a fine head with an expression of slight severity in repose, disarmingly open when she talked, when her whole face was lit by amusement and interest.

She was a born storyteller. Before a couple of hours had past, I knew the names of her employers and of all their sons and daughters and friends and the exact atmosphere of their house in the Ringstrasse and their Styrian country house, and the various characters in the servants' hall, and the details of a fascinating network of quarrels, love affairs, flirtations and crises in both regions. She was full of confidence and kindness. I could have watched her deft sewing and listened to her fascinating tales for ever. Many of them were so funny that I could hear the hotel reverberate with my laughter. She told them with just the right amount of burlesque and mimicry. She had been very fond of these people, especially her mistress, who sounded delightful; but her sense of the absurd presented them, inevitably, in comic roles. After an hour or so, she rolled up her work, straightened the sheets and tucked me in with a matron-like competence. I begged her to go on telling me these stories. 'Tomorrow,' she said, 'bedtime now. Don't forget to turn off the light.' She went out with the piled tray, shutting the door with a long-practised half hook, half flick behind her with one foot, a shoulder skilfully applied as a buffer to stay it from slamming. I was still so engrossed in the adventures and tribulations of Hansi, Max, Friedrich, Konrad, Teresa and Liselotte, and wondering what the sequels would be, that I didn't think about the day's disaster till I was nearly asleep. She gave me a bound volume of *Max and Moritz* to look at. Perfect.

~

I woke up to see a large policeman beside my bed. My rucksack. It had been found! A thief had been apprehended with it hastening along the Dobrudja road. He knew no details. When I got up, would I please come to the station and sign certain documents and make a statement. 'Not now, he's ill,' Rosa said from behind him. 'There you are, you see?' she said to me triumphantly. The policeman went out and came back lugging the familiar burden that I had carted round so many months. I was to check the contents. The last-minute dread was allayed in a moment: there all the notebooks were, tucked down the sides to take up less room. The thief, whoever he was, must have been in too much of a hurry to jettison them. I extracted them with excitement and relief. The policeman saluted and left. While I exulted over this recovered hoard, Rosa was ransacking the rest, flinging out one dirty and crumpled trophy after another with clicks of horror and holding a grimy shirt or fetid sock full of holes between finger and thumb with cries of 'Pfui!' and 'I ask you!' '*Ich frage Sie!*' The things at the bottom, which I hadn't seen for weeks, emerged in a cascade of walnut shells, half rotten apples, dried herbs for making tea, an aluminium egg with salt in one end, red pepper in the other, an onion or two, dismembered garlic cloves (never used), pencil stubs, india rubbers, dust, crumbs, broken cigarettes and tobacco leaves; also, a marvellous trove, a bent but smokeable packet of Nadejda's cigarettes. She finally swept out in a resolute manner with a great bundle.

The contents were slightly varied all the time by a slow process of discard and acquaintance. But now, I think, they were roughly the following. One pair of pyjamas, two grey flannel shirts, a couple of blue short-sleeved ones, two white cotton shirts that could be worn with a tie at a pinch, two pairs of grey canvas trousers, one kept for best, some socks, one dark blue tie and one red one mostly used as a belt, a thick soft white pullover with a high neck, and quantities of different and brightly coloured hand-kerchiefs, starting with red and white spotted ones that navvies carry their dinner in. The great sartorial treasure among all this was a thin, light, beautifully cut grey tweed jacket. It had been fished out of a wardrobe and bestowed on me in Transylvania by a compassionate Hungarian lady whose grandson had been in the Argentine for ten years ('He's getting so rich, he'll never miss it'). It had been made by a very good Budapest tailor and I felt different the moment I put it on, ready for anything almost. With the best pair of trousers properly ironed, I could become almost presentable, though I wished I had a very thin blue suit to cut a dash with in smart urban circles, on the rare occasions that I ventured into them. All this was let down at the lowest level by the ghastly canvas shoes I had bought in Orșova, to which, apart from a pair of gym shoes, my heavy boots were the only alternative footgear.

My outfit was completed by the bad-weather stuff I had been wearing: the brown leather jacket, which had become wonderfully weathered and soft, the comfortable breeches which had also borne the strain well, already a year old when I set out, their strapping, too light at first, long indistinguishable from the rest; and a wide, rather dashing leather belt with a brass buckle that I was very attached to. Those studded boots, the heroes of this walk, resoled and patched, could go on for ever. The puttees probably had a slightly silly and pseudo-military look, but they were wonderful for weather like this, and gave one a feeling of untiring solidity. There was the private soldier's greatcoat hanging on the door, proof against anything. I had always been meaning to get it dyed. (But what colour?) Lastly, in the corner, leant the heavy, beautifully balanced Hungarian walking-stick, given me on the Alföld, carved all over with a twisting pattern of oak leaves: a bit showy, but better than the lost ashplant from Sloane Square that I had set out with, encrusted by shiny aluminium *Stocknägel*, those little figurative plaques that stationers in all German and Austrian towns supply to *Wanderer*. It would have become a glittering and embarrassing wand by now, of which I would have been thoroughly sick but sentimentally unable to discard. I had a great fetishistic regard for its supplanter. The only other article of wearing I owned was the old, rather soft silver medal, the size of a penny, that Nadejda had found at the bottom of the chest and tied round my neck with a leather bootlace. It had a sailing ship tossing in a storm on one side, and on the other an equestrian saint driving his spear through a dragon: St George or St Dimitri. (It was impossible to tell which – they are distinguishable in Byzantine iconography only by the colours of their steeds: a grey for one, a roan for the other.)

Other chattels dug out by Rosa strewed the table: the *prazdnik*-divining kalpack, a roll of red-patterned braid belt from Arad, a shepherd's flute from Transylvania, unplayable by me except for two blurred and doubtful notes, a broken Austrian tobacco pipe with a perched chamois, and a Bulgarian one with a thin earthenware bowl and a bamboo stem like a short calumet that I had self-consciously puffed at for a week or two, a Maria Theresa thaler, a carved round wooden flask for *slivo*, a couple of penknives and the Bulgarian dagger in its sheath, a small compass, sketchbooks, writing materials (pencils from HH to BB), and the two wonderful Freytag's Viennese maps of Eastern Europe. (One, in shreds, is in front of me at this very second, the sole survivor of this random hoard. I had not noticed at the time that they must have been just pre-war, as Bosnia and Herzegovina were included in the Austrian frontier. Bulgaria's frontiers, too, showed one of their brief bulges.) Then apart from the notebooks, there were one or two pocket dictionaries, and some maps that I got rid of when finished. On top of these now was *Crime et châtiment*. I think that's the lot. All this was fairly bulky. That wonderful Bavarian rucksack not only held a lot, but, with its padded frame and its wide straps, seemed light. No need to stoop. Anyway, one of the rewards of this kind of travel was the tremendous health it brought with it. I felt sweated and sunburnt to the bone, thin, muscular, tingling with strength and energy and capable of absolutely anything, a sense of such well-being and vigour that even vast smoking and lack of sleep seemed to have no effect at all.

This being so, I felt a fraud wallowing in bed, and told Rosa. But why not? She said it was still raining, and it was nice for her to have something to do for a change. While she was wrestling with the washing, I luxuriated in the recovery of my effects and scribbled away in the notebook; and when she'd finished, she brought in a dress she was cutting out, and worked at it on the table, more fascinating stories coming out as she snipped and sliced the cloth with huge scissors. I think she liked having company in this rather forlorn building, and I revelled in this marvellous return to nursery spoiling, and the delight of Rosa's conversation and kindness as a just-wrecked traveller might in an unexpected oasis. She had to go out after lunch and I began *Crime and Punishment* against a patter of rain and an occasional siren from the Danube. Sitting up I could see the river grey and cheerless in the rain, but magnificent nevertheless, with strings of barges and log rafts floating downstream. It seemed to have widened enormously since I had last seen it at Lom Palanka a century ago, though the Jiu and the Olt were the only two big rivers which had joined since then, both from the Rumanian shore. On the far side lay the Rumanian town of Giurgiu and the flat plain with a few scattered trees. I had seen the great river so many times since that first narrow river at Ulm that I felt I had a share in it.

Feeling restless, I got up and wandered down to the quays by the warehouses and then back into the town. I was intrigued by the number of Armenian names over the shops, not only because I have always liked them, but for a special reason. Michael Arlen*

---

* Michael Arlen (1895–1956), author of *The Green Hat* and other romances, much celebrated in 1920s London, where he lived. PLF had loved his novels at school.

was born here, under the name of Dikran Kouyoumjian. I asked in an Armenian ship's chandlers if they knew anything about him. 'Yes – yes – yes – let me see,' the old chandler murmured, 'Kouyoumjian . . . of course! There used to be some! But not for many, many years . . .' Yes, he had heard one was a great writer in Europe, yes, yes . . .

The Sephardic Jews were another minority group in Rustchuk. They had prospered in Ottoman times, and the Turks, I think, used to do much of their business through them; they were thought more reliable than the disaffected Bulgars; like the Jews of Plovdiv, they spoke Spanish and had every reason to be grateful to the Turks, as the Ottoman Empire, and Tuscany, were about the only places which welcomed them after they were expelled from Spain in 1492 by Ferdinand and Isabella. The most distinguished member of this little community is Elias Canetti, the author of *Crowds and Power* and *Auto-da-Fé*; but he, like Rosa, had gravitated to Vienna at the age of six, and became Viennese. (I met him two months before writing this, staying under the same friendly roof in the island of Euboea that is sheltering me at this very moment. We talked of Rustchuk, but very understandably my memories were fresher than his.)

A film poster arrested these strollings: a badly painted picture of a fair-haired girl in a man's tailcoat with a cigarette and a top hat at a dashing angle. Underneath, the huge capitals said 'THE BLUE ANGEL' with Marlene Dietrich and Emil Jannings. It was the first night, and starting in an hour. I rushed home and overrode Rosa's objections. There was no time to waste. I was rather impressed by my authoritative tone. She blushed with pleasure at the plan, cooked an omelette at high speed, and changed. I put on my beautifully ironed coat and we set off. The film had been out several years. I knew all the songs and all about it, but strangely, considering my passion for the star, whose only competition was Greta Garbo, I had missed it. Rosa had seen it on a trip to Frankfurt-am-Main when it was first released, but longed to see it again. We were just in time.

On the way back, transported by the film, half depressed and half elated, we passed the rucksack café. I said, 'Come on, a drink!' She said, 'No, no, no. Please! Out of the question. This isn't Vienna. It's where all the *Hochbürgertum* of Rustchuk go.' I insisted. It was the first time I'd seen Rosa anything but completely self-possessed. She sat very straight with her hands deep in her overcoat pockets, looking better and more quietly dressed, I thought, than anyone else. We drank three brandies and were the last to leave, and returned to the hotel singing the songs out of the film. I thought I would try out on her my ridiculous trick of singing backwards: *Falling in Love Again* was my favourite standby; I'd never tried in German. I worked it over in my head as she talked and then said: 'It's much better like this. Listen:

> *Chi nib nov Fpok sib Ssuf*
> *Fua Ebeil tlletsegnie*
> *Nned sad tsi eniem Tlew!*'

Rosa was puzzled. We stopped under a lamp. English or French or Russian: she knew what they sounded like. Was it Swedish? Finnish? Latvian? I told her. 'Sing it again, very slowly, please,' she said. I did so and she listened intently. When I'd reached *sthcin* again, on a languorous note, she let out a great laugh, gave me a pitying look, tapped her temple with a forefinger, and said, in a purposely exaggerated Austrian accent: 'I fear you're completely cracked.' (She said, '*Leider, ganz deppert.*') 'Now once more at the ordinary tempo . . .'

～

When I had sat down, been offered a cigarette and a Turkish coffee and signed for the receipt of the rucksack and its contents in the chief of police's office, I tried to find out what had happened. He was plainly embarrassed that such a thing had occurred in Bulgaria, and apologized elaborately. There were bad people everywhere . . . It was all a mistake . . . His hands fluttered into the air. Rosa's line about my being a MAN OF LETTERS seemed to have borne fruit, to judge by the confused deference. In the middle of these puzzling explanations, there was a sound of people passing through the outside room and the officer broke off to tell them to shut the door. In the middle of the outer room was an unmistakeably familiar face. No mistaking those hare's eyes and red hair! I had felt stricken with guilt about my treacherous conduct on the Rustchuk road ever since. I waved and shouted a hearty and insincere greeting: 'How goes it, Ivancho?'

'Do you know him?' the officer asked in a bewildered voice. I told him we were old friends, and got up to greet him. Never too late to mend. I saw he was wearing handcuffs. The whole thing slipped into place.

I imagined, thinking with unaccustomed speed, that he must have seen me going into the café or through the window of the café, and the whereabouts of the rucksack, and when I had left, nipped indoors and carried it off. No wonder he was less voluble than usual now!

He looked terrible, pale green in the face and with a bad cut on one lip and what looked like the beginning of a black eye. I had heard about automatic police roughness, not in Bulgaria only but in nearly every country hereabouts. His appearance was so utterly woebegone, and there was something rather sinister about his silence. I remembered that I had long ago come to the conclusion that he was off his head. The rucksack was safely mine again and I was having a marvellous time. I also felt that I had so often been in the soup and that he was up to the neck in it, that my presence in the ranks of established authority had a trace of farce; especially of an authority that mistreated its prisoners. In the space of a second I found myself on his side.

I pretended for once to speak even worse Bulgarian than I really did. I took up the officer's words about a mistake. There'd been a *strashni* mistake; a terrible one! I pointed in bewilderment to Ivancho's handcuffs and looked from face to face with outrage. The officer and the two policemen with Ivancho looked equally bewildered. I kept saying he must have been going to the wrong hotel with it, forgotten the name, and frowned meaningly at Ivancho hoping he would take the cue. Then, saying it was a shame I couldn't speak better Bulgarian, I left, after a friendly and ostentatious slap on Ivancho's shoulder, and told them all to wait till I got back with someone who could explain better.

Rosa had just finished ironing. All my possessions stood in a crisp pile. She listened intently while I unfolded the curious tale, and put on her coat. She thought it silly to interfere. After all, he had stolen it. But as I seemed so keen . . . She knew the chief of police and said she would talk to him first, and then come and collect me. I settled in a café a couple of streets away. She was back in an hour. 'Well,' she said smiling, 'it's all right. I said you only spoke very little more German than Bulgarian, that he was a friend and that you had asked him to pick up the rucksack and that he had started out for the wrong hotel when he was picked up. I felt a bit of a fool – I'd been so urgent about their finding it the night before last. Your friend caught on to the idea and said the correct things – far too much. I pretended to be in as much of a muddle as any of them. I'm not sure how convinced the police were but they are certainly confused. I told them again how famous you are and I think they are glad to be rid of the whole business.'

'Do you think they'll let him go?'

'Oh, he's out already. I said I'd take him back to the hotel.' Seeing my look of consternation, she laughed. 'It's all right. I got rid of him. I told him you had left. He's on his way back to Pazardjik.' She paused. 'You are quite right about his being mad. When I told him I knew all about what had really happened, he looked at me in real astonishment. He was convinced, so I didn't press the matter. He's perfectly happy.' We both laughed. She was amazing.

I was catching the boat across the Danube that evening. The weather had cleared up. After packing my rucksack with all my reborn possessions, I paid my bill at the hotel. Rosa had tempered the wind to the shorn lamb to an almost indecently small total. We drove out in one of the Sherlock Holmes carriages to a tavern on a low cliff above the river in a clump of moulting poplars and Spanish chestnuts. Outside was a small concrete dance-floor, now choked with mud and leaves. It was shut for the season, but the driver went to fetch the owner from some nearby cottages, and we ate looking down at the Danube and the flat extent of the Wallachian plain beyond. The wind was shredding the clouds and sending shafts of sunlight and cloud shadows racing like a shifting map on the beautiful and sad prospect of the river and the woods. These gusts drew spirals of leaves past the plate glass window of the empty tavern. All the emotions of the morning and, once again, the imminence of departure, acted as a brake on talk at first, but it didn't matter. I felt I'd known Rosa for ages. But after a couple of glasses of *slivo* which Rosa tipped down very fast and with a grimace as though it were some awful medicine, and long before we had got through those jugs of wine, mostly swallowed by me, we were talking and I was laughing more than ever. Afterwards we found and collected lots of chestnuts, which were bursting out of their felt-lined spiny caskets all over the soaking grass, and sat on a log, looking upstream and wondering how many days the Austrian share of the water flowing past below had taken since Passau, Linz, Krems, Vienna and Bratislava, and for that matter, from its source in the Black Forest?

It was getting late, so we shouted for the driver. He stumbled up from the cottages, jumped on to his perch, cracked his whip, and set off at full tilt. We sang Austrian songs most of the way. The coachman pulled a bottle out of his pocket and waved it behind his back. 'Just as well you're going,' Rosa said, 'or I'd be in an alcoholic's home.' *Wien* was followed by *Adieu mein kleiner Gardeoffizier, In einer kleinen Konditorei, Sag beim Abschied leise Servus,* the *Kaiserjägermarsch, Ich bin von K. u. K. Infanterieregiment, Gute Nacht, Wien* and *Zu Mantua in Banden der treue Hofer war.** 'Do sing *Ich bin von Kopf bis Fuss*† backwards,' she said as we clattered into Rustchuk. The boat looked as if it were moving. I paid the driver as we pounded along, and we exchanged farewells as it drew up. It was nearly dark.

We only got to the quay just in time. They waited a moment, complaining bitterly, while I clambered on board, and the coachman threw my rucksack over the widening gap. 'Don't lose it again!' Rosa shouted laughing. She stood and waved and smiled, the other hand in the wide pocket of her blue overcoat, and I waved back until the little ship was amid-stream and we couldn't see each other waving farewell. There was a greenish sky upstream as we dropped anchor on the Rumanian shore.

---

* 'Vienna', followed by 'Farewell my little Guards officer'; 'In a little café'; 'When you part, say softly Goodbye'; 'Kaiser's Hunting March'; 'I belong to the Imperial and Royal (*kaiserlich und königlich*) infantry regiment'; 'In Mantua was the loyal Hofer captured'.
† 'I'm head over heels . . .'

5

The Wallachian Plain

It was strange at first to be addressed as *domnule* instead of *gospodin*, to switch back from inchoate Bulgarian to inchoate Rumanian, and to see, in lieu of a short *slivo* glass on the table, *tzuika* in a little triangular noggin with its cylindrical neck; on the newspapers and advertisements, instead of Cyrillic, lines of Latin characters with the hovering diacritics – a circumflex and an upside-down crescent that nasalized or muffled vowels, and below, strap-hanging cedilla-like subscripts that turned *s* into *sh* and *t* into *tz*. To clinch the changeover, were it needed – for the difference of atmosphere was discernible immediately with none of these giveaway indices – on the wall was the intelligent, rather puffy face of King Carol* under an appropriately Hohenzollern-looking helmet (sometimes with an eagle on top, sometimes with a waterfall of white horsehair) and below it a gleaming breastplate and over the shoulders the Order of Michael the Brave. Beside him, invariably, was a picture of Prince and ex-King Michael, whom his father, suddenly returning from exile, had displaced from the throne (remaining there until, a decade or so later, the

---

* King Carol II (1893–1953), the scandal-ridden ruler of Rumania from 1930–40. While heir apparent, he had surrendered his future crown to his son, Prince Michael, following an illicit liaison, but returned to oust him five years later. In 1940 General Ion Antonescu forced Carol to abdicate, and Michael returned to the throne.

positions once more reversed): a nice-looking soft-eyed little boy in a jersey or an open shirt and thick hair beautifully brushed.

Sometimes, but seldom – owing, one was always being told, to a coolness between the King and his mother – the fine, rather full features of Queen Marie were displayed, whose immense and lustrous eyes were so incongruously set in her white, nun-like coif and the barbette under the chin that framed her face. But it did not need these emblems, nor the different tricolour over the customs shed nor the eagle on the lei in my pocket, which had replaced the leva's rampant lion, to underline the changeover. There was something quicker, sharper, more brittle and more vocal – more glib perhaps – in the people all round, something very different to the rough-hewn, slow solidity of the ones I had just left. It was the change from the Slav to the Latin world. The dark extent of the Danube outside, with the twinkling necklace of Rustchuk the other side (what was Rosa up to? Having supper? Reading? Polishing? Sewing?) with its dotted line of frontier down the middle, was a far wider gulf than its actual geographic span.

A few dozen miles upstream on the opposite bank, on the same side of Rustchuk as the place where we had lunched, just about where the last of the daylight had vanished, was the site of the Battle of Nicopolis in 1396, where Sigismond of Hungary, who later became Holy Roman Emperor, and a large force of French knights under Jean Sans Peur, son of Philip II le Hardi of Burgundy, campaigning eastwards to check the Ottoman menace, were defeated and captured by Bajazet the Thunderbolt, and held prisoner by him in Turkey till they were ransomed. (Six years later Bajazet himself was beaten at Ankara by Tamburlane and put in a cage, and thirteen years later still many of the same French knights fought at Agincourt.) It is seldom one comes across irruptions of the Western world into the strange and dim-seeming no-man's-land of the Orthodox principalities and Slav czardoms that stretched between the frontiers of the Roman Empire of the Byzantine East and the Holy Roman Empire on the middle Danube. But a few hundred miles south, three centuries before, they became familiar enough from the Crusades, whose first advance took the north Aegean route across Macedonia to Asia Minor. That strange itinerary inaugurated a Western migration that eventually scattered the Levant with cloisters, tiltyards, belfries, kestrelled battlements and cloistered banqueting halls, and slowly turned the Norman paladins of Sicily into satraps among the jasmine: brocaded figures in turbans with hawks on their wrists, more fitting on a Persian miniature than the Bayeux tapestry.

~'

Wallachia, in spite of its name in Rumanian – Muntenia, the mountain country – is, on the whole, plain land. Further north, ranges of hills wander across it which finally rear into the steep, high and grand range of the Transylvanian Alps, the southernmost westward swing of the Carpathians, on the other side of which lay Transylvania, where I had dallied so long earlier in the year. But these southern Danubian marshes were unlike the Bulgarian side where the land sinks to the river in a slow staircase of ledges and breaks off at the bank in a cliff. The river ends, the plain begins, and quite often in this uncompromising flatness, the middle distance was blurred by stretches of marshland, busy with water birds, that looked exactly like the conventional signs for them on maps.

The main road, along which I trudged – there was no point in branching off – ran straight as an arrow from horizon to horizon. Enormous flocks grazed across it. The peasants and the herdsmen were shod in the familiar rawhide footgear – *opinci* in Rumania, *tzervuli* in Bulgaria – but the rest, as it had been in

Transylvania, was all white, with belted white tunics jutting almost to their knees like untucked-in shirts. Again, they were all wearing *cojocs*, those jackets of sheepskin, shaggy-side in, smooth-side out, a jigsaw of patterns and seams; and instead of the flat, hussar-like kalpacks of the Bulgarians, they wore *caciulas*, lopsided cones of black and brown sheepskin. Every few miles there was a tumble-down village of whitewashed houses and reed thatch, the assembly points of long wagons drawn by horses or buffaloes, then the plain. 'Left' and 'right' in Rumanian are *stinga* and *dreapta*. I think that it was on this road that I first noticed the Rumanian peasant words for them when they are addressing buffaloes or oxen. '*Hooisss!*' they utter, in a deep and long-drawn note – and the beasts slowly lurch to the left; '*tchala!*' – and they turn right. Gypsy caravans were much more frequent than on the other side of the Danube, and there were many encampments by the road. I several times kept company with the nomadic ones, but usually defected after a mile or two. I always seemed to draw a blank, which was all the more humiliating when I remembered with what ease other Balkan travellers seemed to get on hobnobbing terms. I did get to know several Rumanian Gypsies fairly well a year or two later in Moldavia, but these were static communities, Romany-speaking but settled in villages where they had lived for many generations – ever since the abolition of feudal serfdom on large estates in the middle of the last century. With the nomads, I seemed unable to break through the begging barrier which they feel in honour bound to maintain.

Further east this plain turns into the real steppe in the Baragan, which lies in the great northward loop of the Danube, and over-flows across it into the Dobrudja the other side: utterly barren and desolate, and in its sinister way very beautiful. Nothing but thistles grow there and these wither and blow about the surface of the steppe, joining with others until they form great globes of moving stuff, like giant thistledown. I only crossed it once, in a car in midsummer. The wind had set these globes racing, and as it grew stronger, gathered them up, with the surrounding dust and whatever sticks and rubbish had fallen from the carts that wend their way across, with a few rotten bits of planking. They twisted into whirling spirals of debris that climbed and spun at a bewildering rate to become thick dust-devils hundreds of feet high, dark with plucked-up rubbish and twirling in ever-varying girths like irregular barley sugar till they frayed out at an enormous height. All the debris which had been plucked into this gyre and rushed up its ascending whirls was then scattered loose along the wind. Three others had sprung up at the same time and all of them whirled mopping and mowing with a loud rushing noise across the wilderness, all leaning in the same direction and appearing to gesticulate wildly with the loose ends of their fraying and widening summits. The plain was still alive with mirages; these four pillars careered across a sunset that the hanging mantle of dust refracted into a vast and tragic drama of orange and amber and blood red and violet, and came to bits in the distance. There are tales of whole wagons being gathered up by these twisting demons, with sheep and buffaloes. The peasants talk of lonely shepherds running across the plain pursued by them, overtaken and spun into the sky and discovered later as smashed and mangled scarecrows. No wonder these things lend themselves to legend; if they are legends . . .

The plain I was crossing was nothing like this; but the desolate tendency was latent in the monotonous, forlorn and rather beautiful champaign on either hand. A feeling of profound melancholy and hopelessness overhangs these plains. In the great tract between the river and the mountains, there is, beyond the wells, nothing to arrest the eye, no skeleton of rock to jut through the even surface, no hint of the variety that quickens the steep leafy world of Transylvania. It is better in summer when it is dressed in sweeping fields of wheat and maize, but even then the melancholy lingers. The villages jut from the surface with something of the uncertainty of mirages and there is a tame, passive docility in the voices and in the expressions of the inhabitants. It is as if history had knocked all the stuffing out of them. Ruled by Orthodox princes, who were often tyrannical and extortionate, and exploited by their own landowning countrymen, they had been deprived, except for occasional abortive agrarian outbursts, even of that stimulus of revolt against an alien conqueror that had acted as a spur and a salve on the mutineers of Greece, Bulgaria, Serbia, Montenegro and the Christian parts of the population of Bosnia, Herzegovina and Albania; and though the Christians of the Balkans were lumped together in common servitude by the Ottomans, they were all in the same boat, and they were spared the domestic serfdom that held sway north of the Danube, and which the landowners themselves, during the liberal trends of the nineteenth century, voted out of existence. There had been romantic Robin Hood-like figures – mostly in the mountains – but, here again, the pandours and haiduks, when they were something more than mountain robbers, were at war with domestic injustices rather than with the concrete, universal, other enemy in a turban, as the Klephts were, and the comitadjis further south. For direct Ottoman rule stopped at the river. But for centuries the two principalities of Wallachia and Moldavia (which only since the mid-nineteenth century have been united under the collective name of Rumania) were vassals of Turkey, and one of the chief tasks of the elective princes who sat on the ancient thrones of Michael the Brave and Stephen the Great was to amass the huge yearly tribute to the Sultan and (a self-appointed duty) enrich themselves at the same time. It is hard to determine whether this subjection to Turkish greed at one remove was more or less onerous to the principalities in general than the more immediately galling Ottoman yoke on the napes of peasants of the Balkans.

When the two principalities were united in the mid-nineteenth century, their joint prince, Alexander Cuza, was succeeded, after a short reign, by Charles of Hohenzollern, who later became King Carol I. This, the old kingdom – as opposed to the new, which was formed by all the provinces awarded to Rumania after the Great War at the Treaty of Trianon – was the Regat: Rumania *par excellence.* The new provinces which were suddenly on ethnological grounds attached to this ancient core, many of which had been detached for centuries, were the Dobrudja south of the Delta, which the Bulgars claimed; Bessarabia, which had been Russian for a hundred years or more; Bukovina in the far north, which had been a far-flung wingtip of the Austrian Empire; Transylvania and the Banat in the south-west, formerly a part of Hungary – thus enormously enlarging the country, increasing its wealth and exciting the irredentist anger of its neighbours, more especially of Hungary and Bulgaria.

It was impossible to say how much the dismal last few centuries – or were they dismal all through history? – had contributed to the fatalistic melancholy that I thought I always detected in Rumanian peasants, and more particularly in those of the plains, or how much the many agrarian reforms, the fragmentation and refragmentation of the great estates, and their piecemeal distribution, had done to mitigate it. Apart from other causes of distress, Rumanian annals read like a catalogue of disasters: the biblical onslaught of insects, the destruction of crops, murrains, fearful plagues that again and again reaped entire populations, the passage of armies, loot, fire and rapine. Above all, in the huge and unannalled centuries before the first monks wrote their chronicles and after the last Roman legions (from whom, with the autochthonous

Dacians, the Rumanians directly descend) had been recalled to Rome, these plains were the halting place and the camp, the vast vacant lot, in which all the barbarians, sweeping west from Asia, and through the Scythian wilderness north of the Black Sea – Goths, Huns, Avars, Magyars, Bulgars, Cumans and Petchenegs – drew rein before plunging south and south-west across the Danube to hasten the death of Rome, and then to batter at the walls of Byzantium, and perhaps take root in the Balkans; or to head west, clean through the mild, shifting flock of Slavs, to challenge western Christendom, threaten Paris, conquer and repeople Spain, or like the Magyars, take root in the Pannonian plain.

But whatever the woes and vicissitudes of history may have been, it is hard to believe that these inert, seemingly limitless flatlands, with their parched and dusty surface in summer and their expanses of snow in winter and the vast sky and those beautiful doomed sunsets every day, could be an ambience for bursting optimism, high spirits or resilience. Rumanian is rich in words expressing shades of sadness; the long-drawn monosyllable of *dor*, meaning a vague, anxious, unfocussed unhappiness and longing (though it can be used in the specific sense of sad longing in love) captures it exactly: '*mi e dor*', 'I have *dor*', 'I long, or pine . . .' with no stated object or cause: it is often on peasant lips. Another word always struck me as being the best word I had ever heard for irretrievable gloom: *zbucium*, pronounced *zboochoum*, a desperate spondee of utter dejection, those Moldowallachian blues. '*Mi e zbucium . . .*' (Although there is no connection between the two words beyond a similarity in the ear, this word always conjures up another Rumanian word – *bucium* – which means 'a long metal horn', of four or five yards, upheld on dutiful shoulders, and turned up at the end – looking very similar to those in use among Buddhist priests and in lamaseries – which shepherds and cowherds blow to summon their flocks in the high Carpathians, sending long, sinister booms of amazing *zbucium*-bearing balefulness echoing down the valleys of the Olt and the Bistritza.)

All this is treacherous ground. We know all about the melancholy of the steppes and the sadness of the plains from many colourful travel accounts: the longing and *Sehnsucht* of open places, and the rustic soul finding its expression in music and things that many a fruity voice, keeping track with a silhouetted herdsman leading his flock into the sunset, has dog-eared beyond any acceptable limit of staleness. I wish it hadn't, for here it is precisely and almost uniquely applicable. Much of Rumanian music and singing, which I loved, embodies all these things, and especially a kind of song called a *doina*. This has nothing to do with the gymnastic changes of tempo from languorous to breakneck in which Gypsies are expert, or the more oriental plangency and the different scale of the Balkans, or the high-pitched, quavering dirges of the Deep Mani. It is an emanation of villages and fields and plains, infinitely slow and with long pauses and unseizable tunes, transportingly beautiful, that one hears out of the window of a train or from behind a rick when harvesters have cut their last swathe or from a village at nightfall as one approaches it on foot, as I did now; stops and listens and understands that the order and scansion that these threnodies have imposed are the only way of making bearable a hovering frame of mind that says that all things to rive the heart are here, and all are vain.

～

The only place to sleep in the first *doina*-haunted village where I stopped that night was the Jewish grocer's shop, which was also the inn. The grocer was a bustling, red-haired man, very dissimilar from the Sephardim of Plovdiv and Rustchuk: an Ashkenaz of the Ashkenazim, known to the villagers as Domnul David. He conversed with his family in Yiddish and with me in quaint nasal German, *Judendeutsch*. Alas, unlike the old rabbi of the Banat, he knew little about the scriptures. I longed to ask him about the exact difference between the Torah and the Talmud, which I was always getting confused, and about the Golem and the Hasidim. There were only little isolated communities here, he said. The place to go was High Moldavia, far away in the north, in towns like Botoshani and Dorohoi – Domnul David's home town – which were almost entirely Jewish. (It is exactly what I did, a year or so later.)

Owing either to Jewish acumen or a general Rumanian inaptness for commerce, and probably both, nearly all village grocers were Jews, as was much of the trade in the towns, except in the Danube delta where the Greeks – notably in Constanţa, Galatz and Braila – were active in business concerns, especially in the barge trade on the Danube itself, where large Greek fortunes were founded. The agents and bailiffs on large estates were nearly always Greeks. Probably as a result of this, they were not always popular. But this was a mild foible compared to the deep-rooted and almost universal anti-Semitism of the Rumanians toward the million or so Jews that lived in the country. The prejudice was even more violent than in Hungary. It was not only that all the vices were attributed to the village innkeepers, grocers and traders; the sentiment had a nearly mystical intensity. The legends of ritual murder were still, at the peasant level, believed. But at a more sophisticated one, Hungarians seemed still more obsessed with the question than were the Rumanians. The books of Jean and Jérôme Tharaud – *La Fin des Habsbourg, Quand Israël n'est plus roi*, etc. – were constantly being given me to read in order to put me right about the part played by the Jews in the Bela Kun revolution. It was not at all uncommon to hear people talking of the plan for world domination – long exposed as a fraud – contained in *The Protocols of the Elders of Zion*. (This plot, according to one genealogically minded Hungarian squire, was being implemented, generation after generation, by Jewish infiltration by marriage of the entire aristocracy of Western Europe, with France in the lead and England as a runner-up. To press his point home, he showed me a rare volume which was often mentioned but seldom seen, called the *Semi-Gotha.* This squat, thick handbook compiled by someone who must have had the singleness of purpose of M. Galtier-Boissière, was of the same format and consistency as the three reference volumes published at Gotha which seemed to form the only reading of some squires who were barely literate in other branches of knowledge: the red-bound *Hofkalender* of royal, mediatized and princely families, the blue-bound *Gräfliche,* and the green *Freiherrliches Taschenbuch.* A privately printed fourth volume was bound in yellow; and instead of the appropriate crowns and coronets of the others, it was embossed by a gold Star of David. To illustrate the spread of world Jewry and the unlikely guises under which it lurked, the squire pointed, with a thin and armorial little finger and an expression of melancholy triumph, at name after name. 'Winston Churchill' was the first he pronounced, Lord Rothermere* the second: rather sadly, as the Lord Rothermere of the day was considered the white hope of Hungarian revisionism. So you can never tell, he said. He was puzzled and hurt when I doubted the importance and accuracy of his favourite book.)†

These hostile feelings were much more deeply rooted in the

---

* Harold Harmsworth, 1st Viscount Rothermere (1868–1940), founder of the *Daily Mirror,* was a supporter of Hungary's claim to revise the 1920 Treaty of Trianon and readjust the country's boundaries. A statue to him survives in Budapest.

† Contrary to PLF's dismissive description, the *Semi-Gotha* was an unbiased survey of those families of Jewish ancestry who were members of the European nobility. The Nazis later used it to identify them.

north, where the Jewish population had increased from about two thousand families to close on a million in a hundred and thirty years, most of them in flight from the appalling conditions in Poland and the Russian Pale, until in several large Moldavian towns, including Yassy, the Moldavian capital, they now outnumbered the Rumanian inhabitants and monopolized the commerce of the province. Small wonder that this indigestible explosion of people caused dismay, resentment and hostility among the inhabitants; there was nothing comparable here to the harmonious and long established position of the polished and much less numerous Sephardim of the Ottoman world; small wonder, too, that the Jews, denied full citizenship and with nearly every route to advancement or honour denied to them, should expand and excel in the only field that was not barred by prejudice. The remote principality in which they suddenly began to proliferate had no middle class; rural society knew nothing between the mediaeval feudalism of landowners – the great and the lesser boyars, many of whom seldom set foot on their accumulations of acres – and a vast and callously exploited peasantry. There was no urban middle class, and, in Moldavia especially, as the country expanded, the Jewish population became a semi-alien bourgeoisie of middlemen and retailers.

Everyone reluctantly admitted that the Jews were honest in their dealings, however ruthless, and faithful to their agreements. I also noticed that nearly everyone, however ill-disposed in general, had one Jewish friend who 'was not like the others', an array of exemptions that must have added up to an imposing total. It was only on later travels in Moldavia and Bukovina that I got to know, talk to and even make friends with Jews not isolated in a Gentile majority. Lack of any need to conform to alien ways had left their way of life absolutely intact: the long black kaftans, broad-brimmed black velvet hats, skullcaps, black, red and blond beards, corkscrew side-whiskers (like those of my host and his son in the woods of the Banat), and a Yiddish largely unalloyed by Rumanian, but embedded with Polish and Russian words as well as the Hebrew studied by the rabbis and divinity students. Here, too, one would hear the nasal intonations and observe the oriental gestures of hunched shoulders and mobile hands raised palm upwards, at their purest. It was in these regions, and particularly in Czernovitz, the capital of Bukovina (which was under the Habsburgs till the end of World War I) that much of the Jewish talent originated which, transplanted to America, has flowered so triumphantly on the stage, the screen, in music and the arts, laced with a humorous twist to be found in no other race, which amounts to genius and supplies the world with all its funny Jewish stories.

Ever since staying with a rabbi in the Banat, I had been bent on learning as much about Jewish history as I could, and I ransacked the encyclopaedias and reference books of Sofia in any language I could understand. I had already been, for too short a time, in an Ashkenazi synagogue in Bratislava, shepherded through the customs that must beset a stranger by a Jewish friend. In Plovdiv, after listening to a fascinating saint's day Mass in the Armenian church, I had hesitated a long time outside the Sephardic synagogue, but, friendless, did not dare enter. (It was not till twenty years later, prompted by a fascination for Orthodox chant and Gregorian plainsong – and their probable descent, especially in the psalms, from the liturgy of the great temples of Antioch and Jerusalem in the time of the Apostles – that I heard Sephardic singing, beautifully executed, in the fine Carolean Portuguese-Dutch synagogue in Artillery Row, in London's City.) So I knew a lot about it: why northern Jewry spoke a German dialect and bore names of German origin – Schwartz, Weiss, Abendstern, Weintraub, Blumenblatt, Goldberg, for instance, or names with

Slav endings, like Moisky or Rabinovitch – instead of their ancient Hebrew ones. Domnul David, as we sat up talking in his general store-cum-inn after the others had gone to bed, was not much help in giving further information about the Maccabees, the Babylonian exile, the Fall of the Temple, the Diaspora and the Khazars; any more than an English grocer, it occurred to me, would know about Danegeld and the Witenagamot; but he was amused by my interest.

But he said something before putting up the shutters, which has survived. We were comparing the Jewish and the Christian religions. 'I'll tell you the great advantage of our religion over yours: nobody can practise Christianity properly and lead an ordinary life. You Christians, unless you are saints, are always falling short of what you should be; you are never in the right for a second, always guilty, always miserable, always, try as you might, in disgrace. But the Jewish religion is made for human beings. There are a few easy rules we mustn't break, that's all. We can practise our religion faultlessly, and still live like ordinary humans. It's easy to be a good Jew, impossible to be a good Christian. But Christians are no more virtuous than Jews, are they? About the same? So what's the odds? And the result? We are happy in our religion, you are all miserable, that's all. We've lots of other troubles, but not religion. *Gott sei dank*. It doesn't attack us in the back, like it does the Goim.'

~

A bracket of explanation is needed just about now, and this brief caesura, in an iron bed under the fly-pocked and leafless calendar of Jacob Bercovici, grain merchant of Galatz, illustrating Judith before Holofernes, is the very place for it.

During the last dozen pages there have been a number of references that hint at a longer acquaintance with Rumania than my summer months, exclusively among Hungarians, or the brief span of this trans-Danubian loop, could possibly warrant. What happened was this. During the five years between the end of this journey and the outbreak of war, I returned several times to all the countries we have so far crossed, with the single exception of Bulgaria, which, after the close of this year, purely by chance, I never visited again. But of all these countries, Greece (which, although it doesn't come into this account, looms beyond the last page) and Rumania were the two that I visited, and lived in, most often. In Rumania I made two sojourns of about a year each. (I might have stayed much longer had not the outbreak of war suddenly tolled like the end of a wonderful summer holiday and dragged me back to what seemed like the spiked railings of a long winter term on the clanging, stamping and shouting squares of the Guards Depot.) Settled in the dales of High Moldavia, I travelled all over the country to the Delta, Bukovina, back to Transylvania, the Dobrudja, Bessarabia and to Bucharest many times. My first memories, therefore, are overlaid by many more, and it is hard to exclude the inklings gleaned later when writing of these first encounters: to attempt to do so would be akin to assuming a spurious naivety. It will be hard to keep subsequent experience out of these earliest irruptions into the Regat. I am almost irresistibly tempted to slip in one or two balloons from a later date in the pages that lie ahead. It is a risky process, but, if I see an apt occasion – a likely paragraph ending or a beckoning gap in the rough and ready joinery of this book – I may, but not without warning the reader, let it rip. After all, I am not likely to pass this way again in print, and there are later impressions of this extraordinary country that I would like to try and recapture. I shall see how it goes.

By this dubious phrase I mean that two main problems beset the very curious and enjoyable task of compiling this private archaeology. The first is a sudden blur, when exact memory conks out and a stretch of itinerary looms eventlessly ahead and no pencil mark on the map comes to my help. This has occurred on several occasions and will again, no doubt. At first these blackouts filled me with distress. I would gaze from page to map with growing misery as the minutes passed and nothing, absolutely nothing, surfaced. Not now. I interpret this blank as an indication that there was nothing, for my private purposes, memorable there. No reflection on the landscape, the villages, towns even – or their denizens. Often I must have wandered through, or just missed, or completely failed to remember, owing to some private defect, buildings of tremendous interest (that I would give perhaps a great deal to see now), whole mountain ranges teeming with history and with natural wonders, political trends and events of momentous importance. This last consideration prompts the thought that even after such a long time-lag, this must be one of the unscoopiest travel accounts ever to see the light. My private let-out here is that this is neither a cultural handbook, a guide, nor a political or military report. (It is impolitic to dwell any longer on these shortcomings.) The cheerful obverse of all these lacunae is that they save us both from drowning in the indiscriminate flood of total recall.

The second problem is the opposite of all this: while piecing together fragments which have lain undisturbed for two decades and more, all at once a detail will surface which acts as potently as the taste of madeleine which made the whole of Proust's childhood unfurl. The haul of irrelevant detail, interlocking trains of thought and associations, and the echoes of echoes re-echoed and ricocheted, is overwhelming, and in the hopes of attaining some redeeming shadow of symmetry and balance, a lot of this irrelevant catch must be thrown away again to swim back to the dark pools where it has been lurking all this time. This, for a writer who is his own worst subeditor, is a harrowing task. At such moments, it almost seems as if the pile of empty foolscap on my left contains what I am about to write in invisible ink, and that each sheet darkens into a concatenation of detail, forgotten until that very second, as soon as it is in front of me, as though the nib-tip were fed by a developing chemical rather than ink; and by the time it joins the stack of manuscript on the right, the balloons of afterthought added to the text are large enough to carry the paper to the whitewashed Greek island ceiling overhead, and many or most of them must be punctured or deflated if any sort of balance or harmony is to be achieved.

A third problem crops up: the anxiety to present an impression of a country which is true, and by this I don't mean a true picture by any absolute standards, should such things exist, but true to the overall impression into which, on any final departure, the innumerable fragments of experience have cohered: a highly personal synthesis which would only be of use to anyone in search of a hypothetical absolute if full allowances were made for the writer's blindness, bias and half-knowledge. But I feel that if I limited these pages to the experiences of this first visit, I would end up wide of the mark. Hence the temptation to slide in one or two post-dated wedges. But this need not worry us for the moment. Whatever hovering compulsion may skulk in the different strata of my memories of Rumania, the details of my arrival in Bucharest are sharply defined; so off we go.

6

Bucharest

Bucharest floated above the level horizon in the late afternoon, a sprawling irregular mass which soon lost whatever shape or skyline it possessed in the fall of night, and in a sense, vanished again. The distant suggestion of a skyscraper or two and a scattering of tall chimneys sank below the rising darkness of its outskirts, and its amorphous aspect became vaguer still through the light, steady rain. Never had the frontier between country and town, always a gradual transition to foot-travellers, been more indistinct. Vague habitations loomed. The mud of the highroad changed by stealthy degrees into a halting, deckle-edged thoroughfare of asphalt, reticulated by wide and planetary craters filled with water. This maze of puddles and the rainy network of tarmac broke up the jagged reflections of fires and flames and windows; then, all at once, everything would be almost dark for a while until, through a clump of dripping acacias, a tier of lights would soar in a small skyscraper, and a bit further on would come the windows of a factory and a suggestion of dynamos pounding away in bright empty halls. Bare rafters and plaster fallen from brickwork, and branches growing through fissured walls and windows, spelt ruin-ation. From a wobbly hamlet hammered together out of kerosene drums, the dim wicks within them shedding a turnip-lantern glow, half-built modern houses would ascend and cease, their angular skylines whiskered with a jungle of rusting metal rods from ferro-concrete already zebra-striped with cracks and auburn stains. Huts and tents, a noticeable increase in disorder, and the tumble and click of forges, indicated Gypsies.

A fluid region; nothing was static; everything was vestigial or inchoate. A smart street of shops would shoot a brightly lit ruler of radiance through the dark, and die away in a faintly discernible cemetery, a midden or a wood.

A panther-like cat peered into a tin and plunged his head in to lick the bottom as though he were trying on a tilting-helmet. The geometry of a brickyard, a kiln's glow, six tethered horses under a dripping wing of leaves. Then it was a question of weaving a path through the carcasses of a hundred dead cars, a thousand tyres, a million bicycle wheels, and suddenly the lighted habitations would recede to the circumference of a vast maidan, which the road bisected in a ragged diameter, with shops and taverns glimmering round the edge in a widening arc of rain-reflecting flares, resembling from the dark centre – across which a random dribble of trucks and cars (one or two of them incongruously smart) as well as the long country wagons, were pitching from shell hole to shell hole like barques in a choppy sea – the lights round a lagoon.

Sharp in the glare of the city behind them, a group of skyscrapers sprouted on the further shore among the syncopated sky signs. At the very centre, in the middle of the road, was a flickering pinpoint which grew, as I approached it, into a camp fire, hopefully kindled in the waning drizzle, and round it, cross-legged, each figure sheltered by a shaggy triangle of sheepskin cape and with their heads topped by tall and bulbous cones of fur, some drovers were quietly supping, their odd silhouettes radiating spokes of shadow across the shell-shocked asphalt, the mud and the flanks of their slumbering buffaloes. As I tramped by, a claxoning Packard with a chauffeur's peaked hat glinting above the wheel, veered cursing and skidding behind the sway of his headlights in the wayside slime, conjuring them in a scream to fornicate with the Devil's mother – '*mama Dracului!*' – while the flame-lit faces munched on with the unruffled ruminance of their charges, as though they had settled for the night in the heart of the Pamirs or the Gobi. These southern tentacles of the capital seemed to belong to a mixture of Samarkand and Detroit.

I headed, moth-like, for the beckoning metropolitan glare, but I must have lost direction, for though the streets were lighted now, the indeterminate maze was still dark and ramshackle. A tram would clank past a crossroads, but never when I was near. I would stick my head into a grocer's or a drinking hole and ask the way to the centre of the town: '*la centru de oraş, ma rog?*' But I always seemed to lose the way and become deeper involved in the tumble-down wilderness. At last I crossed a bridge over a river which can only have been the Dâmboviţa and came upon a long and busy street, but of equal dilapidation. (Could it have been the Calea Moşilor?) There were frequent shop names in Hebrew characters and a few in Armenian script, among the Rumanian ones, a clanking of trams and a sudden swarming of people. It was getting late. Famished after a long trudge, I settled in a smoky eating-house that looked promising: it was called *La Pisica Vesela*, At the Merry Pussy-Cat. Most of the soaring smoke came from a stove where spindle-shaped croquettes were cooking in the flat iron top, after being deftly rolled in the enormous palms of a mild-looking cook.

I swallowed some *tzuika*, and then a large number of those *mititei* and a lot of wine. They were delicious, and there seemed no reason ever to stop eating them; or, for that matter, drinking wine. There was one place in Bucharest, I learnt later, where their excellence was attributed to the Gypsy cook rolling them, it was rumoured, on her thigh. The two most intriguing figures in the room were two bulky men drinking tea. Their bulk was chiefly caused by their thick-padded kaftans of ribbed black and dark blue velvet, caught in with belts at the waist and then expanding voluminously and spreading to the ground from innumerable gathered pleats, from which elephantine knee-boots jutted, and fastening from neck to hem, as closely as an abbé's soutane, with metal buttons. One wore a tall fur hat, the other a black cap with a little peak. The whips leaning against the wall at once connected them with two hooded, high-slung and wide carriages behind waiting horses in the mud outside. But it was not so much their garb that drew scrutiny. Their crass little blue eyes were embedded in wide, soft, smooth faces covered with tiny creases and wrinkles. They conversed in oddly high-pitched voices in a language that sounded at first like Bulgarian but soon turned out to be – judging by its shifting vowels and its liquid sounds – Russian. When they left and bowled away, I exchanged an interrogatory look with the cook. He smiled and said, '*Muscali*' – Muscovites – and the sizzling and the smoke swallowed him up.

My drive for the town's centre had lost some of its momentum. After another rambling and dilapidated furlong or two, the streets grew lighter for a few acres, and I soon saw – from the lighted doorways, the figures that loitered there, the hesitant strolling of civilians and soldiers and the doors in tumbling wooden fences leading into other lighted courtyards with figures leaning on windowsills under the trees – that I was in a brothel quarter of a humble and unsophisticated kind. Yet even so, the intriguing atmosphere which haunts such quarters hung thick in the air. The muddy street and ramshackle boards of the fences contrasted strangely with the lighted rooms where naked bulbs fell on shiny dresses the colours of boiled sweets and an occasional peroxided head of hair with its indigenous darkness beginning to creep back. One courtyard had a festoon of coloured bulbs looped across it through branches. The visiting half of the population strayed rather vacantly past the lights and the beckoning figures, with the indecision of fish in an aquarium, moodily buying walnuts from a blind seller who squatted by his brazier under the acacia. With an intermittent passion for low life, I rather longed to charge in and loiter there too, but felt, with my rucksack and stick and coat, too conspicuous a stranger for the role of auditor – rather than actor – that I aspired to: an observer in a helmet of darkness, a literary Siegfried or Perseus invisible among hempen homespuns. Anyway it was getting late, time to dump all these impedimenta and get to the heart of this new city.

A little further on I saw a small hotel that looked about my level, in spite of its daunting name. It was called the Savoy-Ritz, spelt on the wooden board below the lamp-bracket over the door, Savoi-Ritz. A hawk-nosed, elderly woman showed me to a room that was surprisingly cheerful and snug for this down-at-heel quarter. Hot and cold water: *confort moderne!* Astonishingly, she spoke French with what I had learnt to discern as a Russian accent. I asked her where she came from: Kishinev, she told me, the capital of Bessarabia, which, though formally Moldavian, had been ceded to Russia for over a century. 'What!' I said – trotting out something I had learnt in a reference book in Sofia – 'the town where Pushkin was in exile?' 'That's it,' she said, looking rather impressed. I was washing and combing my hair at high speed, suddenly hell-bent on the bright lights of the town centre. '*Un merveilleux poète, madame!*' I said warmly: I hadn't read a word of him. '*On le dit,*' she said, '*Je l'ai très peu lu . . .*' I asked her the best way to the middle of Bucharest. She looked rather hurt: 'So soon.' She asked me to stay and chat. '*On s'amuse bien ici!*' Surely I would like some company? 'No, no, I am awaited,' I said, untruthfully. She looked puzzled and amused, but set me on my way. A few streets further I stopped one of those elegant cabs. The driver was one of the Muscovites of the Merry Pussy-Cat.

I was amazed when I found myself strolling at last along the pavement of the Calea Victoriei. Amazed, excited, dazzled and rather nonplussed. The smartness of the inhabitants, the grandeur of the cars, those sleek taxis all with a band of yellow and black dicing painted round their glittering black coachwork, the shop fronts with dashing modernistic lettering over them – one of them ultra-chic, containing a single gleaming scent flagon poised on a softly lit pyramid of dove-coloured velvet against a back-drape of ruched, lemon-yellow silk – the ferro-concrete façades, the rainbow tangle of electric signs, the blazing kiosks with their polyglot flutter of periodicals, shallow and softly carpeted steps leading through the turning crystal doors of hotels into interiors of unimaginable splendour, the brightly lit populations of large and luxurious cafés, the massed hooting of a traffic block, a Rolls-load of dinner-jacketed diplomats, with   I observed with an un-analysable pathos – the lion and unicorn fluttering from a metal wand on the mudguard: all the headlamps, the shop front and café windows and electric signs shedding on to the tarmac and paving stones their reflected washes of colour – all this streamlining and glitter and the look of watertight and Olympian security, was overwhelming. I had forgotten about all this. Sofia is so small; the overshadowing mountain, the low buildings and the glimpses of open country at the end of long streets make the newcomer feel that he is in the middle of a country town rather than a capital city. Otherwise the last big town I had seen was Budapest, in April. It was the last week of October now. Seven months and over a thousand miles ago – a stretch which seemed psychologically a great deal more – had been spent among trees and mountains, much of it sleeping out or staying in peasant houses: an utterly different rhythm of life and one which, in spite of my occasional ill-tempered protests, like the sudden onslaught on the way to Rustchuk, I had adored. Now, suddenly landed in the middle of this urban hubbub, I felt alien and uprooted, and filled with the feelings of dazzled bewilderment, uncouthness and solitude that must overcome a peasant in a similar plight.

Actually, I observed, as I tramped about the streets, the town was very far from being a modern conglomeration of skyscrapers – and none of them, incidentally, as enormous as at first they had seemed. The new monsters had sprung up in a city of many styles: 1900s stucco and plaster, rather like an Eastern European equivalent of the same formula in Paris; mid-Victorian, Second Empire, ornate Moldowallachian, neo-Byzantine, with here and there a few charming pillared houses and – as soon as one got away from the central streets – an entertaining disorder of all these interlocking strains juxtaposing each other in a showy, vigorous and tumbledown synthesis. There were lifted eyebrows and murmured invitations in discreet side-streets and everywhere, in squares or under the trees, or clip-clopping nimbly over the tarmac and the cobbles with cracking whips and falsetto cries, were these hooded fiacres with their high-bracketed carriage-lamps and their kaftaned and fur-hatted drivers.

I was inevitably drawn back to the Calea Victoriei. Sentries in blue tunics and tall black fur caps mounted guard outside the gates of the Royal Palace, and further down – or was it in a street branching off to the right? – I gazed in astonishment at a vast stucco palace with many lights poised on brackets, and in mid-air on either side of an ornate gateway two enormous, puissant lions with lights flashing fiercely from their eye-sockets. I think it was a ministry of some kind, but it had originally been built, I learnt later, by that Prince Cantacuzene, one of many, who had been known, for his colossal wealth, as the Nabob. He had been conservative Prime Minister for many years, and the other members of his august and talented dynasty had never forgiven him for this amazing perpetration. I rather liked it.

Cafés succeeded each other. I tried several on one of those

solitary urban pilgrimages, in which one enters, looks round, and leaves, like inserting and withdrawing a thermometer before moving to a fresh patient – and settled in the grandest. It was packed. All was splendour, and the customers too interesting for my kiosk-bought newspapers to compete. The place had the impact of a fascinating nightmare. The first thing that struck me was the great beauty of the women – those enormous eyes! – and then the intricacy of their get-up. Surely nowhere east of Paris was there such a jungle of hats or taller heels or such a complication of pleating and cut and elaboration of detail? And the Tyrian thickness of make-up and the heavy and swooning scents that warred in the air . . . Was it all ludicrously overdone, or was it merely my jaundiced bumpkin's eye? My muddy boots shifted uneasily on the unaccustomed carpet underfoot. The men emerged even worse from this biased scrutiny: those tremendous padded shoulders and vast lapels, the flash of rings and tiepins, the patent-leather reflection in those solid, blue-black helmets of hair, the Pierrot-like pallor of the faces; a lupine predatoriness of expression, a cynical croupier glint in every eye seemed to announce that everything and everyone had its price, including the owner. The older faces looked like allegorical masks of the Seven Deadly Sins. Was it this urban, talcum paleness and softness, the bistred* eyes, a sort of indoor stagey self-satisfaction, after the weather-beaten rustic faces which for months had been the only ones I had seen, that I found so disturbing? They looked shiny and commercial despite their rice-paper cheeks. I had the illusion that the talk of this gleaming and over-upholstered Babylon consisted entirely of sneers. Not at me. (Only, I thought, the white-coated and gold-spangled waiter as he plonked my glass down on the brass round table – or was this an illusion too?) Everyone, in the scores of

---

* Bistre: a brown pigment, best known for its use as painter's ink.

companies, seemed to be competing on a sneering marathon, leaning back with a shoulder and an eyebrow raised, lip curled, waving an upturned palm over what sounded like *He! He! He!*, an unmelodious and jarring note. I hated them. What the hell was all the fuss and the noise about anyway? It was like a ghastly hallucination. Could I have got drunk without realizing it, on my exploration? I felt, even then, as I sat in scowling isolation, that there was something exaggerated in my priggish response to the ambient phenomena. How very surprised and incredulous I would have been, could I have foreseen how attached to Rumania, admittedly not to this one, I would later become.

This sombre mood was interrupted by a small, hairy, horn-rimmed-spectacled man eating sandwiches hurriedly at the next table: could he have a look at my newspapers? When he had glanced through them, he began talking in English, then in very rapid French – a jerky gesticulating, friendly man. He was a journalist on the *Dimineaţa*, and had travelled widely: Turkey, Egypt, Persia, India, Ceylon, where he had been given a lucky charm, the tusk of a stillborn baby elephant, that he had worn round his neck ever since. Look! He unbuttoned his purple and yellow silk shirt, and there it was, about four inches long on a gold chain, embedded in a curly hirsute mass. What was I doing? Ah! Globetrotting! *Magnifique!* Did I like Opera? I said yes. (I had been to exactly four in my life.) Good, good. It was the first night of *La Bohème* tomorrow, and a party for the cast afterwards. Should we meet here? He had to rush back to the paper. After friendly farewells, he put on a green Tyrolean hat and dashed jerkily out.

Outside, a bit later, I had clean forgotten the name of my faraway street; but a lucky fluke revealed, for the third time that night, the same cab driver. He dropped me where he had picked me up, but, as the light over the nameplate was out, I passed the Savoy-Ritz three times before locating it. The hawk-nosed woman opened the door a little, said '*Ah, c'est vous monsieur!*' and let me in. They were shut, she said, it was two o'clock, but come and have a glass of wine or a tea before going to bed; everyone was having supper. I realized (which I had already half suspected) that I had performed the hackneyed act of comic literature, especially in France, of landing by mistake in a *maison de passe*, several important rungs higher than the rough and ready establishments down the road, but by no means grand. Madame Tania, who looked amused, had realized it too, and explained the form. But I was not to be concerned about it; they did very occasionally have bona fide travellers. There was a sound of cheerful talk. Four rather pretty girls in dressing-gowns or kimonos were sitting round a table in a cosy kitchen with an ikon in the corner and a chicken and potatoes in a dish, and we shook hands formally all round. The good looks of Rumanian women, which had struck me so strongly tonight, were a thing that had dawned on me earlier in nearly every village of Transylvania and the Banat. I was given a chair and a glass of wine, and the girls on either side cut off bits of chicken breast and offered them on their forks with friendly solicitude. There was a sound of the front door shutting, and a fifth girl clattered down the steps on wooden pattens, shook hands, sat down, flung her dark shock of hair back, crossed herself and set to. A light-hearted atmosphere of relaxation after the day's work prevailed.

Tania's account of my error, coupled with very good imitations of our preliminary conversation, provoked peals of bell-like laughter. One girl laughed so much I thought she was going to lay her head in her chicken and carrots. How much nicer it sounded than the eerie machinations of the café. They were simple souls. Tania told me where they all came from: one from Bukovina, a Moldavian, a Transylvanian, and a fair-haired and blue-eyed one from Sibie, or Hermanstadt, one of those mediaeval, fortified Saxon towns in the Carpathian passes, whose German nationality

and speech have been romantically attributed to their descent from
the children led away from Hamelin by the Pied Piper. (Swallowed
up by the hillside, they miraculously emerged in this leafy principality.) Safta, the fifth, who was the youngest and rather wild
and unusual-looking, was the object of a mixture of teasing and
spoiling by the other four, and obviously rather enjoyed it. The
teasing was prompted, Tania told me, by funny mistakes in her
Rumanian. She was a Gagauz from the Dobrudja: one of that
fascinating minority of descendants of the Cuman invaders, mixed
with Tartar stock, who laid waste the lower Danube in the Dark
Ages and, according to Byzantine chronicles, drank their victims'
blood out of their skulls. Turkish in speech now, but Christian
in faith. I gazed at her with the reverence of an ornithologist at
the glimpse of an Auckland Island merganser. So, with Tania
herself from Bessarabia, as she pointed out, the household was a
miniature of post-war Rumania. They were, she said, marvellous
girls, and serious (though, I thought, looking round the table,
they didn't look it); they had behaved like angels when she had
been ill a month ago. If only she could find a house somewhere
nearer the middle of the town; above all, away from this terrible
quartier! *Le quartier est terriblement mal famé.* It was called the
Crucea de Piatra, named after an old stone cross that the expansion of the town had engulfed; just mention the Cross of Stone,
she went on, and see what people say! She closed her heavy lids
in disapproval. She told Moldavian Viorica to pour the boy out
some more wine. I had a delightful feeling of being behind the
scenes – a green-room sensation – and a dash of the emotions of
Clodius at the feast of Roma Dea: but a Clodius secretly in league
with the Priestess, an Actaeon intact. I had always wondered what
backstage in such a place might be like; surely not all as cheerful
as this? There was not a hint of professional wooing in all this
extra-curricular relaxation. I was treated with a welcoming

friendliness and also, thanks to my guileless entry, as the best joke for months. Much of the girls' conversation among themselves consisted of imitations of the pompous or pretentious manners and speech of the day's visitors; though many of them were referred to as '*un veritabil domn*' – true gents. Officers were highly thought of, but not all: but lawyers seemed to score highest marks for general bearing. There was a certain amount of competitiveness here, perhaps some boasting. It was fun to be on the other side.

Tania, in her youth, had practised a mixture of singing in cabarets and the same calling as her household. 'You'd never think it with a beak like this', she said, comically touching the bridge of her nose with a bony index-finger, 'but I used to be a great favourite. I used to make them laugh.' Her pre-war travels had taken her far beyond Kishinev, all over the Ukraine and southern Russia: Taganrog, Akkerman, Kiev, Ekaterinoslav, Yalta in the Crimea, and, for a glorious two years before the revolution, to St Petersburg and Moscow and the almost mythical pleasure resort of Yar. It all sounded wonderful. When her active days were over, she was second in command of an establishment in Odessa that really was a splendour: more like a palace. Of course there was the whole grain trade of the Ukraine, prosperous merchants from Greece, from all over the world, and a glittering clientele, really first class: dragoon officers, uhlans, hussars, *chevaliers, gardes* – but St Petersburg was the place for them – counts, barons, princes, even governors. Gypsy music . . . vodka . . . caviar . . . champagne. She dropped her knitting in her lap and her hands lifted in a gesture that seemed to hold all the departed glory of the Czars. And the girls! Beauties from all over Russia, real beauties, especially from the Caucasus and Georgia. Tiflis, that was the place. At this point, I remembered coming across the word *vengerka*, while reading *The Brothers Karamazov* (meaning, in Russian, literally, a Hungarian woman, but colloquially, a streetwalker or other professional). Had there been many Hungarians on the game in Russia? Lots, Tania said, all over the place, but more in the north, in cabarets particularly; the word was still in use. *Curva*, she told me, lowering her voice a bit, was the ordinary Rumanian word. (Years later, a rich Rumanian friend, freshly returned from a motor tour in Italy, told me that the huge inscriptions across twisting mountain roads, *serie di curve*, would mean a row of whores in Rumanian, and had so doubled up her Rumanian chauffeur with hilarity that they had nearly come to grief many times.)

When, enlarging on the glories of Odessa, Tania told me that there were three opera houses in the city, I told her that I had been invited to the Opera next day. The Opera? She glanced at my mud-caked puttees, worn breeches and hobnailed boots; what would I wear? I mentioned the more respectable clothes in my rucksack: not perfect, but better. We'll get the girls to iron them, she said, as she had to go shopping. Apropos of Russia, I asked her: who on earth were these peculiarly dressed, high-voiced Muscovites who drove all the carriages? She began to laugh, and interrupted the general conversation to relay the question in Rumanian. Laughter broke out all round: the *Muscali!* The *Skapetz!* Viorica clicked her tongue twice, making a brisk scissoring gesture with her forefinger and its neighbour in mid-air twice. Tania explained. They belonged to a religious sect widespread in Bessarabia and southern Russia, and their Rumanian headquarters were in Galatz, in the Danube delta. After marriage and producing one or two children, she wasn't quite sure, the men castrated themselves, hence the beardlessness, the high voice and the expanse, and the general eunuch-like style. Their wives were said to submit to some similar ambiguous ceremony, I learnt. Some said the women began to grow beards. (This extraordinary news – at least about male emasculation – was quite true. I visited a whole street of them later on in Galatz. They were coachmen all over the Regat.

In Galatz they were assiduous beekeepers. One of their tenets, I was told, was the belief that Czar Paul, the murdered son of Catherine the Great, would one day return again as the Messiah.) 'They are bad-tempered men,' Tania was saying, 'always cross. I'm not surprised.' A smile hovered on her face. 'Of course, we don't see much of them here . . .'

~

Greta Garbo, Marlene Dietrich, Leslie Howard, Ronald Colman, Gary Cooper, Fred and Adele Astaire and a few Central European vedettes – Lilian Harvey, Willy Fritsch, Anny Ondra, Brigitte Helm, Conrad Veidt – covered the walls opposite the bed with their shiny photos. I gazed up at them next morning through a shaft of brilliant autumn sunlight. There were one or two Rumanian actresses who made good in Paris: Elvira Popesco, Alice Cocea – Madame de la Rochefoucauld – and very good-looking politicians cut out of a newspaper, including Grigore Gafencu, who was to become Minister of Foreign Affairs the next year. My room belonged to a sixth lodger called Niculina who had gone home for a few days to Ploeşti (that curious region of oil wells with flame-tipped iron isosceles) for a niece's christening. Below the window the Bukovinian girl was scattering maize to the chickens with coaxing noises. Beyond, the battered neighbourhood sprawled in the light and lemon-coloured radiance. A large billboard opposite advertised Dorobanti's cigarettes, another, Prince Stirbey's Choice Table Wines. I watched a shrill and hectoring argument between two housewives akimbo on their thresholds and swaying from side to side under the violence of their rhetoric. The devil – which is the same word here as 'dragon' – and the dragon's dam were seldom off their lips in many disobliging contexts. It was a very pure example of what was known as the *mahalajoica* tone of voice, a fearsome note peculiar to the outskirts of towns, the *mahala* or *margine de oraş*, all through Rumania. How different from the soft voices stirring under the roof that sheltered me.

Safta had been sent up to collect my clothes for ironing, and I could hear talk about charcoal for the flat iron, and how the creases should go on the coat and trousers of Petrica, a neo-Dacian form of my first name. There was some question of who was to wield the iron. Viorica seized it in the end, pointing out the danger of too many cooks with a proverb Tania translated later: the child with too many midwives remains with its natal string uncut. '*Copilul cu mai multe moase ramana cu buricul netaiat.*'

How agreeable and exciting were these daily wakings on this journey; in odd surroundings, the proud owner – as one sent the smoke of an early cigarette spiralling across the room – of that unique and utterly unforeseeable object: the day ahead, facet on facet, layer on layer. Not so early today, though. It was nearly noon, and clearly a favourite time of yawning resurrections and leisure for my fellow lodgers, with several hours before they need arm for the afternoon's fray. Viorica and the Saxon girl were playing cards on a sunny landing, speckled with the shadows of a bead curtain that flickered over them like a fall of confetti; the Bukovinian girl was sewing; and sitting on the stairs, the Moldavian was reading aloud from an illustrated magazine to Safta, who was not only weak in Rumanian but could neither read nor write; her high Tartar cheekbones were propped atten-tively on her fists. They immediately left their various pursuits, picked up the beautifully ironed clothes. 'Ah,' said Tania, arriving back with a heavy shopping basket, 'let's have a look at you!' Straightening my tie with an experienced twitch, she said I would do splendidly; nobody would notice the shoes. She told me to try and get back in time for supper. They were going to have bigger and better versions of the pasta I had said I had liked so much. With my morale steamed up by this approval and by waves and farewells as though I were the luck of the house setting forth, I emerged into the sunlit slum.

~

The town, under cloudless sky, was transformed. More advanced than Bulgaria, the leaves were golden, and the whole place wore a sunny and charming aspect. A troop of mounted lancers on fine black horses and in white uniforms, plumes of white horsehair streaming from their helmets, breastplates and pennanted lances, were trotting down the Calea Victoriei.

There were several letters at the poste restante and a magic canvas envelope with some money. I carried them off to a bar. Things were getting better and better. I had written a couple of letters from Giurgiu to people I had met that summer in Transylvania, staying with a neighbour and relation of Paul Teleki's cousin. This sounds rather complicated. This relation, a rich Hungarian country gentleman and, I think, diplomat before the war, had bethought himself after the war of the remote Rumano-Transylvanian origins of his family; alone among Hungarian magnates in Transylvania, he had not only accepted the *fait accompli* of the new frontiers, but had broken out of the self-imposed isolation and boycott of other Transylvanian landowners and, to the disapproval of his neighbours, accepted an important function at the Royal Court of Bucharest and become a power in his new country. His houses, both here and in Transylvania, were always full of diplomats and well-known guests. Two of those had asked me, with – I thought – more than perfunctory hospitality, to let them know on reaching Bucharest in case I needed a bed. Both had answered welcomingly, one – Josias von Rantzau – telling me to ring up the moment I arrived. I rang him up and was bidden to move in at once. This was perfect. But I put it off till next morning, in order to have another twenty-four hours of absolutely independent life in the town, as I always tried to do (usually all too successfully) and also because I thought too abrupt a departure from my present abode might have looked, after their kindness, a bit unfriendly.

I spent a nice afternoon mooching about the town and turned up at the café of the previous night and waited for my opera-loving journalist acquaintance. The denizens of the café were roughly the same as the night before. Significantly my outlook had changed considerably. They now looked merely flamboyantly Latin and picturesque, quite possibly – I thought patronizingly – perfectly all right. In spite of Tania's favourable verdict, I was still concerned about my own appearance; but my journalist friend, when he dashed in wearing a neat blue suit and yellow satin tie, reassured me. *'Quand on est jeune, vous savez! D'ailleurs nous serons tous très bohème – comme il sied.'** It seemed all right in his box, which I think was full of journalists and their wives or girls, though the rest of the auditorium was much more dressed up. What was it that seemed so overpoweringly odd and stirring about all this? The noise of voices, the waves, the elaborate clothes, the greetings and meetings and hobnobbing, the blazing lights and – what seemed to my untutored eye – the blinding luxury of the Opera House itself? The sound of the orchestra tuning, the inhibited rumble of double-basses and the scores of detached bow-strokes, the tentative thumps, the squeak of a reed, the hushed zing and gasp of a cymbal, the quickly muted thud of a drum, all converged into the murmur of a muzzled and muffled zoo. I hadn't been inside a theatre since leaving England. The whole performance, which seemed amazingly good, passed in a mood of trance-like fascination and slight anxiety which was

---

* 'When one's young, you know! Besides, we'll all be very bohemian, as is fitting.'

slowly dissipated by the flask which my friend circulated in the box's penumbra.

The party afterwards began rather stickily with the cast arriving amid salvoes of claps, the prima donna still embracing a quantity of bouquets, and interminable introducing and hand-kissing; but it soon became a great deal more easy-going. With my journalist friend and about a dozen others, I soon found myself eating, off a plate balanced on my knee, what turned out to be a helping of caviar spooned there as though it were mashed potatoes. All, after a while, melted into an agreeable flux. We were sitting with several girls, a splendidly dressed young officer and a visiting French journalist, and one or two others. The journalist asked me where I was staying, and I said at the Savoy-Ritz. He nodded respectful approbation and I remember I thought what an advantage it was to have a good address. My sponsor had to leave to write his piece at the *Dimineaţa*, and disappeared for ever. When the party began to languish, the group to which I belonged in the corner moved on to somebody's flat. It must have belonged to a painter, to go by the properties that filled it and the lights hanging in lobster pots. Brandy in large quantities pumped in a fresh impetus, which was hardly needed by this time, and we danced and sang. All began to blur and smudge deliciously, the lobster pots turned into drowned underwater suns while everyone – but chiefly a high-spirited red-haired girl, the officer (he was somebody's ADC, reckless, funny and looking scarcely older than me), the Frenchman, who was a human dynamo, and I – launched into an orgy of competitive showing-off in singing and dancing. Two noisy Bulgarian songs scored an exotic success. The high-spirited girl was improvising a violent solo dance when bangs on the door from a neighbouring flat reduced the noise to long, very urgent, very enjoyable and very garbled and I suspect rather repetitive arguments about art, literature and history against a musical background softened by two pairs of socks thrust into the gramophone.

The next fragment of memory – a morning beam falling across half-empty glasses and a disorder of records – filled me with a hollow feeling of distress and calamity; morning all over again . . . But the light also rested on two spurred feet projecting from the end of a divan covered with peasant rugs that indicated a warrior taking his rest, then two crossed and gleaming black cylinders with small gold rosettes at the knee, tight dark blue breeches embroidered with foliating black galloons of braid, scarlet braces, a white shirt, and finally the sleeping and dishevelled head of the young officer; and, in another armchair, the crumpled frame of the French journalist. When the red-haired girl, who seemed to live there, emerged with coffee, it transpired that the hard exhibitionist core had all stayed the night, which made things a bit better. When Pierre, the young officer, returned from shaving, I watched him with some envy, slowly and painfully reassemble: struggling shakily with the hooks and eyes of the high astrakhan collar of his astrakhan-cuffed blue tunic, flattening the hussarish soutaches across the chest, arranging the fall of the empty sleeves of the black and blue pelisse he slung on heavy cords across his left shoulder, and correcting the diagonal slant across his back.

He polished his beautifully cut boots with a cushion, and then peered in a looking-glass at the fragile, resplendent cornet reflected there and shuddered. 'Do you think', he asked sadly and slowly in English, 'that I look like an officer and a gentleman?' I said he did indeed. 'Let's hope so,' he murmured lugubriously. He was half Scottish; his mother, he told me, had been a Miss Douglas; rather surprisingly he had an Everyman copy of the *Pickwick Papers* in the pocket of his pelisse.

In the blinding Calea Victoriei, returning salutes was almost too much for him. 'This is terrible,' he groaned. I could understand the torment only too well. But haven was in sight. He turned into one of the side gates of the Palace. After the ordeal of answering the butt-salute of the bearskinned sentry, he was safe. He shot a rueful smile of deliverance over his shoulder through the bars and clinked with dignity across the empty parade ground . . .

Back at the Savoy-Ritz, Tania knew just what was needed; an old, infallible nostrum from Odessa or Kishinev, based on two raw eggs broken into a glass, came to the rescue. She told me to swallow it at a gulp. The others clicked their tongues in commiseration. Their idea of me as a mug, capable of my initial blunder and returning in such a plight, filled them with a frenzy of protective concern. They were full of warnings about the dangers of Bucharest – much better to stay sensibly at home and keep out of harm's way. I, too, was reluctant to leave them, and the harem-like seclusion and the filtered sunlight of late morning. I waved back over the lowered hood of the Muscovite carriage, and their arms fluttered from the open doorway like a sea anemone's tendrils.

~

Josias von Rantzau, who had so promptly and hospitably offered to put me up, lived in a quiet, comfortable flat abutting on the German Legation, where he was one of the secretaries. He was as different as it is possible to be from a foreigner's idea of a German Junker. He belonged to a family that was as hoary as the annals of Holstein, famous in north German and Danish history, and distinguished ever since by a succession of statesmen, soldiers, courtiers and diplomats. One, an exact namesake, had been a marshal of France with Condé in the Thirty Years War. These facts, told me in summer by our Transylvanian host, had made a suitable impression on my socio-historical feelings, if the sentiment may masquerade under so innocuous a name. Tall, good-looking, civilized, gentle, with a quick charm that made him liked everywhere and speaking beautiful English and French, he represented a wonderful change of temperature and climate from the last few days. The only regional clue, should one have been a stranger opposite him in a train, was the pale diagonal of a fencing-scar across a chin already cleft by nature. I had wondered in Transylvania where it had been inflicted. At Heidelberg, I learnt, with the Saxo-Borussia – the Saxon-Prussian student corps – that Bullingdon Club by the Rhine. Josias laughed as he told me and I think blushed slightly as though I had indiscreetly raked up a youthful folly best forgotten. That night, to go to bed in the softly lit spare room with a row of books gleaming in a promising vista, and Harold Nicolson's *Some People* and *Peacemaking* beside the bottle of mineral water on the bedside table, was balm indeed. A picture of Josias's father, dressed as Chamberlain of the vanished Grand Duchy of Mecklenburg-Schwerin, looked benignly down.

No greater solace in a strange capital, after rough or irregular travel, can be compared to staying in a bachelor diplomatist's flat (though some archaeologists run them close), especially if they are as hospitable and welcoming as my present host. ('Please get at all these,' with a wave towards huge cigarette boxes and a glittering drinks table, 'we get them practically free. Do for heaven's sake smoke those cigars, too. I don't know what to do with them all, and please tell Maria if you want anything – any washing, luncheon – she gets depressed if there's nothing to do . . .') Empty all day, it was the dreamed-of refuge for writing and reading, encyclopaedias piling up on divans in warm rooms overlooking the autumn leaves of the quiet street. I was bent on learning as much about Rumania as I could, and, considering the dashing social life, I got through quite a lot; all Seton-Watson's history of Rumania, lumps of Nicolae Iorga and Alexandro Xenopol and for general atmosphere two utterly opposite writers: Princess Marthe Bibesco and Panaït Istrati: *Isvor, Cathérine-Paris* and *Le Perroquet vert* of the first, and *Uncle Anghel, Les Chardons du Baragan* and *Kyra Kyralina* of the other. (How jarring and unwelcome this juxtaposition of names would have been both to Princess Bibesco and to poor Istrati's ghost! These two authors represented, the one in ravishing French, the uppermost layer of the Gallicized Rumanian world; the other, in a self-taught and much less accomplished language, the poverty-stricken miseries and subterfuges of the humblest. The territory between seemed, from a literary point of view, unexplored.) Rumanian, too (perhaps the easiest of the Latin tongues, in spite of the miraculous survival of Roman case-endings that have dropped away everywhere else), began to unfold its secrets. I struggled with the poems of Eminescu, Alexandri and Octavian Goga with dictionaries and grammars, and advanced on the French poems of Carmen Sylva and Hélène Vacaresco's *Le Rhapsode de la Dâmboviţa*. Everything to do with Rumania began to cast a contradictory and powerful spell.

The chief pleasure of this lotus-eating respite was the company of Josias himself: sitting by the fire talking when he got back from work, sometimes with other people, Rumanian, English and French more often than German, and late at night, returning from dinner parties, sometimes the same ones, listening to music or drinking whisky and talking. We became great friends.

There was just a suggestion of sadness in his thoughtful and very good-looking face that disappeared when he laughed, but soon returned again. I wish now I had asked him about Germany and what he thought lay ahead, but, staying with him as I was, I felt reluctant to do so. Anyway, it is always rather ticklish asking diplomats such questions; whatever their private convictions, reservations or opinions, they are, after all, even in private conversation, in honour bound to put forward the official views of the country they represent; it is a question of filling in what is unsaid, never an accurate but always a fascinating process. He was very amusing about all prominent Bucharest figures, but too good-natured to be very damaging. With everyone else, he liked and admired our own minister (this was before the era of embassies everywhere), I was glad to learn. (I had soon met the kind incumbents of the Rolls-Royce with the royal standard I had seen on the first night of my arrival.) I asked him what the German minister was like. He hesitated and said, thoughtfully nodding his head: 'Very intelligent indeed.' Then, in quite a different tone, he began to talk of his predecessor, Count von der Schulenburg,* who had been minister when he had first been nominated to Bucharest. His former chief had since then been made Ambassador in Moscow. He had adored him, he said: they had been great friends and they had often sat up into the small hours talking, just like this. Josias had admired his enormous knowledge and reading and civilization and style – 'another world' – and his breadth of view about Europe and history and politics and diplomacy. He said all this rather sadly and I inferred that he was less happy under the present dispensation. I wish I had asked him how he felt affected, as a career diplomat of several years' standing – Josias must have been thirty, or a bit over – by the momentous change that had taken place in Germany a year ago. (I forgot about Graf von der Schulenburg's name – except a year or so later, looking at the seventeenth-century monument to the soldier of fortune in the Venetian service in Corfu – until during the war when his unconventional career emerged.)

* Count Friedrich Werner von der Schulenburg (1875–1944) used his diplomatic skills trying to strengthen peace between Germany and the Soviet Union. He was executed for complicity in the July Plot against Hitler.

One evening when we had been talking for hours, Josias said, after a pause, rather seriously, fixing me with large, blue eyes: 'Here's a silly question. Do you believe in the English phrase "Right or wrong, my country"?' It took me unawares, and I said I thought I did. (I suppose, though, the answer would be hedged by conditions: only *in extremis*, or in cases where sheer national survival is at stake. The question is far too general.) He nodded thoughtfully several times and the talk took a different turning. This, too, stuck in my mind later as a symptom of the conflicts that must be assailing many Germans like Josias at that time: the antithesis of people like him, honourable, kind, civilized, belonging, like Schulenburg, to a tradition of Western life and thought and a style and manner of being more akin to the time of the Congress of Vienna than to the Third Reich, led by a regime whose every manifestation must have seemed daily more abhorrent. I don't know how they were resolved; when I returned next year, Josias had been shifted to a different post. Several times during this time we spent the evening with a girl called Marcelle Catargi, the daughter of a great boyar, as they were called, who was devoted to him. She committed suicide at the time of the last great and definitive shift of power in Eastern Europe.

A few days after the end of the war, in command of a team of the Special Allied Airborne Reconnaissance Force, bumping over the rubble and the cinders of Hamburg (a sight and a smell which made us all fall silent, and dimmed for a while the exhilaration of victory), I found myself at Flensburg in the north of Holstein. Marked on the map near the town of Itzehoe, was a point reading 'Schloss Rantzau', and I headed for it next day, arriving at dark, to see if there were any news, after so many years, of Josias. It was a large, thick-towered mediaeval building, more fortress than dwelling, standing in a wood. The owner,

Graf Rantzau, an old man with cropped white hair, was having supper by candlelight with his family and servants and many people bombed out of Hamburg. He was only a second cousin. He got up and came out into the yard. 'Dear Josias?' he said sadly. 'Yes, he was in Eastern Europe somewhere. We've no news of him for ages. *Ich glaube, die Russen ihn geschnappt haben . . .*' He made a vague gesture towards the east. 'I think the Russians must have snapped him up . . .'

Nearly all the people in this book, as it turned out, were attached to trails of powder which were already invisibly burning, to explode during the next decade and a half, in unhappy endings.

~

In counterpoint to the sybaritic and bookish retreat of Josias's flat, a life of considerable worldly activity began. Being 'taken up', spoiled and made a fuss of is always agreeable, and something of the kind happened to me now, and I think for three reasons: a) out of a deep and universal Rumanian hospitality to strangers within their gates, b) out of kind hearts, knowing how little cash I had; no chance, or indeed, point, in trying to repay them, and c) from genuine amusement at the whole project. There was a strong bohemian, anti-conventional and un-pompous strain in the section of the Rumanian world in which I now found myself, a leaven which mitigated, and at the same time, in its way, enhanced the pursuit of *l'élégance* and fastidiousness in other directions. Thanks to all these factors, I soon discovered that nobody cared a rap about individual shabbiness; my bourgeois lust for a new pair of shoes, though they still trod beckoning and gleaming through my dreams, died down. (I rather wish it hadn't; somebody told me one could get some made for a pound. 'But', he said, 'if you get a pair, beware of the squeak.' 'The squeak?' 'Yes indeed. In some circles it's highly prized. A sign of smartness

and opulence. *Cu sau fara scartzait?* – the bootmaker asks: With
or without a squeak? The squeak costs more . . .')

If being 'taken up' is always agreeable and exciting when one
is young, at any rate for a while, the contrast now with the
rawness of my recent life stepped it up tenfold. It had something
of the zest of a barbarian padding wild-eyed with longing for
luxury and corruption through the palaces and fountained courtyards of Diocletian, or of a Parthian in Antioch. Notice the
significant change of ethical standpoint from the recoil of my
first hours. This particular stratum of Rumania was by far the
most civilized and sophisticated, and, in a way, the most idiosyn-
cratic society that I had ever encountered. The strangest aspect,
at first, of this great boyar world was the fact that the mother
tongue of its denizens – although they were all, at the very least,
bilingual – was not Rumanian but French, and, as even my rustic
ear could detect, of a particularly pure, cool and charming kind,
and had been so for six or seven generations. I had vaguely known
that the French language had taken deep root at certain levels in
pre-war Russia, Poland and Rumania, but in neither of the first
two instances – judging by overheard conversations between the
equivalent type of white Russians or Poles – to the virtual exclusion of the vernacular.

What had happened – impossible to avoid a few words on
Rumanian history to make it comprehensible – was this. When
Rumania emerged from the almost unchronicled chaos of its dark
ages, as the two principalities Wallachia and Moldavia, its princes
– the voivodes or hospodars – formed their rough courts and
administrations, like those of the Bulgarian czars and the Kraj of
Serbia, as miniature, semi-barbaric replicas of Byzantium, and
administered their lands through the great boyars, the all-powerful
warrior landowning feudal oligarchy to which they themselves
belonged. Though the thrones were officially elective, the tendency

was for them to remain in the same families; in Wallachia, for instance, in spite of intrigues, murders and palace revolutions, the throne remained in the Bassarab family for three centuries. All these princes – monarchs with strange sobriquets like Mircea the Old, Alexander the Bad, Peter the Cruel, Vlad the Impaler, Basil the Wolf – had to contend, with greater or lesser success, with the expansion of Turkey, particularly of the Murads and Bajazet.

Two tremendous figures stand out: Stephen the Great of Moldavia, who fought fifty battles and even defeated Mohammed, the conqueror of Byzantium; and Michael the Brave of Wallachia, who succeeded for a moment in uniting not only both principalities, but all the lands beyond their frontiers where Rumanians lived. But in the isolation after Bulgaria, Serbia and Byzantium had fallen to the Turks, Rumania too was forced to submit; not, however, as an integral part of the Ottoman Empire, but as vassal lands still reigned over by their Orthodox princes, paying tribute to a Sultan who was not their sovereign but their suzerain. But though for a while native boyars such as Brancovan and Cantemir sat on the two thrones, bribery at the Sublime Porte was already becoming the key to the principalities; their places soon began to be taken by Greeks from the Phanar at Constantinople, the seat of the Ecumenical Patriarchate, who were often of Hellenized Albanian origin, and by the Cantacuzenes of the family of Emperor John VI. These, by intermarriage and assimilation, became, early, completely identified with Rumania. As the elections became more mercenary, the oppression more ruthless, the reigns shorter (they all too often ended on the block), the later Phanariots – the thrones interchanged between about a dozen families – remained Greek in sentiment and language, and Greek in the eighteenth century became the court language of the two princely divans at Bucharest and Jassy. The native boyars themselves became more or less Hellenized, to such an extent that the first active blow against the Turks in the Greek War of Independence was struck in Moldavia, by Prince Alexander Ypsilantis and his Phanariot kinsmen and friends.

When, early in the nineteenth century, the twin principalities, through the intervention of the great powers, put a stop to the Phanariot regime and secured the election of native princes once more – Ghikas (Rumanians now for centuries), Bibescos, Stirbeys and Sturdzas – with longer and more liberal reigns, the Greek tongue dropped away and the language of private, aristocratic conversation among the native boyars and Phanariot descendants (who, through intermarriage, had completely merged) became French. Turning away from the old evils of the East, they looked to France and to French liberalism as their beacon. Soaking in French civilization through every pore, the principalities began to emerge from despotism and its more villainous abuses, secured the abolition of serfdom, enlarged the suffrage, and prepared the path for a Western constitution and democratic institutions. After the union of the two principalities under Prince Cuza, and the final severance of all allegiance to the Sublime Porte, the emergence of modern Rumania took place – rather contradictorily – under a prince chosen from the house of Hohenzollern, who became King Carol I. Never, since the time of the Roman Empire, had the region's cultural hegemony been so complete, with the result that the entire ruling elite spoke French. One outcome of the Westernization of Rumania was the eventual break-up, through agrarian reform, of the huge feudal estates of the boyars. Another was a class-separation in which – except in parliamentary speeches or addressing servants – the boyars, quite literally, spoke a different language.

I was fascinated, and slightly obsessed, by these voivodes and boyars as they appeared in frescoes on the walls of the monasteries they were always piously founding – crowned and bearded figures holding up a miniature painted facsimile of the church itself, with their princesses upholding its other corner, each with a line of brocaded, kneeling sons and daughters receding in hierarchical pyramids behind them. Still more fascinating, later portraits, hanging in the houses of their descendants – some by unknown local artists who travelled through the principalities early in the nineteenth century – showed great boyars of the princely divans, men who bore phenomenal titles, most of them of Byzantine origin, some of them Slav: Great Bans of Craiova, Domnitzas, Beyzadeas, Grand Logothetes, hospodars, swordbearers and cupbearers, all dressed in amazing robes with enormous globular headdresses or high fur hats with diamond-clasped plumes, festooned with neck-laces, and jewel-crusted dagger hilts. Bearded like prophets, they loom from the shadows as remotely as potentates in a Persian fairy tale, the only hint of feudal Europe, perhaps, being a crowned escutcheon in which the black raven of Wallachia impales the Moldavian auroch. Their names, too, all seemed to carry a resonance of splendour and remoteness: Sherban Cantacuzene, Constantine Bassaraba, Furtuna Vacaresco, Alexander Mavrocordato, Scarlat Callimachi, Dimitri Cantemir, Duca, Racovitza, Sturdza, Soutzo, Karadja, Mavroyeni, Bibesco, Stirbey, Rosetti, Rosnovano, Moruzi, Balsh, Kretzulesco: strange resonances. The reader at this point might jump to the conclusion that I was suffering from an acute access of class feeling. So might I, though obviously with more reluctance. There's probably worse to come.

～

Historians have been united in execrating the Phanariots. They have inherited the opprobrium that used to load the word 'Byzantine' with suggestions of flexibility, deviousness, lack of scruple, greed and tyranny. But there are signs that the Phanariots, too, are gradually being reassessed. It may be argued that their greed and corruption were laced by zeal for the Orthodox faith and that their share in the foreign affairs of the Ottomans, which the later sultans largely and most unwisely entrusted to them, was dictated as much, or almost as much, by anxiety for the Christian cause as it was by private ambition. It is possible that without their flexibility and genius for compromise, the principalities would have sunk into total subjection to the Ottoman yoke: that all the old national institutions, instead of degeneration, would have been obliterated completely, as they had been in the rest of south-eastern Europe. In nearly every family there was a prince with virtues to offset, in some measure, the vices of his kinsmen. Since the end of their long regime, many of their descendants have been prominent and devoted figures in Rumanian life, both in conservation and reform. But whatever their drawbacks may have been, in the period of their great ascendancy, the eighteenth century, in one thing they were preeminent: they were the only civilized people in south-eastern Europe. The Phanar itself was the last surviving fragment of lost Byzantium, and the courts of Bucharest and Jassy the last, faint, scarcely audible echo of the empire's death rattle.

It was not only on their wealth but on their knowledge of languages and their wider European horizons, in a world of fanatic barbarism, that their oligarchy was based. From the first, when they became Grand Dragomans of the Porte, they were friends of literature and art; the first Rumanian bible was translated by the orders of Sherban Cantacuzene of Wallachia, and with all his faults, a figure as polished as Alexander Mavrocordato, Byron's and Shelley's friend and a leader in the Greek revolt, could have sprung from no other East European soil. They studied in Venice, Padua, Vienna, Paris and St Petersburg and it was mainly due to their civilized and cosmopolitan influence that Western ideas penetrated Rumania. The influence of French ideas, and the total linguistic hegemony of France among the elite, may have gone too far; there were certainly regrettable social side effects; but it did bring a vivifying blast of the Western world, a sort of belated renaissance, into the stifling isolation of the Middle Ages which Rumania was only just sloughing off.

All these different influences, it occurred to me later on (for I knew little or nothing of such matters then), had evolved into a society which was a mixture of late Byzantium and Proustian France. The architectural mood of Bucharest, after it had arisen from its oriental beginnings, was an amalgam of Second Empire and the fin-de-siècle, with a dash of early twentieth-century opulence. The modern buildings were irrelevant postscripts. A strong whiff of the earlier period hung unmistakeably in the social air: a climate which had also been subtly modified, during the last few generations, by a stern army of English nannies and governesses. But it left the bedrock of French influence among the boyars undisturbed, the result of a hundred years of study in the lycées of France and the Sorbonne, and of inhabiting Paris as an alternative capital. In the unregenerate days of enormous estates before the agrarian reforms, many of these now almost mythical-seeming boyars lived in France, completely integrated, and they often intermarried in circles of extreme style and grandeur: a Montesquieu and Castellane existence, combined with a pleasure-loving bent that belongs to the world of cartoons, and, in many cases, to the plays of Feydeau and Flers et Caillavet: packs of staghounds in Normandy, whiskers, curly-brimmed top hats, monocles, and languidly lit cigarettes from gold Fabergé cases with enormous closed crowns and coronets, in the sort of carriages Constantin Guys and Lautrec drew so well. Their wives and daughters, in my mind's eye and in reality, appear with the feathered languor and dash of sitters for Helleu and Boldini and Jacques-Émile Blanche, inhabiting the world of Longchamp, Le

Grand Véfour, Maxim's, Le Rat-Mort, and *la tournée des Grands Ducs*,* and evoking exotic figures like La Païva, La Belle Otero, Émilienne d'Alençon, Cléo de Mérode, Liane de Pougy.

The same life, in miniature, thrived in Bucharest; the most convincing relic of it was the plush, the brass and the chandeliers of Capşa's restaurant. I could never tire of hearing tales of this not yet wholly evaporated epoch. Although it is the last period in history I would have liked to inhabit, there is an absorbing attraction about the robust, undoubting vulgarity and glitter which held Europe in its grip for these decades. The duels, too, which had played a large part in Rumanian, as well as the rest of European life, outside England – and, to a much lesser extent, still did – exercised a morbid, Dumas-bred fascination. Frequently fatal, they were fought with pistols or rapiers which made encounters with sabres in Austria and Hungary – where only slashing was allowed, but no lunging – sound much more innocuous. It was all frantically alien.

What distinguished these people then, and later, from the rest of pleasure-loving aristocratic Europe was their anti-philistinism: a fastidious passion for erudition for its own sake, for literature, painting, music, sculpture and the movement of ideas, that turned their houses into the haunts of Academicians. (Rather like France, again, Rumania has always been a country where a few women, through their brilliance, wit, beauty or hospitality, have played a more important role than in other countries.) The devotion to writing, in particular, went far beyond literary dilettantism and emerged, in many cases, in works of great distinction. Not alas, in Rumanian, a chauvinist might sigh. But at least these extra-territorial exploits released them from the wheel of patriotic nationalism, to which the poetic and literary genius of resurgent nations is indissolubly bound. Paris after all is no mean arena in which

---

* The supposed circuit of fashionable night-spots by Russian grand dukes.

to shine. No wonder that Proust should have been so deeply intrigued by Rumanians in Paris and sought them out as friends. For me it was exciting and impressive to hear the name Marcel dropped so lightly and easily, and to realize that Anna, who seemed to be everyone's cousin, was the Comtesse de Noailles; that Paul, if it was not Morand, who had married Hélène Soutzo, was Valéry; that 'Jean' was Cocteau and that Léon-Paul was Fargue: clues scattered in a paperchase that could be followed later.

I have gone on rather a long time about this because it was so different to anything I had come across in similar circumstances in the Danubian capitals further upstream. In Hungary the candlelit talk at the end of dinner would be more inclined to concern shooting or horses, a serious weighing of the comparative merits of bootmakers and saddlers in London or long discussions about mediatization, morganatic marriages, primogenitive quarterings, *Hoffähigkeit*, the exact degree of cousinage between the Festitich and Fürstenberg families and how many yokes of land the Esterházys owned. So it might, *mutatis mutandis*, in Bucharest, but not for long. But I don't think it would often end up, in the Hungarian capital, with talk about Saint-Saëns and the Goncourt brothers, the points in common between Villiers de L'Isle-Adam and Barbey d'Aurevilly, the link between Lautréamont and surrealism, or what the Abbé Mugnier had told one of the guests about the conversation of Huysmans and what the author had left out in his portrait of him in *En Route*.

∼

Bucharest was not really as big as it seemed when I first reached it. After a week or so, during which I must have met more people than ever in my life before, I felt I had lived there ages. It was also a time of entertaining and parties and tremendous luncheons and dinners, unless it was always like this; anyway, as part of the 'taking up' process or as a sharing of the burden, I found myself at a vast number of these gatherings. I was twice taken out to Mogoşoaia, the old Rumano-Byzantine palace of the Brancovans outside Bucharest that Marthe Bibesco had restored to its former magnificence: a tremendous backdrop for its astonishing owner. It stood on the edge of a wide, sad lake rustling with tall reeds, and flights of water birds settled or soared away over the reflected forest. I thought it was the most beautiful place I'd ever seen. As I went back to Rumania several times, it is hard to remember whether most of these meetings occurred then or later; but thanks to returning several times, some of them I got to know really well and one in particular became my greatest friend. Under the wing of these benefactors, I would gaze with wonder at the figures flitting about the middle distance: Titulescu, the foreign minister, tall and mandarin-like, but with splendid histrionic gestures, and obviously a comic genius of the first order; Grigore Gafencu, one of the best-looking men I've ever seen, a person of enormous charm and courage, who succeeded Titulescu next year, with a funny and charming French wife called Nouchette (I quite saw why the absent owner of my room at Tania's had cut out his picture and stuck it up); Antoine Bibesco, an aloof, Germanesque, leonine, sardonic figure, even, it seemed to me, a slightly sinister one, his wife Elizabeth Asquith, and an omniscient, piercing-eyed prodigy of about fourteen, their daughter Priscilla, who became a tremendous friend later, when she managed to escape from Rumania to Beirut during the war; the already half-mythical Maruca Cantacuzene, who married Enescu, the composer; Rose Covarrubias Nano – a beautiful, tragic, auburn-haired Mexican; Paul Zanesco, a brilliant, funny and very gifted and unconventional young diplomat (both of these last two, alas, died by suicide during the next few years) and his wife Hélène Yourievitch, who later settled in England; Elizabeth and Georghe Cantacuzene, the best architect in the country, hotfoot from a long journey through Persia, accounts of which made me wonder whether to change my itinerary after Constantinople; Dimitri Sturdza, with a nose, a chin and a frown like a Malatesta, a scorching lisp, a virtuosity in comic destruction and great kindness. There was M. Poklevski-Koziell, the Russian minister en poste in Bucharest during the war, whom the Revolution had cruelly stranded here; the polished and monocled Grégoire, brother of Ion Duca, who had been assassinated the year before by the Iron Guard.

I was about to mention beauty again, for as this catalogue lengthens, I am astonished by the stunning looks that surge into the lamplight in answer to their names: beautiful or good-looking for the most part, aquiline masks or engaging ugliness . . . There is always, in such societies, a favourite diplomatic couple. A year before it had been the Hauteclocques, the later General Leclerc's brother and his wife. Now it was the Spaniards, Perico and Lily Prat, and understandably. On we go . . .

But, of course, I can't. Not because it is too much like a list out of the *Tatler*. Quite the contrary, I would like it to continue a great deal longer. But it is best to stick to the rule: 'either out [of Rumania] or dead'.* Of the above names, six belong to the first category, nine to the second. Of the names inside Rumania that should complete this list, one or two have disappeared into a limbo without tidings; the others, about whom their friends know all too well, exist in great distress and poverty, sentenced by geography and the post-war order, and by those that administer it. To enlarge on this pregnant theme would completely change the purpose of this narrative. Anyway, none of it had happened yet: all are still alive and free and holding glasses in their hands.

---

* At the time of PLF's writing, Rumania was languishing under a brutal Communist regime, and naming people still alive might endanger them.

Among the younger ones, two seemed to stand out as paragons: Nicky Chrisoveloni and Constantine Soutzo, both fortunately out, one of them in Athens (I saw him a few days ago). What astonishes me in these reunions over two decades is not the changes that the interval has wrought, but the lack of them, especially as one pieces together the terrible vicissitudes which have intervened on their side. They are heartening instances, in the teeth of all probability, of physical and mental indestructibility. Nicky was half English and had been at school in England, and both he and Constantine had recently come down from Oxford, where Constantine, I learnt with delight, had not taken a valet in high Edwardian style, but, to everyone's wonder, a Rumanian chambermaid. In different ways – Nicky, tall, dark and soft-voiced, and Constantine fair, blue-eyed and extrovert – they seemed spirited and infectious examples of energy and uninhibited enjoyment of life. Both flew aeroplanes – for not everyone, I am glad to record, had been entirely broken by the agrarian reforms. Nicky owned and managed a family bank. Constantine lived in one of the rather charming old houses I had admired on my first exploration of the city, called the Palais Soutzo, where I stayed when my bed at Josias's flat was needed for a family visitation. (The room I occupied, filled with Empire furniture, was entirely circular, the only one I have ever slept in, except a bell tent, a hut in the French Cameroons, a converted oast house and one in the Hôtel de la Louisiana in Paris.) I first remember Nicky Chrisoveloni, late at night, at a young and wild party where everyone was searching for a word in charades. '*J'y suis*', he said – all of our side had dried up – '*concupiscence!*' It was acted out in French with very funny improper elaboration. Another early memory is of Nicky leading a sudden fierce spontaneous *sârba* in double time round the fast-emptied floor of the Arizona, with the Gypsies on their rostrum going mad. That's the way bankers ought to be.

I had slightly guilty feelings, as in Budapest, at accepting so much kindness and hospitality; but perhaps not as guilty as I should have. It was different in people's houses; but what about nightclubs, where evenings often ended? Or meals at Capşa, with caviar flying about and that splendid Danube fish called sterlet? (The food in Rumania was amazing, a very original native nucleus, to which all that was most exciting in Russia, Poland, Turkey, Austria, Hungary and France had contributed their influences.) Everything, fortunately, cost about a quarter of its equivalent in Western Europe. Pricked by conscience at moments like these I would make a frantic flourish with two thousand-lei notes; always, thank God, in vain. These two bits of paper sank to the symbolic role of stage currency.

~

Sinaia. The three syllables send up a wave of bewilderment. I gazed out of the centrally heated room of the villa at the drive and the roofs and the treetops of the other smart villas. I felt as torpid as an autumn fly, weighed down with depression. Somewhere beyond the leafy trimness outside lay golf links and then green Alpine meadows sloping to a blaze of autumn beeches and then the tiers of Christmas trees. A mountain Sunningdale. Nor was there much consolation when one turned indoors: the modish drawing room, bookless except for *Vogue, Harper's Bazaar* and, on a sideboard between two carved chamois, *The Story of San Michele, Ashendon* and a French translation of *Precious Bane;* a hanging print of Vigée le Brun's Marie Antoinette with the Dauphin in her arms and another of Fragonard's *L'Escarpolette;* and, from the two lamp-lit tables a twitter of twilight conversation. '*Deux piques.*' '*Passe.*' '*Un drink?*' '*Oh, que vous êtes malin!*' '*Un petit high-ball.*' 'No bid.' 'Scotch?' '*Tiens, partner?*' '*Très faible – assez, assez!*' '*Comme j'adore la campagne!*' '*Et beaucoup de soda*

. . . encore!' 'Est-ce que vous bridgez chez Julie mardi?' . . . 'Oh, merci, vous êtes un ange . . . ! Trois trèfles . . . turni tome.' In a few hours the smart tailored suits would be replaced by black and pearls, and after another of the slow and delicious meals that acted as breaks between rubbers, the real evening's work would begin. The players were Rumanian, French and English. It was wonderfully tame and restful . . .

The passes in the mountain barrier outside were perhaps the funnels through which, in 1241, the hordes of Genghis Khan had swarmed on their way to tear Europe to bits. I felt rather like one of them. The only thing to see nearby was the royal castle of Peles, about a quarter of an hour away, a mass of battlements and half-timbering and acute-angle turrets, a bold Carpathian Balmoral. Next day I contrived to borrow from my hosts (who were very nice) the enormous Packard in which we had driven from Bucharest, with its tall chauffeur in pale grey livery and leggings, and drive over to Braşov, a romantic and serpentine mountain drive through forests so brilliant that they looked on fire, ending in the little mediaeval Saxon town built in one of the deep passes in the mountainous fender separating Transylvania from the Regat. Very strange it seemed, too, to be surrounded by thick Germanic arches supported on stout pillars, onion cupolas and shingled towers with tangles of *deutsche Schrift* over the shops and the sound of a German dialect in the cobbled streets; strange, too, to feel that I was in Transylvania again, the eastern edge of the mountain principality where much of my idle summer had slipped by.

These Germans, who have been romantically connected with the children of Hamelin, were really Rhinelanders, and some of them Flemings, summoned and settled here early in the twelfth century by the kings of Hungary in seven fortresses of the Carpathians to guard the eastern borders; hence the German name for Transylvania: *Siebenburger.* (In the middle of the century they were followed by the turbulent Teutonic Knights, who were dismissed again a few years later, to move north and eastwards and found the military might of Prussia.) When the new doctrines of Calvin and Luther began to travel eastwards, taking permanent root in parts of the Magyar countries, these towns became outposts of Protestantism, and have remained so ever since: the easternmost wingtip of the Reformation. Further north inside this westward curve of the Carpathians, the Hungarian kings placed another strange population of settlers, even earlier than the Saxons, to defend Transylvania's north-eastern march: the Szeklers. These, though Magyar by race, have been separated from their fellow Hungarians for so long – isolated in an overwhelming sea of Rumanians – that many old tribal customs and an idiosyncrasy of speech survive which their kinsmen lost long ago in the great national Hungarian block further west. They are different enough for people to have thought, in the past, that they were the descendants of Attila's original invading Huns. Like the Saxons, these frontiersmen enjoyed many privileges and exemptions. They were ruled by the Count of the Szeklers, just as the Germans were ruled by the Count of the Saxons; but unlike these, they were ennobled to a man, which freed them from all taxation. These groups, with the Hungarian population much further west, were the three elements which – first under their counts, then under the Hungarian princes of Transylvania, then the kings of Hungary, and then under the dual monarchy, the Habsburgs – ruled Transylvania from the thirteenth century to the twentieth. (It is these arbitrary lumps of population which made the ruling of Rumania's frontiers so difficult and unsatisfactory a task.) During all this immense tract of time the Rumanians, who outnumbered all the others put together and now ruled the country, had not only had no say in the running of Transylvania but no official existence at all; the yoke of serfdom both here and in Hungary proper was even heavier on the Hungarian and Rumanian peasantry than it was in the principalities east of the mountain chain.

The towns here all have three names, the Rumanian, the Hungarian and the German. For the former two, the steep little town all round me was called Braşov and Brasso; the Saxons clung jealously to its first Teutonic name of Kronstadt. Not only the name and the architecture of the town were German, but its speech and the looks of the citizens. It seemed hard to believe that the owners of these florid complexions and blond hair, of the bodices and waistcoats and the felt hats, had had no contact with their distant relations for seven centuries. I wandered about the lanes and dived into bars and taverns, almost rejecting the evidence of my eyes and ears. Beautiful Turkey carpets in the massive and spotless churches reminded one of the important position of the town in the passes through which the eastern trade to northern and western Europe used to flow. But after the market place it was the bars and the back streets that drew one most. How I wished, as I hobnobbed with two cowherds in a pub in the outskirts of the town and listened to their curious dialect, that I had arrived on foot, dumped my kit, and was now deep in one of those unhurried, groping, temperature-taking, gazing and eavesdropping private surveys which always began my solitary sojourns in a new town! Whenever I turned a corner or slunk out of a *Gastwirtschaft*, wondering what next, there, in front of the smart Schwarzer Adler hotel, behind the wheel of that vast limousine, the dove-grey chauffeur yawned. It was getting late. I felt a tremendous fraud as the chauffeur leapt from his seat, saluted and then tucked me in with a fur rug and drove the purring, scarcely audible oblong away over the cobbles. On the way out, we dawdled, in the wake of the car's too melodious horn notes, through a herd of cattle. The drover was one of the ones I had been drinking with an hour before. His blue eyes rounded with astonishment as we drew clear. I waved guiltily, Haroun-al-Raschid unmasked.

When we were gliding through the incandescent forest once more – no potholes on this royal road – with the twilight sliding up the mountainside, I lit one of the splendid cigars Josias had bestowed on my departure. The headlights were soaring through stage wings of leaves and the engine made a sound like a never-ending sigh. Soon only the burning ring that divided the long and carefully husbanded ash at the end of its aromatic cylinder – held, I hoped, with easy nonchalance in the fading pallor of a hand hedonistically adroop over the soft folds of the fur – glowed in the Havana-and-pine-needle and sandalwood-scented shadows. A satrap's progress, the agreeable weariness of a young billionaire. Perhaps this was the way to loll and ponder the beginnings of the Saxons and the Szeklers . . . Nothing had changed when I got back. The intermittent murmur and the chink of ice cubes still wove their lullaby: '*Nous sommes en déroute, partner.*' '*Tout est perdu fors l'honneur.*' '*Deux coeurs.*'

Monday brought liberation. One of a small flotilla, the great equipage bore us down into the lowlands and through the oilfields between Campina and Ploeşti. For many miles, the oil derricks blazed forth their tidings of prosperity like a myriad beacons, and soon we were once more in the heart of the wickedness and delights of Bucharest.

~

Pricked by conscience about this sybaritic way of life a few days later, after being driven (yet again) to luncheon at a country club on the edge of Lake Snagov, some miles outside Bucharest, I set out to return on foot. It was a journey of some miles, at first through lonely woods, all of them a uniform autumnal blaze, then along the straight highway, past Baneaşa aerodrome, and into the capital down a magnificent tree-lined boulevard, the Chaussée Kiselev. How very different from my ramshackle southern approach a couple of weeks before! As it approaches the town, this fine alleyway is lined on either side with large and prosperous houses in many conflicting and sometimes comic styles, leafy tabernacles of the spacious 1900s lying back behind commodious pillared gateways for the easy passage of four-in-hands, tilburies and victorias.

~

It was true about leaving in a couple of days. We were now well into the second week of November and, thanks to my northward swoop, Constantinople was as far away as ever, in fact a long way further off. At Plovdiv it had been almost within my grasp. I had no hard-and-fast plan and no time limit; but the idea of reaching Constantinople by New Year's Day had been subconsciously taking shape as a suitable date for this momentous arrival – say, a month and a half ahead – perfectly feasible, but too short a span for my unhurried rate. I reckoned that I had come many hundreds of miles out of my way; this Rumanian trip was in the nature of a deviant escapade, like my *Lustfahrt* to Prague from Bratislava.

The way on foot would run across the Baragan steppe and then the Dobrudja steppe the other side of the Danube, a flat, barren and sparsely inhabited tract (though a very strange and beautiful one, as I was to learn later on). In wet weather it was almost impassable on foot and there was scarcely anyone there to scrounge a horse from, as I had done in similar circumstances on the Great Hungarian Plain. So why not take the train to Varna, on the Black Sea coast of Bulgaria, just across the Rumanian border? The third class didn't cost much and I would still be hundreds of miles in credit as far as distance covered on foot was concerned; not that I had any doctrinaire objection to getting lifts for short distances – after all, whatever else I was up to (ah, what?) I was not engaged on breaking a record or winning a bet; but I had taken so few lifts that I was starting to nourish a secret pride in the enormous mileage I must already have trudged. But this brief spring by train would only lop off a hundred and fifty miles or less: chicken feed in relation to the totals I had knocked up in my twisting track. I was secretly longing, at my journey's end, to step out and add up each day's march on a really large-scale map of Europe with a pair of dividers, to see exactly how far I had plodded. Happy about this important decision, I prepared to enjoy the two remaining days of unwonted luxury to the hilt.

I struck very lucky. That night there was a marvellous and not very big party given by the Spaniards Perico and Lili Prat at their legation, for Artur Rubinstein. He was a great friend and always stayed with the Prats when he had a concert in Bucharest. After supper he played Chopin for a while, and then dancing and drinking set in at an uninhibited tempo. I thought I'd never seen anyone enjoy himself more, only knocking off dancing to talk at a tremendous speed and very funnily, his conversation scattered with marvellous imitations, abetted by his red hair and a pale, charming face. He seemed to infect everyone else with fun and high spirits. It was a memorable and glorious evening, and a very late one. The last thing I remember was expounding my views on literature with considerable urgency to Julie Ghika and Nouchette Gafencu.

The next night, and my last, was later still. It seemed, during these days in Bucharest, and especially now, as if circumstances had plotted to condone and satisfy each of those fleeting and rather silly longings for a luxurious and dazzling contrast to hovel-dwelling which had suddenly swept over me on that rainy night on the way to Rustchuk. I hesitate to chronicle the enjoyment of surging from the bath and seeing all Constantine Soutzo's lent magnificence laid out on the bed in the softly lit circular room. Borrowed studs gleamed in the stiff borrowed cuffs, and the efficient, black-browed cut-throat of a valet who must have succeeded the maid of Christ Church, pulled in and buckled the flimsy strap at the back of the flimsier waistcoat, while Constantine shouted for him next door, and I slid into the perfectly fitting tails. (It was only the third time in my life I had worn these things.) But then the entry of the cut-throat with a buttonhole carnation in either hand, while Constantine wrestled with the wine and tinfoil of a dark green bottle in the drawing room, seemed difficult to beat. Identical figures, we decided, of foppish robustness, we polished it off standing in front of the fire.

The Palais Stirbey was much older and smaller than the great stucco one with the lions with the blazing eyes that I have mentioned; it was built, I should think, early in the nineteenth century, in a charming Regency style: long rooms with ceilings supported by white wooden free-standing pillars, I think with Ionic capitals, and adorned with lustres of many tear-like, glittering drops; and I remember that the parquet floors, during the few moments that these were empty of dancers, had a very slight wave to them, a faint and scarcely discernible warp, like the marquetry of a casket that age has twisted very slightly out of the true. This charm-enhancing blemish, an infinitesimal trace of some long-forgotten earthquake perhaps, gave a wonderful appearance of movement to the interior, something I have hardly ever seen since: a feeling of simultaneous stasis and flux. From the moment when Constantine put his arm through mine – how clearly one remembers kind gestures like this! – and abetted my beginnings with the friendly ease of which some people have the gift, the whole evening leaves a memory as though it had unfolded itself somewhere in the country, and not in a town at all.

~

A marvellous awakening, rather like an earlier one, with borrowed plumage scattered, coffee filling the round room with wonderful fumes, then a whiff of leaves burning damply on a bonfire, the muted sound of trams outside, horses' hooves and claxons, the voices of Gypsies crying their wares, and finally the clash of rings along their rods and a swish of curtains letting in rainy light and a good morning murmur from Constantine's cut-throat servant! Seton-Watson's history of Rumania by the bed, *Crome Yellow*, finished yesterday for the third time, an overflow of maps . . . Of course! Now Ion, the servant, was laying out, as I had asked him to last night, leather jacket, breeches, puttees, those uncompromising boots, gaping rucksack, staff, scrip, cockle shell – all a palmer's gear at the end of a stay in a castle – as carefully as if they were some exotic uniform. I could hear Constantine on the telephone, talking to a mechanic about the overhaul of an aeroplane, planning a boar-shoot, fixing a dinner date several days hence, a pause, loud laughter. End of the holidays . . . At lunch time, the rain was battering on the windows. After finishing the autopsy of the previous night, Constantine asked if I would really set out next day, to Bulgaria, if it were raining like that: why not stay on a bit?

7

To Varna

After the un-Kim-like life of the past three weeks, the wooden
seat and the dim light in the third class carriage, and the rain
falling desolately over the plain outside, were a dejecting contrast.
The train stopped at every station, sometimes with long waits
by the deserted platforms of remote halts. There were only a few
peasants on board, all with that bewildered refugee look that
overcomes country people in trains: women with coloured
kerchiefs and Anna Karenina bundles on their laps, and men
with their hands – blunt instruments temporarily idle – hanging
sadly between their knees, with the looseness of turtles' fins. They
didn't know what to do with themselves, and I felt rather the
same, fumbling my stick, so long abandoned, with the rucksack
squatting on the seat beside me like a toad companion. I thought
about Bucharest. Infected by all I had heard from Hungarians
and Bulgarians, I had dreaded it, in spite of the fascination that
had tugged me there: how unbelievably kind they had been! I
could hardly believe that all those faces and rooms and streets
had been packed into so short a span. I wondered sadly if I would
ever meet any of them again. The country outside the window
seemed so remote and shapeless and without landmarks.

Much later, we were all shaken from our fitful dozing and
herded out. The name of the station came as a bit of a shock.
Giurgiu on the north bank! I had somehow thought we would

cross the Danube much further downstream by the great Cernavoda Bridge, and so down the Black Sea coast through Constanţa, Mangalia and Babadag, and here we were on my old route!

I was the only passenger on the ferry boat. As we crossed the river towards the lights of Rustchuk and the familiar quay, things seemed to cheer up. I made a dash for the hotel, with the idea of staying the night and telling Rosa all my adventures over another lovely meal on the cliff's edge next day. At last an unknown, sleepy woman came clip-clopping down the stairs. No, Gospodja Rosa was in Sofia for a week. I left a note with her stand-in, and wandered glumly to the station to sleep on a bench till the train started, and at last climbed into the carriage like a somnambulist and back into a slow and jolting limbo, and a cold one. I felt terrible. Could it be a delayed-action result of the whole string of tremendously late nights and heaven knew how many drinks of every different kind, hammered home by the Rubinstein party and the Stirbey ball, a whole century ago? Thank God, I was usually and most unjustly spared the full retribution of *katzenjammer* and *gueule de bois*, like a foot soldier with a charmed life whose friends fall thick about him. Anyway, neither evening had come anywhere near the pace of the night after *La Bohème*, and surely hangovers should be plucked from one's luggage like contraband when crossing the border from one sovereign state to another, even though undeclared?

Much later, I was woken by dawn rising along a navy-blue sierra of mountains and down ravines with threadbare poplars, pricking through the mist under a pure, watery sky of still unshed rain, shot with pale shafts of sunlight. The leaves shone with dew. Like Rumania, but a bit later, all the woods had burst into fire while I had been away. I ate some cold *mititei* saved from Giurgiu in a twist of greasepaper, and watched the Balkans much lower and more shapeless than further west, but beautiful nevertheless, curling towards us. This would be the third time I had crossed these mountains, and I began to feel I owned the range. I had just crossed the Danube for the tenth time (not, of course, counting the bridges across it between Pest and Buda): more than once, at Ulm, in its nonage; over and back at Bratislava; across it again from Czechoslovakia to Hungary at Esztergom; at Budapest; then from Orşova to Vidin on the steamer, and now Rustchuk – Giurgiu and back. The branching and reedy wonders of the Delta, bursting with birds, were still unknown, and the stream's lovely beginnings at Donaueschingen; but I was beginning to have a sensation of familiarity with the tremendous river, the real hero, or perhaps the heroine, of our continent. These inklings about the geography of Eastern Europe were like the early fumblings of a blind person getting the hang of a complicated text in Braille, as though I were beginning to feel the asperity of ranges and the sinuosities of rivers under the palm of my hand.

The train lurched and clanked along the Balkan passes. In a few hours I was pacing along the main street of Varna and then gazing down at an expanse of pearly water, ruffled at the edge and crinkled with little waves as it expanded to infinity: the Black Sea!

~

Loitering through the town about lamp-lighting time, I was wondering where to find Gatcho when I heard a shout from the other side of the road and a familiar figure charged across. We seized each other like Orestes and Pylades. A familiar figure, but only just. His cap, tilted at a killing angle, was one of those shallow pillboxes worn at German universities, with a narrow black and white band round the edge and a small shining peak. He saw my look of amazement and raised the cap with a comically woebegone look to reveal a totally shaven pate. Nothing of his unruly black shock remained. He couldn't stop laughing. I had noticed several chaps similarly shorn and capped since my arrival and hadn't realized that they were fellow alumni of Gatcho's at the Handelsschule. Words showering out of us, we headed for a café and exchanged our adventures. Not much had happened to him, he said, he had come back to Varna soon after I had left: and what about my doings? I told him all about the theft of the rucksack and Rosa's wonderful intervention. 'I bet they beat him up,' Gatcho said, 'and a good job too.' I short-circuited the argument about this (too early for a clash), and moved on to Bucharest. My stay at the Savoy-Ritz was a great success. Gatcho grinned from ear to ear as I told him. Remembering his prejudices, I underplayed all my worldly goings-on, but stuck up for the Rumanians: they were not at all the ogres the Bulgarians thought they were. I had done the same thing, vice versa, in Rumania, like the mouse that helped in Aesop's fable. To little effect, though. 'Savages,' had been the dismissive Rumanian comment, and 'Robbers!' was Gatcho's. After an exchange of fruitless argument, I slithered off into demands about our acquaintances in Tirnovo. Two of them were here – but not Vasil the spy-hunter, Gatcho said with a smile. In fact, we all had dinner together, and I slept on a camp-bed in his digs at the outskirts of the town. Why didn't I stay on and return with him to Tirnovo for Christmas? 'Turkey awaits!' I said importantly, pointing down the coast.

Thanks to the word 'student' on my passport, a rather agreeable life began, and I had all my meals at a students' restaurant frequented by Gatcho and his friends, with even my own napkin in a ring. A pre-Advent fast was in progress, which the students and the people who ran the place took rather seriously, and the food consisted mainly of spinach-like herbs, mache lettuces, cabbage, cauliflower, and two of my favourite things, bean and lentil soup, eaten with wonderful black bread, and plenty of wine.

When Gatcho was free, we wandered about the town, and into the fascinating quarters where the Tartars and Circassians had lived their primitive lives. These Tcherkesses had been brought here by the Turks in the middle of the last century, and had taken root. There was nothing remarkable about the town, except its marvellous position poised above the sea, with cliffs running north and south under a fleece of woods and the waves lapping on shingle and sand immediately below.

North of the town, among tall trees, stood the Stanchoff villa, and beyond it, Evksinograd, half villa and half rustic palace, where the royal family spent their holidays in summer. About twenty miles north, along the same coast and the other side of the border, Queen Marie of Rumania* lived off and on in her romantic oriental retreat at Balchik. I wondered if these two sets of Coburg cousins ever defied the prejudices of their subjects and slipped across by motor boat for tea.

Gatcho and his friends gave a lot of thought to the *studentkas*, the girl students, who, like them, had come to study in Varna. They, too, wore student caps very like the boys' ones; they looked terrible on some heads, rather dashing and Apache-like on others. These romances were nearly all, I think, platonic, owing to two things: the close chaperoning of the girls, who were nearly always lodged under the Argus-eyed vigilance of kinsmen, and the pan-Balkan attitude to technical virginity. Its absence in peasant circles was a matter of repudiation and bloodshed, and the prejudice is just as deeply rooted in the intelligentsia. It is much less a question of morality or ethics than of tribal feeling, and it must be largely an heirloom of the fierce seclusion of their women which

* Queen Marie (1875–1938), wife of Ferdinand I and later estranged mother of Carol II. She was a powerful ambassador for Rumanian post-war interests. The royal houses of Rumania and Bulgaria were related to one another (and to Queen Victoria) through the Saxe-Coburg-Gotha family.

prevailed for centuries among the occupying Muslims. This strictly localized physiological fixation, and the rough and ready tests by which a bride's inviolacy is gauged, must have led to boundless injustice. Gatcho told me that the terror of lost maidenheads tormented both their owners and their potential destroyers with the dread of family retribution (and perhaps gunshot weddings – though girls had been known to act in bad faith here). The would-be seducer might naturally be diffident, even without these sanctions, about landing his momentary benefactress in the soup for life. Love affairs, then, even the most innocent ones, had to be conducted with great secrecy to avoid even the appearance of danger; the rare occasions when they were less innocent called for as much strategy and resource as the capture of a city. Even so, when the lovers had outwitted all the hazards, drugged the watchdogs, as it were, bribed the guards, and talked the duenna round, the gloomy tribal veto lay between them like a sword: a curse only to be exorcized by the physiological equivalent of a mediaeval theologian's device to transgress the spirit of a text while keeping the hallowed wording intact.

At this point, to cheer Gatcho up, I told him of the Rumanian name for these fell diseases which had first caught my eye on a doctor's plate in Arad: *Boale Lumeţşi* (the first word is a dissyllable, the second, *Loomeshti*: literally, 'ailments of the world' – 'world' is *lume* in Rumanian) – rather lyrical-sounding words for a thought to send a shudder down young spines. '*Boale lumeţşi* . . . *boale lumeţşi!*' We uttered the syllables in slow, elevated and almost dreamy tones, as though they were a charm or an exorcism. *Weltliche Krankheiten* . . . the ills of the world . . .

Our talk wandered round these and kindred themes. He knew that the Bogomils had supplied the English language, at several removes, with the most widespread word for sexual heterodoxy. The practice was almost as prevalent, it seemed from what Gatcho said, as in Western Europe; perhaps slightly less. In the usual way of the Levant, whatever blame there was, and that not very severe, attached to passivity; not on moral grounds, but on the score of abrogation of virile prerogative in a world where toughness is prized. But the cruel hostility of England is absent. The idea of people being thrown into prison for sexual unorthodoxy, unless accompanied by factors which would equally put a heterosexual offender behind bars, seems to them as barbarous and atrocious as Balkan atrocities to us. All through the Balkan peninsula, homosexuality conjures up an image that sharply conflicts with Western symbolism. Instead of a sinuously fluting timbre of voice, the word evokes a tall and burly figure, often with a cudgel, talking in a slow bass voice, twirling vast bristling moustaches and surveying his fellow men with a burning, shrewd and speculative eye.

These platonic love affairs of the young, then, found their outlet in two ways. At the sunset hour, when all southern Europe pours into the main street to slowly promenade in the falling dusk, the sexes, except for family parties, are as sternly segregated as they are on either side of the nave in church, usually walking in opposite directions so that sweethearts are only within striking distance for a few palpitating seconds a mile. The two streams of strollers become a tangle of furtive oeillades, lovelorn glances, fluttered lashes, hungry looks and, when nobody is looking, of love letters hastily changing hands. These tightly folded billets were the only other means of contact. Gatcho was deep in one of these pen-friendships, and, since he made me his confidant as a complete outsider, I was able to marvel at the high-flown, euphuistic fervour on either side. Sighs, tears, pining away with love-longing, veiled or overt threats of suicide, sleepless nights with tear-sodden pillows (Gatcho slept magnificently) were the normal currency of these letters; and poetry, in which all nature

– the swallow, the lark, lonely seagulls and nightingales leaning their breasts on a thorn until the heart itself was transfixed – was pressed into service. Gatcho, reprehensibly, was involved in three separate romances of this kind; two were stylistic exercises, but the heroine of the third, Ivanka, was more serious. She was pointed out during the evening promenade, a very pretty girl from Shumen, and Gatcho took me to have a formal coffee and *slivo* at her uncle's house on her aunt's name day, a perfect opportunity for letter-swapping.

The odd thing about all these romances is how seldom they end in anything, let alone marriage. Marriage is nearly always a matter of dowries and family arrangement in which neither party has much say, and sentiment, usually, very little. The same rule obtains in all these countries. It seems to work very well. All this puts the vast quantity of songs about love – I think it even outstrips war as a favourite theme – in a strangely theoretical, abstract category. These feelings, as it were, spin in the void, like an elaborate machine that cogs into nothing more solid than air. Gatcho admitted that it was so. But I rather envied him the excitement of the whole thing, the illicit correspondence, the hot-house *Schwärmerei*, the subterfuges and collusion, which can, in a way, be an end in itself.

There were signs indicating that the old order was beginning to relax, and, to weaken my sweeping thesis, Gatcho did actually marry Ivanka two years later, against considerable opposition by both families who had other candidates lined up, and lived happily ever after; at least, until I last heard from him a year before the war.

～

Many things lodge Varna in my memory. One was an old man who must have been picked off by the first cold of winter; at the end of a lane on the edge of the town, a long object was being thrust through a window; a coffin, as I saw, when it was safely on the shoulders of the bearers. I stood back against the wall as the vested priest and the mourners – a few of them, old women mostly, wailing piteously – thronged the narrow gulley. The coffin passed within a foot of me, open, containing an old man in a black suit with patent leather shoes, specially bought, as I learnt later, for the occasion, and probably smarter than any he had worn in his lifetime. A few flowers were tucked round him, and a satin ribbon bound his gnarled hands together. The head, with hollow cheeks, cavernous eyes, and a toothless mouth slightly agape, looked smaller than the head of a live person, as though death had shrunk it; and quite different. It rocked on its pillow with the bearers' gait. The little group, with its tall candles blown out by the wind, turned the corner. The sad chanting and wailing died. Two small boys carrying a coffin lid that was too heavy for them brought up the rear, arguing importantly and possessively about which way up it should be carried.

About ten minutes later a more prosperous group was moving along the main street. Passers-by stopped, uncovered and crossed themselves. Acolytes carried processional crosses radiating a forest of gold and silver spokes which they gyrated slightly on their staves, so that the metal rays jangled together with a sound like shaken tinfoil. In the middle, carried slowly and at a slant that was almost perpendicular, a small, flower-lined coffin contained a pretty little girl of about four in a stiff white party dress with a wreath of white flowers round her carefully combed black hair in which big, white satin bows were tied. Her pallor gave her the look of a wax doll on display in a window where everything had been remembered except the pink on the cheeks. The chanting this time was in Armenian and the whole company disappeared at last into the Armenian church. (The hats of the Armenian clergy only differed from the cylinders of the Orthodox at the summit. The latter were flat on top; the Armenian *kati-mankia* were roofed by a fluted cone.)

Gatcho was dumbfounded when I told him, soon afterwards, that I had just seen corpses for the first time in my life. How could I have possibly reached the age of nineteen without having seen dozens? I explained about closed coffins. What an odd idea, and what an unreal life we must lead. I had felt rather shaken.

Mr and Mrs Collas, the British consul and his wife, lived in a house high up with a wide view of the Black Sea. I had several cheerful meals there, borrowed their books and received many kindnesses from them. After a few days Judith Tollinton, whom I had stayed with in Sofia, came to stay for a day or two, and we went for walks along the cliffs, playing analogies and other elaborate guessing-games while the falling leaves blew about in the cold sunny air. One evening, when we had all sat up late, I think playing paper games, I set off for Gatcho's after a final whisky and soda, as usual clutching a couple of those round tins of Player's bestowed by the kind Collases.

Now something very odd occurs; so peculiar indeed, and so unfinished, in that I still don't know what it was about, that I hesitate to set it down. But it is hard to leave out. I walked back to Gatcho's house where I was staying. It was about midnight. The key wasn't in its usual place. Obviously Gatcho had forgotten it. The light was on, so I called his name once or twice, then threw some gravel at the window. There was no answer: he must have gone to bed with the lights on. So I shinned up a drainpipe – Gatcho's room was on the second floor – opened the window and lowered myself inside the room on my tiptoes as quietly as I could. Gatcho wasn't in bed, but sitting on the edge of it fully dressed, glaring at me with a brow clouded with histrionic thunder. I cheerfully asked what had happened about the key. Gatcho shouted: 'Go away! I hate you!' He said this so dramatically that

I thought it was some elaborate joke, started laughing and walked to the middle of the room. He stood up and shouted still louder: '*Ich hasse Dich!*' And then louder still, 'What are you laughing at?' I clapped and said, 'Bravo, Gatcho!' At this Gatcho picked up the huge Bulgarian two-edged knife that was lying on my bed with a lot of other stuff, pulled off the sheath and stood under the lamp, with the knife-grasping arm flung out wide, at right angles to his body, the raised tip pointing at me. His eyebrows were painfully high, his eyes wide and fixed and his lips so tightly pinched together that they scarcely showed. At last I understood that there was no question of a joke at all and seized his right wrist with both hands. There was a moment of deadlock. He made no effort to attack with the knife, but resisted my forward thrust. This sent us both crashing to the floor and the knife clattering across the room. I extricated myself, picked up the knife and flung it into the garden through the still-open window. In this sudden violence, we had upset the *mangali*, a huge brass brazier with heavy rings used for heating the room. The floor was covered with burning charcoal. Without saying a word, we set about collecting this scarlet scattering with whatever was handy and pouring it back into the righted *mangali*. Meanwhile a din of feet pounded up the stairs. Kiril and Veniamin, the two Tirnovo friends who lived below, burst in and asked what the noise was about. 'Only the *mangali*,' we said, our eyes fixed on our task, 'Come and help.' When the coal was all restored and the others had gone, we both sat down on our beds saying nothing, and Gatcho sank his cropped brow in his hands. There was a long silence. Then we looked at each other in bewilderment. When we were more composed, I asked him what on earth had happened. Gatcho answered, 'I don't know. I truly don't know', then after a pause, 'Please forgive me.' We shook hands ceremoniously. 'I wouldn't have done you any harm. Please don't ask me any more.'

It seemed hopeless to do so just then. We went to bed, wished each other a forlorn goodnight, and blew out the light.

What had happened? Of one thing I was quite certain. Even if I hadn't made a dive for the knife, Gatcho would never have plunged it into my gizzard. He hadn't attacked, and he had released the knife at once. He was just as strong as I was and he could have put up – had he wanted – a far longer fight. It was obviously my imperceptive and no doubt whisky-sprung and jarring laughter that had made him seize it in exasperation. But what had started it off in the first place? There had been not a flicker of previous trouble and we had parted cheerfully before I had set off. Nor had there been a trace of any sentimental discord, rivalry over *studentkas*, or friction of any other kind. Could I have talked too much about hated Rumania? I thought I had been careful about that. Or boasted beyond endurance about my smart new friends in Bucharest? Surely I would have had enough tact not to go wrong there. Could I have seemed to abandon Gatcho and his companions these last few days for English friends in exalted consular circles? It couldn't have been this. I was certain, too, that it wasn't a question of overstayed welcome, which after all it might have been. (I suddenly began to wonder how much of a nuisance I might have proved to countless people during the last year: had I been a perfect pest all across Central Europe? A deep subsidiary gloom set in, that made it almost a relief to return to the dominant question.) Perhaps I had stopped him from working. But that was just what I hadn't been doing these last two nights; anyway, Gatcho was an even more confirmed noctambulist than I was, just as bent on excess and injudicious conduct; in fact I think we had what schoolmasters so damningly call 'a bad influence on each other', in this respect. At last I came to the conclusion, peering at the dark ceiling, that I must have said something tactless, perhaps during some exchange of heavy-handed teasing, or even something quite innocent which had passed unnoticed at the moment and been misunderstood later: one of those unintentional, feud-launching words that cannot be expiated, wiped out or explained, which after rankling and festering had exploded like a delayed-action bomb. The result could have been one of Gatcho's blind rages which I had seen wreaking havoc on others . . . Was I letting myself off too lightly? Suddenly Gatcho asked if I were asleep, and apologized again. I said I was sure everything was my fault. 'No, no, no!' 'Yes, yes!'; a maudlin exchange, but much better than nothing. We both feigned sleep.

It was much better, but far from all right next morning. We were both ill-at-ease and avoiding each other's glance. As we squatted by the *mangali*, pushing the two long-stemmed Turkish coffee saucepans into the charcoal, I said, 'Gatcho, I don't know quite what has happened, but I think I ought to find other rooms. I'm sorry for being a nuisance.' (I was waiting for the post again.) He seized me by the arm, almost upsetting the *mangali* again, and cried, 'Oh, no! Please, please don't! Think of the shame to me!' He meant the crime against Balkan hospitality. I begged him to come and have lunch at a café I had discovered and had turned into a writing and reading headquarters during the day on top of the cliff. No more was said before he left, except: 'Please, don't tell the others.' (As if I would!) On the way out, I went to look at the drainpipe. The knife was sticking in an upright of the woodshed wall, flung with enough violence to embed it nearly an inch. I put it back in its place.

The café was in an exactly similar position to the place where I had lunched with Rosa outside Rustchuk, except that instead of the Danube lay the Black Sea. Nobody seemed to come there. The old *kafedji* said he had got some sausages and could find some potatoes to fry when the time came. I spent a miserable morning there trying to unravel the events of the night before, but without success, peering out at the rain-dappled waves till Gatcho turned up on a borrowed bike. We chucked a first glass of *slivo* down our throats and poured out another. Our openings were nearly identical and embarrassingly contrite. Me: 'I'm terribly sorry, whatever I did. I didn't mean to.' Gatcho: 'I'm terribly sorry. I didn't mean anything. I must be mad. Don't let's talk about it', followed by an awkward pause overhung by a giant question-mark. I got busy with the wine and the conversation became less stilted. Gatcho asked me questions and I answered. I realized that we were running briskly through nearly all the subjects we had touched on since I had arrived in Varna. Gatcho listened in silence punctuated by grave nods. I feared I might repeat the same error, like the man in comic stories asked back into a house years after making some monster gaffe, and doing the same thing again. If only I knew where the snag lay! I talked a lot, but more thoughtfully than usual. There was no point at which, in spite of watching carefully, I could detect a sudden movement of détente, but the atmosphere did thaw. Afterwards, looking over the cliff, I realized we were walking arm in arm – it reminded me suddenly of Constantine at the ball – as though nothing had happened. It had somehow come right.

All was back to normal. I asked him two days later what the reason had been. He said, apologetically, that it was merely his lunatic temper. But I know it wasn't. I had said something which had been misunderstood. Once cleared up, I think he felt shy about admitting how trivial it was.

The explanation of this odd incident has gone on too long. But, though much in a narrative like this had to be jettisoned, I couldn't quite omit it, however inconclusive – I have thought about it often since, and always with mystification – and, once embarked on, to curtail it would have presented it wrongly. Not for the first time, I concluded despondently, I have wounded somebody badly without meaning to; nor, alas, for the last. But I wish I knew exactly how.

~

. . . for a long walk in St James' Park. The Admiralty from the Regent's Bridge looked like a palace in an illustration in the Russian Fairy Book, pearl and ivory coloured, the pinnacles and domes floating above the thinnest of mists, but the only sign of autumn was a lonely spray of gold in the green leaves of one plane tree, like Whistler's solitary lock of silver hair. I was peacefully watching the pelicans (how sooty they get!) when a friendly old tramp with a nose like Mount Vesuvius in full eruption and a pink and positively magenta cloth cap asked me if they were . . .

. . . and the mean rainfall in Nepal is the heaviest in the Himalayas, 82% per annum, so I will be glad to return to Simla. The dress of the King and the court officials is most picturesque. I was interested of course, in a subsidiary of the Rhaeto-Alpine system of unwarped sedimentary with a superstratum of friable schist and faults of jurassic gneiss and hornblende. I hope you observe . . .

These letters from my mother and father, many times re-forwarded, and picked up that morning, must have been delayed on one of their many stages. My mother's letters, dashingly written at top speed, were (and still are) long, charming and funny. I surprised the café-keeper several times by laughing out loud, till I got to the finish ('everything, even the Cromwell Road, must come to an end, so . . .') With the letters, as always, was a thick roll of weekly magazines and interesting or amusing cuttings from newspapers, comic juxtapositions, *Times* crosswords and so on. I answered them with long travel accounts (which, borrowed back for the first go at this book, also, unfortunately, went astray like the notebooks). Letters from my father, much shorter and more formal and punctilious both in writing and content, were rarer events. My parents had separated about twelve years earlier, and even before that he only returned to England for six months' leave every three years, with the result that like many Anglo-Indian parents and children (in my case, one who had never been to India, though my mother and sister were born there and my father lived there nearly all his life) we were, in spite of determined efforts on both sides, semi-strangers.

My childhood was spent in London, in my mother's very exciting company, with my sister Vanessa, who was four years older, when she was not in India: first of all, when I was about five, in Primrose Hill Studios, where one could hear the lions roaring at night in the zoo. These studios were entirely inhabited by sculptors and painters, and my mother persuaded Arthur Rackham to paint the door of our nursery-schoolroom with a picture of Peter Pan in Kensington Gardens sailing down the Serpentine in a bird's nest. Then for years we lived in a rather fascinating flat high up at 213 Piccadilly, where I could watch across the Circus a staccato sky-sign shaker pouring a cocktail into a glass with a cherry in it – GORDON'S GIN THE HEART OF A GOOD COCKTAIL! – from my bed. In summer she would take a cottage at Dodford, in Northamptonshire, on the edge of one of the smallest and remotest villages anywhere, beside a brook flowing between steep, fox-haunted spinneys. Here my mother was absorbed in writing plays under the name of Aeleen Taafe, plays which never really struck lucky, though they seemed marvellous and tremendously exciting to me, especially read out loud. They were mostly about India, extremely adventurous and romantic, and not written without knowledge.

Her family, a mixture of Irish and English, had been there for three generations. My grandfather arrived there, as a midshipman in the East India Company's navy, in the thick of the Mutiny and was greeted on landing by the appalling sight of mutineers being blown from a cannon's mouth. My grandparents owned some large slate quarries in Bihar and Orissa, and when they were in India they lived in Hickey and Thackerayish splendour with even more than the usual army of servants, and unnumbered horses: an Elysian state vanished for many a year. Unlike many Anglo-Indians, my mother not only learnt to speak Hindi and Urdu perfectly, but to read and write them, and gathered much more than a superficial knowledge of India. (When, later on, she and my sister would suddenly break into an unknown tongue as we were walking across some sodden Midland field, I would try to drown them by bawling in Latin, but this was not nearly arcane enough to either of them for real revenge.) Beside this went random but enormous reading, passionate devotion to horsemanship and, above all, the amateur theatricals which seem to have played such a tremendous part in the life of Calcutta and Simla; these first started my mother's long-standing devotion to the theatre in all its aspects (which perversely and sadly has always filled me – I mean the backstage part of it – with an instinctive recoil. Wrongly perhaps, because it got me out of a hole once during the war in Cairo, when I had landed into some sort of trouble. Halfway through the rocket which a rather nice elderly general was perfunctorily administering, his brow clouded thoughtfully. 'Could it have been your mother that I saw playing the lead in *The Maid of the Mountains* in Simla in 1913? It was? My dear boy, I've never forgotten it! She was wonderful! I'm afraid she'd never remember a fogey like me, but please send her my regards.' His old eyes misted over and the forgotten rocket sizzled out. I was very relieved and extremely touched.) This post-Kipling existence of reading, languages, gymkhanas and acting, unfolding under deodars, was half hindered, half abetted by my grandmother. She was a very fair portrait painter, rather of the Burne-Jones school, and she had left a picture of my mother at that time: a beautiful girl in a white dress with her head bowed in a posture of entirely deceptive meekness in order, I think, and quite rightly, to display the long Pre-Raphaelite cascade of flame-coloured hair.

This London–Northamptonshire life, which lasted all through my calamitous schooldays, was enlivened during a year or so by a sudden passion of my mother's for the air, involving long drives to Castle Bromwich aerodrome and then anxious waits while my sister and I watched her disappear in minute Moth biplanes, and then, worse still, solo. Fortunately this period died away without disaster. But far more exciting than the delights of London and the country were journeys to France, and to the Bernese Oberland for skiing, which had us all three in its grip. (My mother was married when she was eighteen, so there was much that we could share.) But better even than this, or France, or the museums and picture galleries of Paris and London, which she knew by heart and filled with excitement, or the endless plays, were my mother's gift for reading aloud: quantities of Shakespeare and poetry and scores of books ranging over vast tracts of English literature, sometimes for hours a day – and much of it, as I was four years younger than my sister, only just within reach, which made it doubly mysterious and memorable, and leaves a deeper impression than anything else in those years. There was a great deal of reciting and singing to the piano and dressing up. What was so extraordinary in all this fun and stimulus and charm of decor was that it was all achieved, though I didn't know it for years, on scarcely any cash at all, by a genius for improvisation and stage-management: a miraculous and absolutely successful emanation of a very imaginative, inventive and strong personality.

Rather unexpectedly, beneath the shimmering, unconventional play of the surface waves lurked sunken and adamantine ranges of inherited and unquestioned conviction. On occasions they could rip the keel off a craft sailing too confidently there. Sometimes these submarine hazards seemed to change position and this would lend incalculability to the scene, a feeling that one would never learn the art of navigating this in all its niceties. Clouds would suddenly assemble in unexpected quarters, charged with distress and bewilderment – not too stiff a price to pay for the charm, generosity, stimulus, enterprise, fun and excitement that was the normal climate, let alone her forbearance and kindness about my troubled career which might justifiably have filled anyone else with despair. I think her own rather headstrong and turbulent career as a girl charitably tempered exasperation with a secret sympathy, however much it had to be repressed for decorum's sake. A many-faceted character evoked every reaction except tedium. It was her high-spirited style and sense of the absurd in this long letter that made me, to the Bulgarian café-keeper's puzzlement, laugh out loud again and again.

To say that one letter-writer could make something alive and captivating out of an ordinary London day and the other, somehow, drain the diamonds and aigrettes of a Himalayan court of their gleam, is not a fair comparison. It may indicate a shift in tempo and temperature, but it is interesting for a different reason. My own letters to my father were as formal and lacklustre as his. Due to the scarcity of leave from India and the small overlap with them that summer holidays afforded, we hardly knew each other. We met for the first time when I was five and since then, for the rest of our lives, we spent – placing all the communal periods end to end – about six months in each other's company, for as long as our lives overlapped. It was never much of a go, and I think we always parted with secret relief, after trying hard on both sides. I wish we had met as total strangers when I was grown up, because today, if I saw him sitting in a hotel, say, in the Italian mountains, I would have longed to get to know him for the very reasons that filled me with malaise at the time.

He was enormously tall and thin, with a distinguished and scholarly look, heavily spectacled, and dressed and equipped on the occasion which I have in mind – these occasions rare enough for each one to leave an indelible impression – in a way that indicated his interests as plainly as *armes parlantes*. We were in Baveno on Lake Maggiore in April, preparing to climb the Monte della Croce just behind, and I think I was eight or nine. He wore heavy boots, carefully oiled and dubbined with tags that stuck out behind, thick green stockings, pepper-and-salt knickerbockers and an old-fashioned Norfolk jacket of the same stuff, belted, with pleats on the pockets and intricate leather buttons, a watch attached to the buttonhole in the lapel by a leather thong. In the pockets went lens, compass, maps, sandwiches, a bar of chocolate, an apple and an orange, a notebook, sketching block, pencils, killing bottle, guides to the regional botany and avifauna, and – slung about his long form – a japanned vasculum on a wide web baldrick, field glasses and a collapsible butterfly net. An alpenstock leant nearby. All this was all right, I thought, standing hard by like a reluctant page at this accoutring; but I dreaded the two coming items. The first was a geological hammer, the head of which was marked – as my father was in the service of the Government of India – with that scarcely perceptible broad arrow that stamps all government property. It was a favourite joke of my father's that the only people to possess such imple- ments were he, his colleagues and the convicts on Dartmoor, for breaking stones. I knew it was a joke, *but did everybody else?*

When he stuck it through the belt of his jacket, I always prayed that the arrow side was not the exposed one. On this occasion, it blazed forth. Pretending officiously to adjust it more comfortably, I tried to reverse it, when my father said in an austere and cavernous voice from high above: 'Paddy, what on earth are you up to?' I lost my nerve and left it, trusting the English people in the hall wouldn't notice, although I had eyes for nothing else, and that the Italians might not know . . . The second item was almost equally dreaded: a vast semicircular cap, I think originally destined for Tibetan travel, like a bisected pumpkin of fur, armed with a peak and with fur-lined earflaps that were joined (when tied under the chin which was worse still) by a disturbing bow on the summit.

I had just got the sack from my preparatory school (which was why I was hanging about in Italy in the middle of the spring term, with my father, for once, having to put up with the second of these recurring calamities), but not soon enough to have escaped the indoctrination of prep schools, which, unlike public schools, turns children – all of them, till then, near-geniuses trailing clouds of glory – into frightened, insufferable little conformist prigs. (It is in these children's Potsdams, not in public schools, that old England's sociological winding sheet is woven. If these beastly places were all blown up, the humanistic liberation, which is, unexpectedly, latent in public schools, would be given a chance at last.) When we were in the street and the hat in position, with the Lombardic sun shining on the broad-arrowed hammer-head, I lagged behind, miserably hoping that nobody would think there was any connection between us, longing to be demolished by a merciful lightning flash, until I was reproached for dawdling in kindly, sepulchral tones. I smiled, while thinking of this in the café in Varna, and of how closely my outfit now approximated his.

My father, at that time, was Director-General of the Geological Survey of India, and remained so for many years, responsible for the mineral welfare of the whole subcontinent, and constantly travelling, when he could get away from Calcutta and Simla, all over it (always, I imagined as a child, from a faded photograph, sitting gravely solar-topeed behind an aukus-wielding mahout, on an enormous elephant, through landscapes of jungle and mountain). Letters would arrive from Bangalore, Ceylon, Sikkim, Waziristan . . . A true Darwinian naturalist, the whole physical world absorbed him. I used to boast at school how he had discovered a snowflake and a caterpillar with eight hairs on its back and a mineral called Fermorite, a claim which would often bewilder and silence other boasters by its oddity. For one of these feats the Royal Society had made him a Fellow. Somehow we always failed to click. I think I found him too austere, remote and frugal, and his naturalist's instincts ensured a scientific passion for classification: for instructing me, later that day for instance, whether the gentians we found just below the snow line on Monte della Croce were bicotyledons or monocotyledons, without a word about the colour. I called for wilder music and for stronger wine . . . I dread to speculate what he thought of me, a permanent long-distance nuisance and source of perplexity and expense. He had been rather tolerant otherwise about the misdeeds that I have darkly hinted at now and then; and he had accepted with philosophy the reversal in his plans implicit in my present travels. Perhaps he felt that they were the beginning of the dissolution of our remote link, which, in fact, they turned out to be.

About our only common ground was the fondness of both of us for puns, which, if they are long and elaborate enough, is not dead in me yet. A great and rather unexpected talent of my father's, and one which seems to belie the impression I have written, was a wonderful gift for storytelling. Night after night, in the hotels of Devonshire, Switzerland or Italy which were our habitat when he was on leave, these complex and exciting serial-sagas would hold us and the other children staying there (all of whom, disguised under intriguing names, were woven into the narrative) silent and spellbound on the floor in pitch darkness.

I put the two letters back into their many-stamped envelopes, each with its conflicting redolence, so different one from the other, and both so unconnected and remote from the Black Sea and Balkan scene that lay all round.

~

The café, my new headquarters on the cliff above the Black Sea, where nobody but me ever seemed to come, was little more than a hut among trees, with a single wide window. I used to gaze down through it at the Black Sea – bright blue in the winter sunlight, steely grey or cobalt, traversed by racing clouds, shivered by raindrops, churned by the wind in sudden angry waves, and once invisible under a twirling mist that turned all the trees and the beetling shrubs along the cliff's rim into a ghostly forest – and repeat its names slowly and with delectation, over and over again, in English, then in German, Rumanian, Turkish: Schwarzes Meer, Marea Neagra, Kara Deniz, and, deepest and darkest of all, the Bulgarian Cherno Moré. It seemed that ancient Greek navigators changed their original name for it – the Pontus Axeinos, the hostile or anti-stranger sea – into its opposite, 'Euxine', 'the welcoming one', to placate sudden and terrible storms, on the same superstitious principle as the Furies were named 'the kindly ones'. It is ballasted with thousands of wrecks. I would look north along the tufted cliffs towards the Dobrudja and Constanța, the ancient Tomi, where Ovid was exiled by Augustus for writing the *Ars amatoria*. (If only in the *Tristia* he had written more about his surroundings!) Then came the vast flimsy wilderness of the Danube's mouths fraying out like the unravelled strands at the end of a long cable, and Bessarabia, and then Russia. It all seemed very close. Odessa, the Crimea, the Sea of Azov – Krim Tartary and the whole sweep of the Scythian empire, the dark land of the Cimmerians – Novorossiysk, and, almost opposite my table, Colchis, where Jason stole the Golden Fleece: a long sail for the *Argo* from Mount Pelion. If my forefinger could shoot out like a telescope several hundred miles long it would strike the Caucasus, fumble its way through the valleys of Imeretia and Mingelia and into Georgia, through the Lermontoff world of Tiflis, touching the tip of Mount Ararat and dipping, on the other side, in the Caspian. The Elburz mountains, Azerbaijan, Persia – all this seemed suddenly close and accessible. A southern swing of the forefinger brought it in line with Trebizond, the ancient kingdom of Pontus and Paphlagonia, the coast of Asia Minor, all northern Turkey, and at last, south and a bit to the east, about a hundred and fifty miles away as the gull flies, to the Bosphorus and, on its bank, the many-named city I was heading for. A wild and fabulous spirit overhung these waves, as though this coast were still the end of the world, the forlorn ultimate border of reality beyond which a cloud of legend, rumour and surmise began.

'I've tramped Britain and I've tramped Gaul, and the Pontic shore where the snow-flakes fall'* – the lines were seldom out of my head these days. Another literary association of the region, to set beside Ovid and Pushkin, was the tumulus marking the grave of Mazeppa, a lonely mound among the tangle of the Danube's outlets. I had been told about this in Bucharest, and quickly read Byron's poem, and my thoughts of the plain sweeping

---

* The line is from an imagined Roman marching song in Rudyard Kipling's *Puck of Pook's Hill.*

from the river and across the Ukraine to Kiev were incomplete
thenceforward without the Géricault-vision of Peter the Great's
hetman of Cossacks lashed naked to the back of a wild horse
galloping with streaming mane and wild eyes and nostrils across
the crepuscular steppe.

But Varna, and particularly the rolling wooded country inland
from my lair, is especially singled out by a larger disaster. Here,
in November 1444, the young King Wladislaw of Hungary and
Poland, with the great Janos Hunyadi, Prince of Transylvania,
and Vlad the Devil, Prince of Wallachia, advanced with their
joint armies against Murad II: rashly, for, as Vlad told the young
king, 'the Sultan, when he goes hunting, has a greater retinue
than the whole of your army.' And so it turned out. The hosts
of the second Amurath and of Wladislaw Jagiello (who was of
the great Lithuanian dynasty that reigned over Poland, Hungary
and Bohemia) fell upon each other. After a savage battle the
Christian army was cut to bits. Dead knights and men-at-arms
littered the slopes, among them two bishops and Cardinal
Cesarini, the facilitator of the engagement, in spite of a truce,
on the theory that it was no sin to break faith with infidels.
Prisoners of note were ransomed, the rest butchered by the
Ottomans. It was a defeat of tragic moment to the whole of
Christendom, the last attempt of the West to block the advance
of the Turks. The field was now clear for the Ottomans, and,
nine years later, Constantinople was captured.

The young king himself fell in the heart of the melee with
his horse stuck full of arrows. A janissary called Hidja Hirdir –
odd how these names have been handed down, like that of the
first janissary to leap through the breached walls of Theodosius
later on – struck off his head. It was put in a pot full of honey
and Murad despatched a runner with it to his capital at Broussa
to announce the great victory; it was pulled out of the pot on

the outskirts, washed in a brook, stuck on a pole and carried in triumph through the cheering streets.

Outside all had turned different shades of glimmering, sunless blue. When the *kafedji* had lit a lamp and put it on my table – dusk started now about five – I could see its ghost on the inside of the windowpane and my own fragmented lamp-lit reflection and, through them both, like two scenes on the same photograph, the fading blues of the headland and the sea and sky. Loose in this void of darkening blue, the yellow pinpoints of a ship's portholes advanced from the north-east, perhaps those of a Russian tramp-steamer; from Odessa, it might be, or Kherson, Yalta, Novorossiysk. The only bit of the Black Sea coast I knew nothing about at all was the stretch immediately to the south. I would soon find out, as I was setting off next day.

~

'These', Gatcho said, pointing to a just discernible zigzag of trough-like hollows, 'are trenches from the war, when they thought the Russian Black Sea fleet might try a landing.' They were choked with threadbare brambles and bracken, a wavering blur along the cliff's edge. It seemed a long time ago, just about a year after we were all born: eighteen years of dust and mud nearly effaced them. Somewhere out at sea, the mutiny on the *Potemkin* had taken place. It was Sunday, a brilliant, cloudless, but freezing cold day, and Gatcho and the other two Tirnovo boys who lived below, Kiril and Veniamin, had accompanied me about ten miles on my southern journey. We had slunk out of the town like malefactors long before daybreak. The misty jets of our breath in the wintry air, shooting from the heads of our silhouettes, had been the first symptoms of dawn. We had just finished some bread and cheese and drunk a bottle of wine under a hawthorn bush. I had been puzzled by Veniamin's name – it turned out to be the Orthodox version of Benjamin (the B turning to V and the J to I): a fat, sleepy, nice boy who had brought a pistol with him and surprisingly succeeded in shooting a hare, an enormous one, now grasped and dangling by its hind legs, its ears sweeping the ground. It was time for them to start back. All had been well after Gatcho's and my lunch together, better than ever, as it sometimes is after a row. The night before, all of us had sat up till late in a deep wine-cellar, drinking by candlelight in a narrow alley between enormous shadowy barrels.

We had been arrested on the way home for singing arm in arm in the street – by two policemen, who were, it turned out, far drunker than our merely cheerful selves. The officer in charge of the police station, when he turned up and found us quietly droning *Die Lorelei* on the bench in a cell, let us out at once. Immediately after we had left, a policeman friend of Veniamin's told us, on our way out of the town, that our two captors were flung into the cell we had just vacated, which sent our spirits soaring.

It was time for them to turn back. We all embraced and waved many times as I watched the red crowns of their three student caps and the trailed hare dwindle along the dunes. We exchanged letters intermittently until the war, but I never saw Gatcho again.

8

Dancing by the Black Sea

It was the first day of December. Treading along this windy rim
of the continent, I saw that much had changed since the last bit
of my journey between the northern mountains and the Danube.
I ate up the miles at a great pace. Inland to the north-west the
Balkan range rose in milder slopes than those I had crossed – three
times, now – but far away, at the other end of this brilliant
morning, I could just see those western heights now gleaming
with an ice-bright and blue-shadowed line of snow, and, to the
south-west, a faint and a faraway shimmer of the Rhodope.
(Perhaps it was just about here, at the end of the wide funnel
between the two ranges, that those migrating storks had struck
the Black Sea coast on their way to Africa.) All the tiers of slopes,
the soft hills and valleys that rolled away inland, were now feathered with young green grass and some frothier vegetation leaping
out of the ground with the abruptness and the optimism of
mustard and cress from a flannel. The hammer-blow of the
Bulgarian winter, although the late autumn had come to an end
at last, had not yet fallen, and these pale emerald or moss-bright
sweeps across the damp russet earth spread a fiction of early spring.
The hills seemed empty of men though I caught rare glimpses of
perched villages inland, their chimneys balancing above them
floating veils as thin and blue as un-inhaled tobacco smoke. Into
the still, cold air an occasional tall thread rose swaying and

expanding from distant bonfires, as though Hurons were signalling from range to range. A steep, ploughed hillside would uncoil symmetrical waves of damp and dark red furrows, all of them hispid with young green between their ridges, sometimes reaching to the very edge of the cliff. A few cataleptic kraals of muffled hives were scattered in the undergrowth, silently waiting for the spring heather. Slow landslides of flocks streamed across the slants of pasture, only the travelling clink of their bells across the clear air hinting that they were on the move, grazing their way across Bulgaria at a glacier's pace. Some of the fields were white with gulls, peacefully standing in the grass or among the furrows, bent on a brief inland holiday. In this open country, the only other birds were magpies of which one at least was usually fidgeting in the middle distance, standing in a field or flapping across the path. The cliff track would sink every so often into a deep combe where a stream wound into the sea over a crescent of sand or shingle, the valleys twisting upward in long hollows, often filled with woods, bald now except for a few threadbare patches of foliage, the pewter and pearl-barked walnut trees and the spidery distaffs of the poplars dominating the others. The ground underneath was deep in dead leaves which a gust of wind from the west would send flurrying downhill and out over the water.

In one of these inlets, close to the sand's edge, a man was sitting on the doorstep of a lopsided wooden hut with a little boat beached under the bushes beside it. His flat and high-cheekboned face was a skeleton leaf of benign wrinkles. We smoked a cigarette together and talked of the coldness of the day and the brightness of the sun, and beamed between our stilted clauses. He was an old Tartar fisherman living by himself, the only human being I saw all day. But the bare branches were dark and bowed under the weight of many hundreds of hooded crows, looking baleful and ragged and filling the air with their croaking and cawing. A clap of the hands would send them spinning into the air in a sudden clamour as the released branches sprang upwards, whirling overhead like a load of flung soot, and then, with one accord, streaming up the valley and over the hills in a long blur for a league or so, before swinging back to put the naked spinneys in mourning again. Somebody had told me, probably wrongly, that these birds – suddenly ominous by their enormous numbers – lived for a hundred years or more. If it were true, some of them could have feasted on the fallen during the Crimean War; perhaps a few Methuselahs, I thought rather fancifully, might have flown south across the Ukraine after following the retreat from Moscow . . .

As the miles mounted up, the scene grew emptier. Then rising woodland blotted out the interior. The dark slope of trees sank to the sea's edge and the path snaked through them halfway up, easily climbing and falling and running across small tilted glades full of white and red anemones, and white ones streaked with mauve.

Attuned for nearly a year to nothing but hinterland prospects of plain and mountain, my eyes, alighting now like a stranger's on the stepped woods and the shore below, found something so improbable and extreme in the beauty of this interlock of vegetation and sea that it appeared an illusion. The cold air was afloat with the smell of herbs.

Myrtle and bay and arbutus, with dark green leaves interspersed with big, soft berries as scarlet as strawberries, climbed downhill through thickets of lanceolate evergreen leaves and others as round and flat as the sea-grape; and tall trees jutted among them – could they have been ilexes? – roots looped in plaited arches from the slope like those in Japanese paintings, and blue-black boughs heavy with shade. Downhill at the end of plunging tunnels of trunks and branches and over the foliage of the ledges, the lowest stems of which seemed almost rooted in the sea, the European continent fell to fragments in spikes and small tufted islets far below, standing in translucent, pale green water, which darkened as it receded from the rocks to bottle green and the blue of a peacock's neck feathers and fled away to the skyline. The almost still water was stirred by incoming creases as slight as a breath on silk, just enough to hem the join of rock and water with a thin bracelet of white, but too little to interfere with the symmetry of the semi- and three-quarter circles that the rocks sent spinning slowly out to sea again. Only the ghost of their sigh floated up through the mews and the wheeling sunlit wings of the seagulls. Headland followed headland, each pair of them enclosing their secret bay in a south-westerly recession of plumed capes, dwindling at last to dim threads that either the sea or the sky could claim. Late in the afternoon, sunbeams penetrated the wood at an angle exactly parallel to the slant of the coast, filling the clearings and striking the tree-boles and the foliage with layers of wintry gold, hanging rafts of light in the leaves, falling through the wood in long spokes and breaking up the loops of shadow over the surface of the water with horizontal windows of radiance. Celestial light floated under the branches: evening in the Hesperides. The solitude, the peace and the hush were complete. Was this quiet ecstasy that roved the air a murmur of promise, at this cold north-easternmost corner of Thrace, of what – beyond the Black Sea and the Bosphorus and the Propontis – were waiting in the Aegean: of what Greece and those remote islands held in store?

~

A trio of cormorants or shags had flown along over the water earlier in the day. I saw them later swimming in one of the combes, craned necks and swivelling beaks suggesting the periscopes of submarines. Now a dozen of them were standing scattered on the rocks ahead, their wings half open in their limp and quasi-heraldic pose. I took a path branching downhill and following the coast nearer the water to see them closer. They took wing all together and flapped off in an urgent wedge over the water, which was streaked with zinc and lilac.

After a mile or so I was picking my way along a track which was becoming rockier at every pace. By the time it was dusk, all trace of it had vanished and I found myself alternately wriggling through the undergrowth and scrambling over the rocks and sometimes both simultaneously. The going seemed slightly better over the rocks, so I advanced jumping from slab to slab, circumventing pools, bestriding fissures and climbing up damp ledges and down irregular causeways, hoping for a break in the rocks and the vegetation that might lead uphill again. Soon it was quite dark, except for a blazing mass of stars, which were little help in this confusion of boulders and water. I remembered a torch in one of the pockets of my rucksack, and continued with its strong beam, picking my way over the steepening rocks, determined, if it grew any worse, to turn back. Advancing, immediately after this decision, I found myself slipping on a steep, scaly ledge, then sliding down a slant like a barn roof. Then came a drop and a jolting bang that landed me in a pool up to my waist. When I had got out, I found myself sitting, jarred and shaken with a cut on my forehead and a split thumbnail, on the edge of a still deeper pool, shuddering with the sudden icy cold. I could tell that the pool was deeper because about twenty-five feet down lay my torch, burrowing a brilliant tunnel of light through sea anemones and weeds and a flickering concourse of fish. Behind me soared black walls of rock, and in front the same dark, rocky-looking upheaval running out to sea and leading, it must be, to the cape I had seen before night fell. I thought dazedly of what would have happened if, in my rucksack and overcoat and heavy boots, I had followed the torch into the depths. Should I take off my heavy stuff and dive for the drowned torch? I was already shaking all over and my teeth were chattering; it was out of the question. Should I wait there till it was light? The sun had only just set: it would have meant sitting on this rock for twelve or thirteen hours in the freezing night under these brilliant and useless stars. Fortunately I could just discern my stick, floating and recoverable on the shallower part of the pool. In case, by a wild chance, there were somebody on this deserted coast, I decided to shout. But what? I had forgotten, if I ever knew it, the Bulgarian for *Help*. All I could think of was a formal cry of 'Good evening!' '*Dobro vetcher!*' I shouted again and again, but, as I expected, with no reply, except a returning *vetcher!* from the rock face.

The only thing was to go on. With a reluctant Hylas gaze at the lost light and the glittering mob of fish five fathoms down, now jerking, jostling and going mad round this fallen portent, I began to fumble my way forward, tapping the rocks with my stick, feeling my way along the landward wall of rock: sliding, crawling on all fours, climbing up ledges draped with popping and slippery ribbons of bladderwrack, filled with dread of what lay the other side, wading waist-deep and afraid that a sudden chasm should open; stopping on a rock every now and again to send up my reiterated cry of desperate affability. I was close to despair. The only hope was not to think at all beyond the range of my groping fingers.

The stars were no help. They faintly indicated large masses in dim silhouette, but by contrast seemed to leave immediate detail in even denser obscurity than if a bank of clouds had hung between them and the sea. But after an eternity of this slithering and pawing advance, a few constellations appeared in front where all had been black before, indicating that I was reaching the cape and, after another unending period, rounding it. Inland, the end of the stars meant that the mainland was blocking them out. There was no other hint, nothing to say whether the height was miles inland or close at hand, or whether it was a steep cliff or gentle slope: a huge black nothing. I shoved on, preferring recklessly to wade now; the water, oddly, was not so cold as the night air; but when I began crawling up the rocks again, my clothes turned to a plate armour of ice and lead. Within a few minutes of each other, both my bootlaces broke as though by collusion, and my boots turned at once into buckets that dragged like anchors underwater and into squelching and retarding fetters up and down those leaning blades of rock. I felt so beaten and exhausted and hopeless that I lay down on a ledge of basalt, getting my breath back with fleeting visions of brief entries in daily papers recording youth's or student's mishap on Black Sea, but no foul play suspected; until the cold warned me that if I didn't go on, I would give up the ghost. After another cycle in hell, lowering my half-unshod foot on to what I thought was the surface of a pool, I found the solidity of sand and the grate of pebbles underfoot. Another pace confirmed it: I was on the shore of an inlet. Rounding a black buttress of cliff, I saw, a little way up the beach, a ragged rectangular line of light, queerly surrounded by many other bright cracks and chinks through which light leaked. I sloshed across the pebbles, pulled open an improvised door, uttered through rattling teeth the last *dobro vetcher* of the day and walked into the other side.

A dozen fire-lit faces looked up in surprise and consternation from their cross-legged supper on the ground as though an enemy agent had just landed, or a sea monster or a drowned man's ghost had crossed their threshold.

Ten minutes later, changed into gym shoes and canvas trousers, two shirts and several layers of jersey, all miraculously dry, with a sheepskin shepherd's cloak, and my fur kalpack, justified at last, rammed over my ears, I was crouched on a stool in front of a blaze of stacked thorns that reached the height of a bonfire, with three or four slugs of *slivo* burning inside me, sipping a second glass of tea brewed from some mountain herbs, two inches deep in sugar, and still shuddering. One of the denizens of the place had washed the blood away and rubbed stinging *slivo* over my

hands and face and feet; another had plied a towel from my rucksack. Recovered from the first shock of this bleeding, chalk-white,
bedraggled and sodden apparition, they had leapt to my help like
Bernardine monks. It took me some time to focus and segregate
the figures moving about in the firelight and the shadows and the
smoke of this strange concavity.

They were a wild-looking lot. Six of them were dressed in the
customary heavy, homespun earth-brown or dark blue, but so
patched and tattered that it was hard to distinguish the parent
colour, and shod in the usual crusted apparatus of swaddles and
thongs and canoe-tipped rawhide moccasins, one of which looked
as if it had been abraded for several decades. Knives were stuck
into their voluminous scarlet sashes, and they were hatted like
me, in battered and threadbare busbies that had moulted most of
their fur. An old man with a tangled white beard seemed to be
the dominating figure. A second group of four wore more ordinary
clothes, though equally patched and worn, and blue jerseys pocked
with holes. Ancient sailors' caps with once-shiny peaks were askew
on their matted hair. They all of them looked exactly what they
were; shepherds and seamen. One of the sailors, who must have
been about forty, had only one hand and a star tattooed on the
back of the other. His comrades were a few years older than me.

The extraordinary place all round us, which at first had seemed
little beyond a fire-lit hollow, was a large cave. It arched high
overhead but did not go very deep into the cliff side. Much of
the outer wall was formed by natural standing blades of rock;
boulders and a rough, mortarless masonry of stones filled the gaps,
branches and planks completed it, and flattened tins stamped with
the name *Socony-Vacuum* in Cyrillic letters. The flames picked out
the springing fans of shrub high on the rock face, with clusters
of stalactites, and summoned loose gear out of the shadows that
told of the cave's dual function: a rowing boat on its side, oars,

rudders, fishing lamps, long-shafted fishing spears topped by barbed spikes like eight-toothed metal combs, anchors, geometric fish-pots, creels, bait-buckets, corks, gourds and loops of net. A small primitive anvil was clawed on to an embedded tree stump.

On the other side of the fire a significant change of paraphernalia set in: cheese baskets on planks, leaning crooks and a dangling grove of heavy orbs – cheese poured liquid into goatskin bags, hairs innermost, the white drops pitter-patting from the bottom. A large cauldron of whey simmered over a second fire. Now and then the old man with the beard leant over it and stirred and skimmed. Lastly, across the dark reaches at the further end of this vast chamber, ran a breast-high barrier of bleached stones and furze. From the gloom behind it came a sudden cracked and derisive cachinnation that shook me out of the torpor of my own woes. In answer to my question the old man picked a burning brand from under the cauldron and held it up: the brief oval of his flame revealed a thicket of spiral-bladed horns and the imperial beards and the matted black-and-white striped pelts of fifty goats. A flourish of the torch kindled the momentary flash of a hundred oblong-pupilled eyes, another wave of falsetto jeering, a clicking of horns and the notes of a few heavy bronze bells. A black patina of smoke and soot gave a polish to the bosses and spikes of the cave. The rocks that leapt from the floor were used as irregular tables or backs to lean against for the floor-dwelling population. Half a dozen dogs wandered about this grotto or slept. A big white one, lying with lolling tongue and his forepaws expectantly crossed, surveyed the scene through feloniously close-set eyes, one of them surrounded by a black ring. The sand and pebbles underlay a thick trodden layer of goats' pellets and fish scales, and the precinct reeked of goats, fish, curds, cheese, tar, brine, sweat and woodsmoke: an abode harmoniously shared by Polyphemus and Sinbad.

They had been finishing supper. The remainder of the lentils was ladled out and handed me in a tin plate, while one of the fishermen poured oil in the frying pan, laid a couple of fish across it, and in due course plucked them out sizzling by their tails and laid them where the lentils had been. I had thought I was beyond eating; but these delicious fish were demolished in no time. What were they called? '*Skoumbri,*' the fishermen said; 'no, no!' cried the others: '*shumria!*' (It was mackerel.) There was some friendly teasing about this: the shepherds were Bulgars, the fishermen Greeks. One of them apologized, saying that they had, alas, finished all the *slivo* and the wine. I remembered and fished out Gatcho's parting present: two bottles of raki from Tirnovo, one of them safe in Nadejda's wooden flask, the other mercifully intact as well. In spite of an occasional shudder and a rattle of teeth, I began, as the food and drink piled up inside, to feel marvellous. The circulating raki ignited a mood of nautico-pastoral wassail, and by the time the second bottle was broached all these wind-battered and weather-chipped faces were singing Bulgarian songs, some of which I had heard before and one that I knew. I had noticed something hanging on a peg which I had taken to be a goatskin bag for milking ewes. It was a bagpipe; but its owner, the old bearded man, said he thought it was broken. When he inflated it, the drone through the horn trumpet died away in a loud groan. This death rattle called forth an answering dirge-like wail from the white dog with the black monocle, briskly silenced by a backhanded cuff. A crease in the parchment bag had split. I managed to mend it, to everyone's laughing approval, with a strip of adhesive tape.

As the drone swelled, one of the younger fishermen began a burlesque Turkish belly-dance – I think called the *kütchek* – learnt, he said, in Tzarigrad, Constantinople. It was very convincing, even to the loud crack that accompanied a particularly spasmodic wrench of haunch and midriff, produced by the parting of the two interlocked forefingers of either hand as they were held, with joined palms, above his head. The comic effect of this dance was all the greater owing to the husky and piratical appearance of Dimitri, the dancer. 'He needs a *charchaff*,' one of the shepherds cried, and bound a cheese cloth round the lower part of Dimitri's face and across the bridge of his nose like a yashmak. The rolling of his smoke-reddened eyes above this veil turned him to a mixture of virago, houri and the Widow Twankey.

Meanwhile Costa, another sailor, was preparing a further elaboration in the shadows. Knotting a length of cable into a loose ring, he slipped it round his legs just above the knee, then, holding his thighs wide, he twisted it hand over hand till only a loop remained into which he stuck a thick log of wood two feet long, held in position by the twisted cable like the arm of a roman catapult. When he advanced into the firelight with the same rotating motion as Dimitri, the log swung in circles, suggesting a Priapus in repose, a sight which evoked an outburst of uninhibited laughter from us all. A mock pursuit of the veiled Dimitri began, the sudden widening of Costa's thighs tightening the cable and swinging the log into the horizontal, then letting it fall again rhythmically. Further widening of the thighs raised the log into an ithyphallic stance, and to keep it at this angle entailed moving by leaps, a gait which was half that of a grasshopper, half of a predatory pasha bent on rape. He plucked one of the shepherd's knives from its sheath and clenched it between his teeth. The bagpipe howled louder and louder, and the spectators clapped in time to the beat. Dimitri gyrated in even more uncouthly skittish postures. Sweat stood out on Costa's brow with the effort of maintaining the seesaw motion of the log. The flames threw ribald shadows monstrously enlarged and distorted across the wall of the cave. Finally, in a sustained and culminating blast of bag-piping, with his legs splayed in the knees-bend position, he circled his writhing partner in a sequence of gyrating leaps, allowing the log to thump the floor after each bound before hoisting it once more to its soaring perpendicular. At last, with a long scream, the hoarse and panting pibroch finished, subsiding at the end with the wail of a slaughtered ox; the dancer collapsed melodramatically, laughing and out of breath. His partner Dimitri broke off too, tore down his yashmak and strolled to where Costa was recovering. Then with an offhand 'You won't need this any more', he plucked the log from where it lay in its loosened harness and pitched it into the flaming thorns where it sent up a shower of sparks, and Costa let out an ear-splitting howl of pretended pain. This last touch brought the house down. The raki went round again. The place was an uproar of laughter and shouted toasts.

Egged on by the others after a while, Panayi, the fourth of the fishermen, extracted a long, wrapped object from the boat. The removal of the cloth, when he rejoined us on the floor, exposed an instrument halfway between a lute and a mandolin, with an inlaid sounding-board; the gleaming shell of its bowl was ribbed with ivory and ebony; but the unusual length and slenderness of the neck, slanting from his cross-legged lap as he screwed the pegs into tune and plucked the seven wire strings with a hen's quill for a plectrum, gave it the air of a court musician's instrument from a Persian painting: an incongruously delicate and polished thing in our rough-hewn den. When it was in tune, the player showered minims and crotchets into the grotto in a long and elaborate pattern and a succession of jangling chords in different keys, and, after a pause, launched into a regular tune with a slow, heavily stressed and almost lurching rhythm that slid insidiously into the bloodstream until even the musician himself, stooping over the strings or gazing straight ahead, seemed to be mesmerized by the spell of his own music. He was a tall, muscular, battered man of about thirty with large grey eyes. After a few bars, he and the older man began to sing. It sounded like a deep-voiced lament, with many telling pauses and repetitions, and at moments it was purposely grating and strained and full of oriental undulations. The older man accentuated the beat by slapping the drum-like side of a gourd float, steadying it with the stump of one hand and striking it with the star-backed palm of the other.

Before long Dimitri and Costa were on their feet again, involved in an intricate dance very unlike the cheerful and bawdy stampings they had just improvised. The dancers were side by side, linked at a stiff arm's length by a hand on each other's shoulder, their unsmiling faces hanging forward chin on breast like those of hanged men. Nothing could be less carefree or orgiastic than the perverse mood of the steps, the premeditated hornpipe, then an abrupt halt. This was broken by movements as slight as the bending and straightening of the knee; the feet, flat on the ground with heels together, opened at an angle then closed and opened again. The right feet were then lifted and slowly swung backwards and forwards. A left-foot jump brought their torsos seesawing in a right angle to balance a simultaneous kick on the ground behind them with their right. Then the dancers swept forward for an accelerated pace or two, braked and halted with their right legs lifted, knees to heels sweeping parallel to the ground in slow scything movements, and falling again. Their hands smote beneath them in a double clap, then they were almost on their knees, hands on shoulders again, gliding off sideways, then rolling forward once more at their smooth and unnaturally timed pace. The softness, the hypnotic-seeming control and union, the abrupt surging, the recoveries and the arms falling loose for an identical pirouette before joining again, the fastidious shelving of stereotype – what on earth had all this sophistication to do with Balkan or peasant simplicity? Then there was the planned anticlimax, compensated by a drilled outburst when, in any other dance, all would have been decrescendo and subsidence. The sudden asperity and vigour and speed were muzzled and hushed in mid-swoop, like the flash of steel unsheathed halfway up the blade, then allowed to slide back with a soft subsiding click of hilt on scabbard. The subtle and complex beauty of this peculiar dancing in relation to all the dancing I had seen in recent months, and coming hotfoot on the straightforward bumpkin fun of the first performance, was as much of a surprise as would be finding unheralded in a collection of folk verse a long metaphysical poem in a highly elaborate metre and stuffed with conceits, tropes, assonances, internal rhymes and abstruse allusions. I think it was just as new to the shepherds as it was to me.

At the end of the dance, Dimitri joined us by the fire and swelled the accompaniment with his own voice and another gourd. The next dance, on which Costa now embarked solo, though akin to its forerunner, was even odder. There was the same delay and deliberation, the same hanging head with its cap on the side, a cigarette in the middle of the dancer's mouth. He gazed at the ground with his eyes almost closed, rotating on the spot with his hands crossed in the small of his back; soon they rose above his head like a vulture's wings opening, then soared in alternate sweeps before his lowered face with an occasional carefully placed crack of thumb and forefinger as the slow and complex steps evolved. The downward gaze, the absorption, the precise placing of the feet, the sudden twirl of the body, the sinking on alternate knees, the sweep of an outstretched leg in three quarters of a circle, with the arms all at once outflung in two radii as the dancer rose again in another slow circle, gathering pace till he spun for a few seconds at high speed and then slowed down in defiance of all the laws of momentum – these steps and passes and above all the downward scrutiny were as though the dancer were proving, on the fish scales and the goats' droppings underfoot, some lost theorem about tangents and circles, or retracing the conclusions of Pythagoras about the square on the hypotenuse. Sometimes during these subsidences, he slapped the ground with one hand and shot into the air again. A leap, after a few grave and nearly static paces, would carry him effortlessly through the air to land motionless with knees bent and ankles crossed. He would rise from this crouched posture, his trunk flung forward like a pair of scissors closing, the smoke from his cigarette spiralling round him. These abrupt acrobatics and calculated flashes of strength were redoubled in effect by the measured smoothness and abstraction of the steps that bracketed them. This controlled acceleration and braking wove them all into a single and solemn choreographic line. Perhaps the most striking aspect of it was the tragic and doomed aura that surrounded the dance, the flaunting so quickly muffled, and the introvert and cerebral aloofness of the dancer, so cut off by indifference from the others in the cave that he might have been alone in another room, applying ritual devices to conundrums reluctant of yielding their answers, or exorcizing a private and incommunicable pain. The loneliness was absolute. The singing had stopped and nothing but the jangle of the wire strings accompanied him.

On a rock near where I sat was the heavy, low round table that I had eaten from. Revolving past it, Costa leant forward: suddenly the table levitated into the air, sailed past us and pivoted at right angles to his head in a sequence of wide loops, the edge clamped firmly in his mouth and held there by nothing but his teeth buried in the wood. It rotated like a flying carpet, slicing crescents out of the haze of woodsmoke, so fast at some moments that the four glasses on it, the chap-fallen bagpipe with its perforated cow's horn dangling, the raki flask, the knives and spoons, the earthenware saucepan that had held the lentils and the backbones of the two mackerels with their heads and tails hanging over the edge of the tin plate, all dissolved for a few swift revolutions into a circular blur, then redefined themselves, as the pace dwindled, into a still life travelling in wide rings along the cave. As Costa sank gyrating to floor level, firelight lit the table from above, then he soared into the dark so that only the underside glowed. Simultaneously he quickened his pace and reduced the circumference of the circle by rotating faster and faster on the spot, his revolutions striking sparks of astonished applause through the grotto, which quickly rose to an uproar. His head was flung back and his streaming features corrugated with veins and muscles, his balancing arms outflung like those of a dervish until the flying table itself seemed to melt into a vast disc twice its own diameter spinning in the cave's centre at a speed, which should have scattered its whirling still-life into the nether shadows. Slowly the speed slackened. The table was once more a table, looping through the smoke five feet from the floor, sliding out of its own orbit, rotating back to its launching-rock and unhurriedly alighting there with all its impedimenta undisturbed. Not once had the dancer's hands touched it; but, the moment before it resettled in its place, he retrieved the stub of the cigarette he had left burning on the rock, and danced slowly back to the centre with no hint of haste or vertigo, tapping away the long ash with the fourth finger of his upraised left hand. He replaced it in his mouth, gyrated, sank, and unwound into his sober initial steps – the planned anticlimax again! – then having regained his motionless starting point, straight as an arrow and on tip-toe, he broke off, sauntered smoking with lowered lids to the re-established table, picked up his raki glass, took a meditative sip, deaf to the clamour, and subsided unhurriedly among the rest of us.

How I wished I spoke Greek! I could catch a word here and there, loose in a flow of incomprehensible Romaic, as they talked among themselves. And how was I to find out, with my clumsy rudiments of Bulgarian, the origin of these dances, the roots of their unique and absolute oddity, even should the dancers know themselves? Panayi was swaddling his instrument for the night; its incendiary work was done, but its message still twanged and paused and twanged again in all our veins; Dimitri had drifted off into sleep for a moment, lying with his head on his arm, and the one-handed elder had clapped the neck of the raki bottle to his eye, as an admiral would a telescope, to see how much was left. Costa, the dancer, was smoking and smiling with the easy air of a geometrician who has proved what had to be proved: *quod erat demonstrandum*, the smile seemed to say, under the peak of his old cap, pushed forward to shield his eyes from the flames.

It was only later, in Greece, that I was to learn a bit about them: that some scholars place the birth of the first dance in Tatavli, the butchers' quarter of Constantinople, and the second one among the Tzeibeks, a wild tribe in the mountains of Phrygia, and think it possible that they date from Byzantine times. Others seek their origins much further back in Greek history, and ingenious and rather seductive mythological analogies have been evolved for the different phases of these two dances. Others, however, blind to their strangeness and their complex perfection, and abhorring their possible echoes of Turkish slavery, seek the true descendants of the warlike Pyrrhic dance in the much more straightforward and dashing chain dances – with the leader of the chain performing dazzling feats of agility – which the Klephts, who resisted and fought the Turks, danced in the free mountains for many centuries. (These dances are as much an emblem of this warlike spirit as are the white pleated kilt, the curly-tipped and pom-pommed brogues, the yataghan and the long gun.) Such critics are right in finding nothing warlike or simple in the two dances I had just seen (known jointly, with their music and singing, as *mas ta rebetiko*). They are, in fact, the quintessence of fatalism and morose solitude, a consolation and an anodyne in individual calamity, and with the songs that accompany them create a hard metrical and choreographic counterspell. They have another black mark against them: they are linked with low life in refugee quarters, with drunken cellars and hashish-smoking dens and waterfront bars, with idle hours spent over the nargileh, and with a dandified trick of flicking those tasselled and time-killing amber beads. Traditionally they are accompanied by a sartorial style, now largely obsolete: pointed shoes, peg-top trousers held up by a red sash, the jacket worn loose on the shoulders with sleeves hanging – and by twisted moustaches, a quiff falling over the forehead, and the cap aslant on the back of the head. With this goes a relaxed gait, a languid syncopated flick of the beads round the index finger held in the small of the back, a cigarette in the corner of the mouth, a faintly derisive smile, a poker face, an unflurriable deliberation of gesture and a dangerous ironic light in the veiled eyes.

The urban figure in whom these attributes unite is usually known as the *mangas*, and though time may have modified his mid-nineteenth-century dress, the spirit, the manner and the mood remain intact. The *mangas* drawls in a deep, rasping and ironic tone, and, worse still, in an arcane lingo of cant words which are largely unknown outside the fraternity, laced with impropriety and strange oaths. Touchy on points of personal dignity, rancorous, sceptical and unimpressible, at least outwardly, the *mangas* have a rigorous code of honour and conduct among themselves which has nothing whatever to do with the official legal code. They are unshakeable in friendship and, when committed, strangers to treachery. A deep melancholy accompanies the classical canon of this proletarian dandy, as it does with more modish dandiacal postures; and, like them, it is the outward expression of a philosophy: independence, contempt for bourgeois values, readiness for any wild scheme, reluctance to accept jobs as employees (especially as grocers, though butchers for some reason have a dispensing glamour and dash), scorn of drudgery; smuggling or any similar illicit activity is ideal, even sometimes more advanced illegal practices; but *mangas* are never pimps, and very seldom out-and-out bad hats. A murder in *mangas* circles is much more likely to be prompted by an insult or a love affair gone wrong than to be a by-product of full-time criminal activity. To be crossed in love, as part of the melancholy stance, is almost a *sine qua non*. No relaxation of mien, even at times of great joy, is allowed to mar the outward scowl: a rose may express it symbolically, placed behind the ear or held between the teeth at the same angle as the ousted cigarette. This antisocial way of thought, however, is free of the juvenility which seems to turn the devotees of similar groups in the West into stuffed babies until they are ripe in years. *Mangas*, on the contrary, seek masculinity and a wary adult independence. When their crust of frowning aloofness is broken, and their guard down and the maddening banter lulled, they are often spontaneous, enthusiastic and – despite the opposite intention – extremely naive and transparently innocent. They have many variants, and many different names mark their degrees – *rebetis, mortis, dervisis* (dervish), *koutzavakis, meraklis* – all these are *mangas* subspecies (and the word *mangas* can, incidentally, also be used, in tones of affectionate derision, to mean nothing more than 'rascal' or 'scamp'). The temptation to enlarge on them for several pages more is almost insuperable, but as I knew nothing about them at all at the time I am describing, and not a single word of modern Greek, I had better stop at once.

Or almost at once. It was the link between Costa's and Dimitri's two dances, and the characteristics of their usual exponents, which led us astray. The other great dancers of the *hasapiko* and the *tzeibekiko*, as the two forms of *rebetiko* dances are severally called, are seamen, particularly those that ply between the islands and the ports of the Levant in merchantmen, tramp steamers and caiques. The preoccupations of sailors on shore and of waterfront *mangas* easily dovetail, overlap and merge. Critics of these dances may be right in dubbing them oriental, but they are wrong to call them un-Greek. Whatever their origins and wherever they are danced,

I have never seen or heard of them being performed by anyone but Greeks, and particularly Greek sailors, in Constantinople, the Danube delta, Trebizond, Smyrna, Beirut, Alexandria or any other harbour of the Levant or the Archipelago – or ever considered to be anything but Greek. In the Piraeus and Salonika and Patras, at any rate, they have long been known, but semi-underworld; since the last war, alas, they have come into the open and been exploited, losing much of their integrity and mystique; but not all. To me they seemed at the time, and they still seem, to be exactly that amalgam of Greece and the Orient which is covered by the word 'Byzantine', appertaining to the city which was the heart and soul of the Greek world for over a thousand years. Others have thought the same; others place *rebetiko* earlier, and some would demote its origins to the day before yesterday. Any of them may be right (though probability, I think, weighs heavily against the third of these verdicts), as there is not a shred of ascertainable evidence in any direction, or any real reason there should be. This being so, I have my own private subdivision of the Byzantine hypothesis. For me these dances epitomize the last two hundred years of Byzantium, when the Empire, pillaged and dismembered by the Crusades, survived with the certainty of catastrophe looming at the end. The steps seem to symbolize all the artifice, the passion for complexity, the hair-splitting, the sophistication, the dejection, the sudden renaissances, the flaunting challenge, the resignation, the feeling of the enemy closing in, the abandonment by all who should have been friends, the ineluctability of the approaching doom and the determination to perish, when the time came, with style. It is tempting to add to all this a metaphysical trend of late Byzantine times, the introspective, navel-gazing detachment of the Hesychasts. I yield to this temptation. I don't mean that these dances are a literal mime of the late Byzantines, of whom, unlike the emperors, caesars, sebastocrators and logothetes, history says little. On nobody does a longer, more resplendent or more tragic history weigh as heavily as it does on the shoulders of the Greeks. The atavistic spring is long and tightly coiled inside them. So, should my almost baseless and incorroborable inklings be true, any half-literate, hashish-bemused *mangas* in the Piraeus, or any Greek fisherman in a cave on the Black Sea coast (marooned by frontiers among an alien majority), is not really twirling and halting and soaring to interpret the woes of poverty or bad luck or the pangs of disprized love – at least not in the direct way that the words of the songs indicate. He is the unsuspecting microcosm and interpreter of older and heavier sorrows.

Nothing of all this – except, perhaps, a vague inchoate feeling – could have been in my mind while the cave-dwellers, after a final all-round gulp of raki, began to settle for the night. I was to sleep at the nautical end. Costa and Dimitri hospitably spread a layer of fresh leaves close to the fire, rolled up a coat as a pillow, and piled blanket on blanket and laid the old shepherd's cloak on top of me. I was as snug as a tortoise. '*Kryo?*' they asked. '*Studeno?*' Cold? – they had learnt four or five words of English on their travels. 'No.' Only an occasional tremor at increasing intervals reminded me of my earlier mishaps; later impressions had smothered them. I made out that the Greeks were three cousins and an uncle. There was nothing in the least guarded, apathetic or *mangas*-like about them. The trance-like melancholy of their steps had evaporated with the last fumes of the dances and the music. Their identical grey eyes were wide with humour, curiosity, alertness and intelligence. I thought I had divined an extra warmth in their welcome and their horny handshakes earlier on, and I interpreted it, as with Nadejda's grandfather, as a late symptom of Greek feelings towards Lord Byron's countrymen. I was right. Dimitri said as much. Uttering the words '*Lordos Vyron?*' he raised his bunched fingers in a gesture of approval. Costa, shielding his action from indiscreet glances, placed his forefingers side by side; '*Grtzia – Anglia!* Good!', then he opposed them endways on and tips touching in antagonism: '*Grtzia! Bulgaria! Tk, tk!*' he clicked his tongue and threw back his head: not so good. The shepherds were all right though, I gathered; they were friends.

This day, starting in the dark in Varna, had been the longest and oddest of the entire journey so far, but I couldn't sleep for a long time. Plenty to think about, especially about unknown Greece and the Greeks, coming nearer every day. There was an occasional clank from the fifty goats at the further end, and the fall of a burning log now and again. Beyond the twelve-trope harmony of snores I could just hear the faint gasp of the Euxine a few yards off. The firelight ebbed from the walls and the stalactites, and the logs sank to a glow. Through a high gap in the cave's outer wall, three quarters of Orion blazed like a slanting lozenge of ice-crystals. A slight clatter roused me as I was on the brink of oblivion, to observe the spectral, tip-toe figure, confident everyone was asleep (ah, but they weren't!), of the dog with the black monocle, nimbly licking the last of the lentils out of the saucepan.

~

The storks, sculling equator-wards earlier in the year a hundred fathoms overhead, can only have had a slightly more aerial vision of this empty uncoiling and dropping-away of capes. The headlands had hoisted me into mid-air again, each time shooting skywards through layers of gulls, out of these bights of sand and shingle at the head of deep corkscrews of ravine. The interior billowed to the distant mountains, and everything was emptier than ever of mankind. Driven inland by the lack of habitations or shelter, I had slept in a small village (could it have been called Dolni Chiflik? – the map is blurred and torn here by a fold) and stocked up with bread, cheese, onions and garlic. The winter had now swollen the dry garlic cloves with soft green hearts, putting out shoots through their papery husks. Munching these, I blasted my switchback trail south-west. The ordeal by water, thanks to the therapy of the measureless cavern, had left no trace. The old Cyclopean shepherd had replaced my broken bootlaces by slicing a half-cured goat's hide into strips; with my boots braced by these shaggy thongs, I felt I could confront anything. The shepherds and fishermen, two days before, had prophesied snow, and I had been secretly longing for it ('the Pontic shore . . .') but that freezing razor-clarity which had seemed to presage snow relaxed into milder sunshine, wandering cumulus and light intermittent rain as gentle as the quality of mercy. There was something consoling about this soft unfolding landscape, the low hovering glint of the sierras, and the sea ruffling under the wind. Sunlight and rain alternated, and often the two of them together in that union, propitious to rainbows, which is known in some places as a fox's wedding. Occasionally the scene would dissolve in vapour. The desertion of this winter world held a seldom-failing ravishment, a stilling of the nerves and a smoothing-out of the mind. If my head were a small sun, and my glance its ray, how many miles would it have to travel through the veils that the sky suspended, before throwing more than the most unconvincing of watery shadows? Winter serenity, the peace of hibernation had descended, when ideas and inspiration fall with the quietness of dew.

The autumn forest came frothing down to the jagged cliffs and the rocks for a few more miles next day. Vast deserted bays looped one after the other between the thrust of the headlands. The Khodja Balkan rumbled away into the interior to join the far-off assembly of Bulgarian mountains along the watery skyline. Here and there the valleys widened into small fens, and on one of these, spiked with tufts of reed and sedge like the conventional sign for marshland on a map, an old man all in brown sat reflected in a flat-bottomed boat with a gun across his knees. A party of waterfowl, alerted perhaps by my approach, rose from the mere and as they flew over his head, he raised his gun, a tongue of flame shot out and a moment later a report like a bomb exploding shivered the air. For a second or two smoke hid the marksman. When it blew away, no rewarding drop of a felled bird ringed the water, and he busied himself over his weapon. Spotting me, he rowed alongside and asked if I had a cigarette. He could take me a short cut across the swamp. I stepped into his leaky punt, and he went on recharging – an elaborate job, as his gun was a muzzle-loader with a very long and rusty barrel. He poured in what looked like a pound of powder from an old brass flask, then a handful of buckshot and alternate bits of newspaper and rag for wadding, driving everything home with a ramrod. The barrel was secured to the wood with lashings of twine, bands of rusty tin, and an old handkerchief knotted round it like a bandage. 'Here they come!' he said, after half a dozen strokes, and leaving the oars free on their tholes he lifted his terrifying fowling piece at the returning birds. There was a deafening bang, a blaze like a rocket and all was dim with smoke. He materialized once more, shaking his fist at the vanishing and undepleted wedge and shouting '*Pezerengi!*' – the Turkish word for pimps. His gun looked even closer to disintegration. When it was ready again, we sculled to the other side and I was glad to get out. A quarter of an hour later, I heard another detonation, and looked anxiously down: my benefactor was still alive, and comminating yet another flight of elusive pimps.

The path followed a stream bed and a turn brought me almost on top of a wild boar drinking, a dark grey matted creature with curling discoloured tusks. It turned its snout in my direction for a moment, then trotted away through the brambles into a wood. I had never seen one before. I crossed the road to Byala, and a long dusty track led, in the late afternoon, to the unpromising village of Avantlar, so I rashly pushed on. It was only two hours, they told me, to another village. The sun set and I must have gone astray, for it was much later, after a long trudge through the dark rolling heathland till I saw one or two dim lights twinkling. It was a grim hamlet called Hadjikoë; but only grim in aspect. I asked a shadowy figure in the main street where the khan was. There was no khan, he said, in a strange accent, but he took me by the elbow and led me to a dark cottage, tapped on the door murmuring, 'Rustum!' Who was it? 'Suleiman,' my guide answered. When a light appeared I saw they were both Turkish, and in half an hour I was sitting with them and a squatting, cross-legged group of fellow villagers – Djem, Abdurrahman, Mustapha, Mehmet, Hassan Ali and Selim – on the planks of a rickety loggia, eating bread flaps and fried *pastourma*; naturally, no wine. There had been a barefoot, shadowy flitting of black veiled figures in the background: a *mangali* – full of glowing charcoal – had been handed out, then, after a flickering and crackling of thorns, a low round table already laden with its dizzily powerful plate-load. It was the first time I had tasted *pastourma*, an Asia Minor version of pemmican or biltong. (A couple of months later, I asked a Greek refugee tavern-keeper from Iconium how this amazing stuff was made. His eyes sparkled. 'You get a camel or an ox, but a camel's best,' he said with elliptic urgency, 'then you put it in an olive press, and you tighten it up till every drop of moisture has been squeezed out. *Every drop!* Then cut it up in strips and salt it, then lay it in the sun for a month or two – best of all, in the branches of a tree, so that the wind cures it as well – but in a cage, of course, so the crows can't get at it.' Then it is taken down and embedded in a paste of poached garlic and the hottest paprika you can find on the market, reinforced by whatever spices of the Orient are handy. When this has again been dried to a hard crust, it has nearly the consistency of wood: it keeps for years. Thin slices, cut off with a razor-sharp knife, are normally eaten raw; occasionally it is cooked, when the aroma, always unmanning to the uninitiated, becomes explosive. The taste is terrific and marvellous, but anathema to many because not only is the ordinary smell of garlic squared or cubed in strength – breath emerges with the violence of a blowlamp – but a baleful redolence of great range and power surfaces at every pore; people reel backwards and leave an empty ring around the diner, as though one were whirling in incendiary parabolas.)

As I grew better acquainted with the taste of *pastourma*, a specious and flimsy theory took shape about its origins. Turkish cooking, like Turkish architecture, is really a coalition of the civilizations of the races they invaded and conquered on their journey to the West: nearly everything can ultimately be traced back to the Persians, the Arabs and the Byzantines. Perhaps *pastourma* is the last culinary survivor of the days before the Turks irrupted into Western history. Dried meat is true nomad food, a primordial technique developed, perhaps, in the steppes of the Ural and the Altai, where camels were numbered by the hundred thousand: imperishable, palatable and sustaining. A secondary theory offers itself. The Turks' kinsmen, the Huns, are said to have lived on raw meat which they treated by strapping it between their saddle-flaps and the shaggy flanks of their steeds. Steaming and soaked with sweat when they unsaddled at nightfall, this meat must have had a saline pungency that the Seljuks missed when at last they drew rein for good to exploit their vast conquests. Perhaps like their modern cousins the Kirgiz, and the Scythians in Herodotus, these hordes washed *pastourma* down with the fermented milk of their mares and she-camels. Could the violent salting and seasoning have been improvised as a substitute for the tang of sweat, now that their horses were at grass and their camels away on peaceful caravans: a means of recapturing, in consistency and savour, the fierce zest of the draughty meals of the Ghuzz tribesmen of Alp Aslan and Togril Beg? The Sultanate of Rum must have reeked with this fare, and when they expanded in further invasions, a following wind would have spread terror even before the thundering of their hoofs and war-cries could be heard, causing their foes to quail and scatter while they were still out of bowshot.

The wick lit up a flickering ring of mild and rather sad faces. All of them, except for one or two, were content to sit and drink in the giaour in their midst with a blank, startled but unwavering gaze. Their battered fezzes were turbaned in twisted rags, all except the white-coiffed hodja, Suleiman, our host. Their wide sashes of scarlet, their threadbare homespun, were so tattered and patched they scarcely held together. Decay had been at work on some of their wearers too, nibbling away at a nostril, effacing an eyeball with glaucoma, stippling features with pockmarks and cratering them with the Baghdad boil. One old man, with ears projecting like wings that flushed pink when the light was behind them, sat and peered raptly into eternity, grasping the opposite big toe (for all slippers had been shed) with either hand as though it would have been fatal to let go. This group must have been the loneliest and most moth-eaten fragment of the vanished Ottoman Empire in all the Balkans.

Their Bulgarian was almost as inchoate as mine: England sounded as remote to them, and as vague, as Samoa or the Aleutians. Only the old hodja, I could just make out, had been to Istanbul, long, long ago, before the Balkan wars. He boiled minute saucepans of coffee one after another in bubbling thimblefuls.

When I asked about Atatürk – Kemal Pasha – the chat grew more animated. A few of the younger men seemed dimly in favour of him. But the hodja, who had grown up when Sultan Abdul Hamid was still Padishah and Caliph, flung back his head with clicks of denial again and again. The argument became exclusively Turkish. For the hodja, I gathered, Kemal was little better than an infidel. The shift to Latin characters from the sacred script of the Koran, strong drink, the dissolution of the dervishes, prayers in the vernacular, the proscription of the fez and the unveiling of women – all this was Satan's work. So I was astonished, when bedtime came, that the hodja led me, accompanied by the others bearing blankets, pillows and a water-pitcher, to a barn-like building, which turned out, by the light of a lantern, to be the mosque, or rather a tiny building leading off it, where they spread my bedding on a mat. I think their houses were too humble to possess the traditional division between the *haremlik* and *salemlik* for accommodating guests. After a brief and silent prayer, these kind scarecrows left me with a graceful and aspen-like flutter of goodnight salaams. I slept under a faded poster dating from the 1890s which, judging from the primitive coloured illustration of a steamship with the crescent at the masthead and another of the Kaaba Stone surrounded by the faithful, all in a faded tangle of typographical arabesques, had been an advertisement for the hadj to Mecca. I was bewildered that they allowed what they must have considered the uncircumcised to pollute so hallowed a place. Rain began pattering on the tiles as I fell asleep. I was woken at daybreak by the hodja creaking up his rickety spiral and putting the horrified djinns to flight.

⁓

It must have been a few miles further south that I caught a first momentous glimpse of Sarakatsans. I heard them long before they came into sight: a trembling and clanging on many notes rolled through the damp air. A drop in the bare headlands revealed a score of conical huts gathered like dark beehives on the edge of a green slope crested with a spinney, and from the summit of each of these bulbous cones of skilfully woven reeds and osier, a feather

of smoke rose into the rainy air. Up the hillside, tilted by the slope
to offer a bird's-eye view inside, ran great zariba-like goat-folds of
thorn and thatch. Dark figures moved about among the wigwams.
At the centre, among scooped wooden troughs for the watering
of a multitude, stood the tall forked upright of a well, pivoting a
cross-beam three fathoms long. There were a number of horses and
mules and donkeys, a mare or two with foals trotting beside them,
and the barking of many dogs, but these were all outnumbered
hopelessly by the thousands of sheep and goats, each of them
contributing, by the sound of the iron or bronze bells slung round
their necks, to the constantly changing mineral tune that pervaded
the damp landscape. There were many more goats than sheep, grey
and striped, some of them almost white, shaggy and twirly-horned,
but the greater part of them a dark purplish brown to black. I made
a beeline for the heart of this hubbub. The shepherds, tall wild-
looking men, were as varied in colouring of eyes and hair as their
flock. Some had grey or blue eyes, and on the heads of a few of
the young ones, low black pillboxes slanted askew on a tangle of
uncombed hair, bleached pale by the sun. But now all their faces
were deep in the pointed hoods of the shaggy black homespun
capes, hanging almost to their feet, as stiff as cardboard, each bristle
streaming with rain. They carried staves as tall as spears, which
slotted into elaborately carved crooks. There was a guarded alertness
about their bearing and their glance; they were clad and sashed in
stuff almost as uncompromising as their cloaks; *and all in black!*
The women, some with their babies slung like papooses in wooden
cradles while they spun the yarn from their carved distaffs or clacked
and shuttled at the looms in the wigwams, were plaited and coiffed
and dressed in amazing clothes of black and white pleats and zigzags
that were as stylized as the garb of the queens of playing cards.

The place reeked of horses and goats and curds and woodsmoke.
Everything was made of twisted branches, thorns, reeds and timber;

all was pegged, plaited, woven and lashed with thongs; there were cauldrons of copper and iron, wooden buckets and casks, skins turned inside out and lashed at the lopped necks and legs to make squelching containers, all dripping with milk and whey. The noise and bustle were tremendous. I might have been in the Ark; and as I sipped a cup of hot and foaming milk that a kind herdsman provided from a leather bag, I thought that these black-hooded and cloaked figures, these black and white zigzagged women, these conical huts and their teeming tintinnabulation of flocks through the rainy woods of Rumelia comprised the most mysterious community I had ever seen. There was a legendary air about them, and about the whole scene, now made stranger still by sunbeams breaking through the fleece of clouds in dozens of pale concentric spokes. The raindrops seemed almost static in the still and bell-reverberating air, a slow confetti of microscopic sequins. There would be rainbows soon.

'*Karakatchan!*' an old Bulgar carrying a plough on his shoulder had answered when I first caught sight of them from afar; and then, after a pause, '*Grtzki*' – and Greek was the language I heard being bandied urgently from one black monolith of a herdsman to another, each flourishing his lance of a crook and marooned in his calm grazing backwater, or in momentary eddies of goats flowing in every direction across the lift and dip of the foothills; and those sudden insurrections of sound were the last notes to survive when they were all several furlongs behind me and the camp had shrunk to a small and fictitious-looking cluster of smoking cones at the other end of the glassy atmosphere.

But I was still thinking about these people, in a state of great excitement, for a league or two. The Sarakatsani – *Karakatchan* is only the Bulgarian name for them – are a fascinating community. Greek in race and speech, they are the only complete nomads of the Balkans. They are scattered all over northern Greece. These ones had been sadly lopped off from the rest of their fellow tribes in Greece by the frontiers that sprang up after the Second Balkan War, across the wreckage of the Ottoman Empire. Some authorities argue that these nomads are the direct descendants of the earliest Greek wanderers to settle in Greece – except that they never settled: they live in the high mountains in summer; in autumn their vast caravans and flocks descend to the green lowland grazing, to return to their mountains when spring comes. This camp was typical of their winter quarters: grassy, well-watered lowland pastures far from roads and villages and the civil authorities they hate everywhere, and safe from the snow and the wolves of the Rhodope mountains that were their summer haunts.

(I was to see much of these people in the coming decades. Though I couldn't know it, I was to stay in their huts in three months' time, leaving for a moment the squadron of Greek cavalry whose advance I was accompanying during the Venizelist revolution that broke out in March, climbing to one of their Macedonian eyries on horseback. It is tempting to enlarge on the Sarakatsans; but as I have done so at considerable length elsewhere, we must push on.)*

~

Isolated shepherds with little flocks, looking very tame after the Sarakatsans, were the only other people I saw for the remainder of the day; these, and bumping along the invisible track, an *aralia*, one of those little Turkish carts, flat as a tray, with a low balustrade of spokes all round, drawn by an old horse. A Turk sat cross-legged in the front, and behind him, all cross-legged and so heavily veiled with *charchaff* and *fereje* as to resemble black cocktail shakers, his four wives.

* See *Roumeli*, pp. 3–63.

I had wandered some distance inland; when I got to the sea again, the ripple of headlands was bare and looking down from one of them in the late afternoon, I saw eleven dolphins leaping and gambolling in the bay, all shooting up into the air together in semicircles, then diving, plainly visible through the clear water, streaking along the sea's floor like greyhounds, to surface again through spreading rings and leap clear in a wild ecstatic game. The plops and the tearing noise of their passage came clear to the clifftops. I gazed at them entranced for half an hour until, on a sudden whim, they all turned east and went spiralling away towards the horizon, hell bent for the Caucasus. The roll of the hills was beginning to subside, and, as it grew dark, a little gathering of lights began to tremble below through the dusk. It jutted out to sea in what appeared at first to be a small island, but, as I approached, it turned out to be joined to the land by a narrow panhandle of causeway with a wide bay on either side. The coast had taken a sharp turn to the south-west a few leagues back, and every few seconds, from the cape to the north-east (which I had somehow managed to cut off on my meandering course), the revolving beam of the Eminé lighthouse – Eminé Bunar – flicked off and on.

A strange, rather sad, rather beguiling spell haunted the cobbled lanes of this twinkling, twilight little town of Mesembria. Only secured by its slender tether to the mainland, the Black Sea seemed entirely to surround it. At a first glance, churches appeared to outnumber the dwelling houses: little Byzantine churches, as I was beginning to recognize by their cupolas and the string course of faded red brick and tile among the masonry, some of them half in ruins, embedded by heaps of rubble and choked with weeds and brambles, all of them shut and silent and dead-looking. The place had been a Greek settlement for centuries BC, and in Byzantine times, a prosperous city; captured by the terrible

Czar Krum, recaptured by the Byzantines, the churches had mainly accumulated under the Palaeologue and Cantacuzene emperors, falling at last to the Turks only a little while before Constantinople itself. But till early in this century, the citizens were purely Greek. Dark doings had diminished their numbers and when, after the Balkan wars, the little outpost was allotted to Bulgaria, their numbers fell still more through emigration and exchange. But still some remained, languishing and reluctant to leave their habitat of two and a half thousand years; like the Sarakatsans and the cave-dwelling fishermen, secretly counting, perhaps, on the impermanence of political boundaries. In the few winding streets and the coffee house, it was Greek rather than Bulgarian that I heard spoken, and Greek too among the little fleet of beached fishing boats and the russet festoons of looped net. For it was an amphibian place. The water lapped at the end of the streets, hulls and masts broke up the skyline, there was even something of the shipwright's trade about the jutting timbered upper storeys of the old houses, which confronted each other across the lanes like the poops of galleons anchored stern to stern. So muted, ambiguous, watery, with the dimness of the afterglow contending with lighting-up time, the town might have been at the bottom of the sea. The sound of the water sighed in every street and shop and room as though the place were a seashell. A shell, in a different sense, was exactly what it was.

One of those projecting upper storeys was my shelter for the next two nights, and the intervening day: an aged Greek couple, whose children and grandchildren had taken wing, put me up. Inside, the resemblance to the sterncastle of an old ship was doubly compelling. Everything was panelled, the ceiling was coffered in lozenges and, like Nadejda's house in Plovdiv, a divan ran round the raised end of the living room. Through its poop-like windows and their infinity of small panes, there was only the Black Sea. I sat scribbling here most of next day, setting down all I had seen along the Euxine coast. It was, and is, hard to capture the charm of the journey along this almost deserted coast, and its pervading atmosphere of peaceful seclusion and consolation. This little floating town, where all was decayed, warped, waterlogged, rusted, falling into ruin and adrift with watery magic was the very place for it. After a walk along the sedgy shore the other side of the isthmus, I wrote a stack of letters. (Hard to believe they would, eventually, find their way to their various destinations all over Central Europe; what about London and Calcutta?) When I had finished, the smooth sea outside slid away to the horizon under an elaborate mackerel sky which was less like a shoal of fish than the looped roof of a tremendous emir's tent, each loop tinged an extraordinary lilac hue. Under it, trailing three dinghies, a schooner under sail glided on stage, heading for Ancialo or Burgas with a cargo of fish – I could see them flashing on deck as the sailors stooped over their catch; and all round the vessel, like the whirlpools of snowflakes unloosed by upending one of those glass globes containing a miniature ship, circled a screeching cloud of seagulls.

As we sat by the brazier before going to bed, I tried out the few bits of Homer I knew by heart on my host and hostess, and a couple of bits of Sappho. I suppose it was rather like a Greek, in an incomprehensible accent, hopefully murmuring passages of *Sir Gawain and the Green Knight* in Middle English to an old fisher couple in a Penzance cottage. Even so, the verses seemed to have a sort of talismanic value to their ears, and caused pleasure rather than the nonplussed tedium its English equivalent might have evoked in Cornwall. I struck luckier with Fauriel's Greek folksongs, in the collection of Nadejda's grandfather. They knew several of them, and my hostess Kyria Eleni – an alert old woman with wide-open blue eyes, dressed and elaborately kerchiefed in black – even sang a few lines here and there in a quavery voice. Once I had got the hang of the modern pronunciation of the vowels and diphthongs, with the fact that all hard breathings had evaporated and that all the accents merely indicated where the stress of a word fell, I saw that reading it aloud, though halting at first, would soon become plain sailing. I could also break down the construction of the sentences; even, now and then, and in spite of the deep demotic, the ghost of an inkling of their drift. Old newspapers hinted their meanings a stage more easily, as through a glass darkly, but with a battered missal I found on a shelf, it was almost face to face. All this was full of promise for the coming months; for, Constantinople once reached, I was planning a private invasion of Greece. But, infuriatingly, we were still confined in conversation to my halting and scarcely existent Bulgarian.

This dabbling with the mysteries of Greek caused many a sigh. They had never been to Greece, and now (unlike me) never would. They seemed glad to have a guest once more. I felt that my being English played a part in their kind welcome. At all events, when I tried to offer some money before setting off next day for Burgas, they both started back in horror as though the coins were red hot. I slept on the divan, under the twinkling ikon lamp. There was a silver-covered ikon of the Virgin (I was beginning to notice these things) and another of SS Constantine and Helen, holding up the True Cross between them; also two faded marriage wreaths intertwined in a glass case, carefully kept from their wedding day in the later decades of the last century. I could hear the water lapping all night, and when I woke up the silver ripples reflected from the sea were eddying all over the wooden lozenges of the ceiling, and now and then one of the gulls would settle on the sill and walk up and down before taking off again.

～

'I say, what *have* you been eating, old boy?' Mr Kendal, halfway across the room with welcoming hand outstretched, stopped dead in his tracks. On the way from Mesembria, still unapprised of its social backlash, I had cut up the last slices of the *pastourma* the Turks had given me and eaten it under a carob tree, looking down at the low marshy country and the salt flats, and the far-off moles and cranes of Burgas. Now here I was at the British Consulate, whose windows commanded an enlarged version of the ships and the long mole I had seen from afar.

Scores of times during the last year I had found myself cutting an incongruous, perhaps alarming figure, a shaggy and travel-stained bull, as it were, in the china-shop of civilized surroundings – and this time I had tried to do something about it before meeting Mr Kendal, to whom the Tollintons had promised to write from Sofia. Fishing in my rucksack in the battered cara-vanserai of a hotel, I soon saw that little could be done: my jacket and trousers looked like old rope after the fall into the pool. There was nothing for it but to stick to my tattered puttees and breeches and hob-nailed boots. I brushed off as much of the dust and caked mud as I could, got a small boy with a brass-embellished portable shoe-cleaning shrine to give my boots an unwonted glitter, stuck my head under the tap, brushed my hair and put on a tie under the leather jerkin. I had stumped off to the Consulate feeling uncouth but semi-respectable, and all in vain.

Not that it mattered a rap. Mr Kendal's old tweed jacket with a leather watch-strap from the buttonhole to the breast pocket, the grey trousers and (I think) the regimental tie, the jovial and rosy face, robust build, clipped moustache and sandy hair which had retreated early from the scalp, all combined, in my eyes acclimatized to the Balkans – with the Lion and the Unicorn over the door and the grave glances of George V and Queen Mary from their frames on the wall – into a whole so unmistakeably English as, perhaps, to fill me with fears that my shabby mien might be letting the side down. But the amused and friendly tone of voice, and above all, an expression of transparent kindness in the bright blue eyes, routed all such thoughts at once.

He sniffed. 'I've got it! *Pastourma!* It's the strongest I've ever smelt.' A little later, in the living part of the house, Mr Kendal handed me a drink, saying he was a hero not to be using tongs.

Under these circumstances, the fact that I was out of my hotel room and established in the nursery of their daughter Cecily that night, says much for the kind hearts of Tony Kendal and his wife Mila. It was, for another twenty-four hours at least, like having a polecat as a guest. Mila, soft-voiced and quiet, radiated a benignity which was the complement of Tony's exuberance and high spirits. Her father, who turned up for a day, was a retired Bulgarian general: a tall, imposing old gentleman with a white moustache, and a glance sharpened by scanning fields of fire from the Balkan passes.

These days in Burgas, and the days immediately before them, are one of the stretches of this journey which are fairly amply covered in the intermittent journal so strangely recovered, two and a half decades after I had lost it and long after I had embarked on this book. So, instead of piecing these fragments of lost time together by memory, all of a sudden I am surrounded by a windfall of day-to-day jottings, too rough and abbreviated to be used as they stand. But at least, from here to the end of the journey and this book, I know roughly what happened during the day and where I slept at night without having to put it all together like a jigsaw in which some of the pieces are missing or broken, or rubbed clean of their pattern. In some ways, this abundance is a bit of an embarrassment: to make use of it all would mean a change of focus, a shift in key from all the foregoing and a temptation, for instance, to enlarge on this stay in Burgas at undue length.

The temptation is all the stronger because I remember my time under Tony and Mila's roof as one of the most cheerful of the whole journey. I see from my notes that the delights of wandering along the Black Sea coast had been accompanying a slight but growing feeling of loneliness, brought on by the shortened days, the beginning of December, and the dash of melancholy that Balkan winters always bring me. There were sudden, fleeting onslaughts of homesickness that I had forgotten about, and had thought myself, in retrospect, immune from. No need for loneliness or homesickness now: the Kendals had numerous friends among the inhabitants of this little multiracial port in which many of the races of the Balkans were represented; and yet, in another sense, although

[ends]

The text of 'A Youthful Journey' stops in mid-sentence. Although Paddy reached Constantinople a few days afterwards, he never recorded it other than in his Green Diary: a record which, he admitted, was 'a bit of an embarrassment'.

Strangely, even in this diary, he recounts nothing of the leftover Byzantine glories of the old capital (no word, even, of Haghia Sophia or the great walls of Theodosius) and little of its Ottoman splendour. He mentions a fleeting friendship with an attractive Greek woman, some consular parties and various rendezvous with social contacts in the city. But the entries are all cursory. It was strange, above all, that he never contacted Professor Whittemore, whom he had met in Sofia, and whose ongoing work uncovering mosaics in Haghia Sophia would have given Paddy an unparalleled insight into the Byzantium that was starting to fascinate him.

Perhaps the end of his journey was weighing on him with the traveller's bewilderment of at last reaching his goal, and the uneasy question of his future. He had been prey to infrequent depressions. Did he think of writing a book, or journalism, or even the army again? When asked, he said he did not remember. Or perhaps the great city disappointed him in its dilapidation and overwhelming Turkish presence (although this was less than it is now). Later he was to write that he never left Istanbul without a lightening of the heart.

Yet his surviving diary excerpts – a few of them follow – are largely cheerful.

1st January 1935, Constantinople
So tired after journey and whoopee on New Year's Eve, slept till six o'clock in the evening, then, waking up, thought it was only the dawn, having overslept twelve hours, so turned over and slept again till Jan 2nd morning, thus New Year's day 1935 will always be a blank for me.

2nd January
. . . A lovely day, the sun shining on the Golden Horn, and the town full of a hundred sounds . . . Had luncheon in a little Armenian restaurant, where French-speaking proprietor made my hair stand on end with tales of Turkish persecutions, then wandered round again by docks; what quantities of cats! Late at night, date with Maria, and we went and drank beer together in a little restaurant. She is really lovely, ideally lovely, and we sat and chatted in perfect happiness. Dear Maria! Saw her home and sauntered home in the Turkish moonlight, Stambul and her minarets looking wonderful . . .

3rd January
Phoned up Djherat Pasha, for whom Count Teleki gave me an introduction at Budapest, he invited me to visit him that day, so

I took boat from under Galata bridge . . . Pasha splendid, bristling moustached chap, very English country gent – spoke good French (looked as if he might have massacred a few Armenians in his day). Talked of Armenian, Balkan and the Great wars . . .

6th January
Went by car to carpet museum, home to tea, and then drank beer together in Fischer's. We will become good friends, I see. Talked about everything in the world. Constantinople is a good background to romance, in evening tiff with Maria ripened to quarrel and I went to bed in a rage.

9th January
Went to Stambul bazaar, fascinating, look at thousands of carpets, swords and yataghans etc. I bought a cigarette holder with amber mouthpiece . . .

11th January
Lay lateish in bed, then got up and went to luncheon with Bob Coe from American embassy . . . We sat on the veranda overlooking the Bosphorus; perfectly peaceful, the caiques plying up and down . . .

Between the 12th and 23rd of January Paddy's diary lapses altogether, for reasons unknown. By the time he resumed it, he had taken a train out of Constantinople to Salonika, and was about to board a boat to the great Orthodox monastic state of Mount Athos, where, for the first time, his diary becomes fully written.

Mount Athos

Taken from Patrick Leigh Fermor's 'Green Diary', written at the time

24th January

I left Salonika last night; Patullo and Elphinstone came along with me to the boat, and we bought some bread, and salami and cheese by the harbour gates. I was glad they came, as it was already sunset, and it's very lonely starting off on these journeys alone. The ship was surprisingly small; very dirty and overloaded with every kind of cargo, all of which was hauled on board in a surprisingly unworkmanlike way. The boat was a shambles inside too, with enormous banks of coal in the passages, and peasants lying in their blankets in despondent groups everywhere. We stood in the passages and smoked, and chatted, waiting for the bells to ring to announce departure, so they could get off; but the boat was nearly two hours late, and they nearly came away with me, which would have been rather serious for Patullo has to join a troopship for Hong Kong in a day or two at Port Said.

It was quite dark when we eventually pushed off, and P. and Elphinstone scuttled over the gangway at the last moment and we shouted through the darkness at each other, till our voices were inaudible. I hope I meet them again sometime.

Although I was Third Class, one of the ship's officials, seeing the lights of Salonika dwindle in the distance, kindly told me I could go Second, as the Third travellers have nowhere to sit down, except on the decks, where they sleep and eat too, huddled like cattle, trying to keep the cold out. I was glad I didn't have to.

I had some coffee and ate my provisions, and then for a few hours smoked and read Lord Byron's *Don Juan* – I bought Byron's verse yesterday, very cheap in a little bookshop. I think it's grand stuff, though not all poetry. Finally I got a few hours sleep on the cushioned bench, with my martial coat over me, feeling rather excited, as one always does starting a new venture.

This morning, I woke up just after dawn, and ran to the upper deck. It was one of the most glorious days, sky and sea light blue, plenty of waves and clouds, and to starboard, not half a mile away, the mountains and the pine-clad slopes of the Kassandra peninsula. I keep trying to recreate it all as it must have been in ancient Greece – hardly any different, except that our vessel would have been a long galley, with painted sails and sweeping oars. Walking round and round on the deck, I thought of the triremes of all the empires that have sailed these same waters, and called to mind the tales about Perseus, Jason and Odysseus, and the Tyrants of the Archipelago; the piracy of Mithridates, and later the Roman galleys packed with legionaries for Thrace or Paphlagonia; and the laden ships of the Eastern Empire at Byzantium. Later, in the time of Marco Polo, came the Genoese and Venetian galleons, sailing to the furthest corners of the Levant, and the Moorish and Arabian corsairs who plundered them, and the ships of the Ottoman Empire, trading from the Sublime Porte right down to this morning. I wonder just how much has changed; one thing however is reassuring: these pine-clad mountains and golden strands are the same as those on which the heavy-helmeted hoplites stood looking seaward, the Macedonia of Philip and Alexander.

We called at one little village on the western shore of the Kassandra peninsula, by an island: the houses were so small and white they looked like children's toys; the fishermen rowed out in boats, and took off sacks of flour, loading it skilfully amidships. They were all fine, tall chaps, barefoot. They have to buy all their corn, as the tongues of the Chalkidiki are so rocky and barren that cultivation is impossible. Rounding the peninsula was magnificent as it was steep and rocky, with landslides and jagged cliffs sinking sheer into the water, and many caves, islands and arches; two eagles were sailing lazily about halfway down, their shadows following them on the cliff face. The water was very rough here, and a little fisherman's sailing vessel was tossing wildly to and fro in it.

Rounding the cape, I suddenly saw the goal of my pilgrimage, Mount Athos, a huge, ghostly white peak, as pale and wraithlike as the skeleton moon in the blue sunlit sky; the lower slopes were entirely hidden by a level stratum of white cloud; the Greek name for it is Ἅγιον Ὄρος– the Holy Mountain – and as I now see it across the glancing waves, it does not look as if it belonged to this world. Austere and aloof, I had no idea it was so enormous. The slender monasteried peninsula, of which it is the highest peak, is quite invisible in the clouds.

We are now sailing along the eastern side of the Longos or Sithonia peninsula, which is all bare rock, and, except for an occasional cluster of huts in a crag-sheltered cove, uninhabitable. It is now evening and the sun is sinking to the horizon. We seem miles from the ordinary world, and there is a softness in the air as the sun goes down. We have yet to sail to the most inland point of this slender gulf, where we turn about for the little port of Daphni, on the Holy Mountain itself. I will always remember this evening. Now the clouds have floated away from the wild slopes of the Athos peninsula, and we are still too far off to distinguish any of the monasteries.

2 hours later

It's quite dark now, and from the quarterdeck I watch the sun setting, and the glow fading from the white peak of Athos, until the snowy crest seems but a detached cloud in the deepening sky.

Seven dolphins joined the ship, and are swimming just before the bows under the antique bowsprit. They are the most beautiful creatures, lithe, active and swift, sometimes leaping clean out of the water and sinking back again with the utmost grace. Their speed is really amazing, and to see them cutting their way through the green water is unforgettable. I hope they bring us luck, as the sailors say. They remind me of the Arion legend.*

It is quite dark now, but the sky is ablaze with stars. The only constellation I can pick out is the Great Bear. It seems to have completely changed places since I noticed it in Bulgaria, and is oddly standing on its end.

I have been reading the part of *Don Juan* where he is shipwrecked in the Aegean, eventually to be sold as a slave in Constantinople. We reach Daphni in another hour or two now.

25th January, Xeropotamos

I fell into an uneasy sleep leaning on the table in the cabin, despairing of reaching Daphni, but at one o'clock the steward shook me, and told me we were there, so I got my kit together, paid for my coffees, and went down the little ladder over the side, into a dinghy that was dancing up and down on the waves.

* In Greek legend the poet Arion, thrown into the sea by pirates, was saved from drowning by a dolphin.

It was pitch dark and cold, and the old whiskered fisherman who rowed me ashore looked very chilled in the lantern light. Daphni is a small fishing village, rather like a Devonshire one, with low stone buildings, thick walls and massive outdoor ladders and steps to the houses. I was the only person who disembarked here, and had to wake up the inn, where my bed was made up in a small, bare room overlooking the sea. They gave me some bread and cheese and red wine, before I turned in, and when I did, I slept like a log.

I lay long abed this morning. The scene outside the window was glorious – little fishing boats were putting out to sea, one or two fishermen sitting and smoking on the low sea wall. The sea a resplendent blue. The mountains sloped steeply down on all sides, so that the two score houses cluster in a little semicircle facing the sea. To the left, the coast receded as far as one could see, with here and there a monastery perched like an eagle's nest among the rocks; in the distance the blue coast of Sithonia was just visible.

I went to the little sunlit police station on the quay – one of the policemen had taken my passport last night – and one of them wrote my name down in the book, and told me I could collect my passport whenever I left. The road to Xeropotamos lay along the coast, climbing along the hillside. It was all cobbled with a low deep wall facing the sea, a luxuriant growth of slender trees making it shady and pleasant. The whole atmosphere is exotic – trees with smooth, glazed leaves whose names I don't know, inland the tree-covered hills sloping steeply upwards, and the road skirting many little combes and inlets; later it curved inland over a high-arched bridge, which crossed a little stream which tumbled down the mountain's side half a mile off in a long white plume of water. It is a dry, rather sleepy land, with lizards basking on the sun-warmed rocks, and with grateful shade under gnarled cork trees. Halfway up the mountain I sat on the brink of a little stone spring and looked at a sailing vessel putting out from the bay of Daphni, now small in the distance. A monk passed me, leading two laden mules; he had a sweeping beard, and his hair was bound in a knot under his black cylindrical hat. The horses were both geldings of course, as not only are no women permitted on the Holy Mountain but as far as the monks are able, all female creatures are excluded too; for centuries, no mares, sheep, she-goats, bitches, cats etc. have lived here, and all the flocks that I saw cropping what grass they could among the rocks, watched by a shepherd boy with a flute, were of rams and billy-goats.

After another half-hour's climb, the high, sunny walls of Xeropotamos (named from the torrent that runs by its gates) came into view, with the jutting, beam-sprung upper storeys, tall chimneys, and gleaming cupolas of the chapel.

A tall, grey-bearded monk was talking to a deacon in the courtyard when I entered, and seeing me he came and shook hands, and after some words of welcome in Greek, he led me to a little janitor's lodge, and insisted on my taking off my rucksack, while several of the monks came in and sat round the fire. They seemed very interested, and the conversation went on through an Albanian monk, who spoke Russian and could translate from my Bulgarian into Greek. One of them pushed a little brass saucepan of Turkish coffee among the glowing cinders of the log fire, and, when prepared, gave it me in a little round handleless cup.

They pulled out their spectacles and examined the Patriarch's introductory letter with interest. One of them took my kit, and led me through several flagged courtyards, and up several flights of stairs, into a sunny wing obviously reserved for guests.

One of the brothers, with a clever, sensitive face, gold teeth and straggly black beard, and somehow unmonastic air, told me in perfect French that my letter had been taken to the abbot who would come himself in a moment. He came a bit later, an elderly man, with a venerable white beard and hair and a fine presence. He was very kind indeed, and we sat down, and he asked me all about myself. A brother brought a tray, with the usual spoonful of preserved fruit, Turkish coffee and glass of fruit-spirit, the ratification of welcome all over south-east Europe. We all three got on very well, and he seemed very interested on hearing I was keeping a journal about it all, and produced a book, with illustrations, that he had written himself about Mount Athos. I was very interested, and he suddenly astonished and delighted me by presenting me with it. I thanked him profusely and meant it, though it was limited to a repetition of *efharisto poli*. He wrote something in the flyleaf, and then produced his visitors' book for me to sign. There were several other English names in it. The Crown Prince of Sweden was the name directly before mine.

The French-speaking monk and I had a long chat sitting on the deep windowsill, overlooking the Aegean, and he told me he had been many years in Paris studying music, but had finally abandoned it, owing to poverty. He is an extraordinarily nice man, who seems to have been told to look after me. We had supper together, brought by one of the monks, an odd-looking one, young, with a huge jet-black beard and moustache, and large dark, tragic eyes under curving black brows, and smooth pale olive skin. An extraordinary being. Our meal was very simple: beans, fried potatoes, bread and red wine – *mavro krassi* – but very good.

The very black-haired monk had taken my kit into one of the cells reserved for guests, a nice light one, with whitewashed walls, a big luxurious bed laid with clean sheets, a sofa, table and chair; he was just putting some more logs into the blue-painted stove, and the lighted oil lamp on the table made the room look very snug. The embrasure of the window is very deep, owing to the thickness of the walls, and looks down on to a deep well of cloisters, across whose cobbles a monk occasionally walks by in his sweeping black robes.

It is very late now, as the French-speaking monk and I sat by the fire chatting for quite a while after supper, since when I've been sitting and writing by lamplight. My first day at Mount Athos has been splendid, and I am surprised by the real solicitude and kindness of these hospitable monks, who seem to be really delighted to have guests, and to take endless trouble for their happiness.

26th January, Koutloumousiou
I read *Don Juan* pretty late last night, and so woke up at almost ten this morning, having slept gloriously. The black-bearded monk soon turned up, with some coffee and bread which he put on my table, after wishing me *kalimera*, 'good day'. Father Giorgios, the French-speaking monk, came just as I was finishing shaving, and we had a chat together over a cigarette, and in the end I decided to make my way to Karyai that day, in order to report to the Chapter of Monasteries, and get an official letter to all the monasteries.

The two monks, after lunch, wished me farewell, and I set off up the lonely stone track winding through rather sad woods of ilex and acacia, looking rather like bible woodcuts of the Mount of Olives. The road climbed steadily, past many small streams and boulders, and, with increasing height, the trees all became firs, with traces of snow still on their branches. The sun gleamed on the roofs and painted walls of Xeropotamos, among its terraced vineyards and cypresses not far below. A monk on a mule soon overtook me, and hung my rucksack and overcoat on his wooden saddle. He dismounted several times, to try and make me take his place, and was very sorry that I wouldn't take it. The monks really are true models of unselfishness.

After about an hour's climb, we reached the top of the slender peninsula with the blue Aegean on both sides. Directly below lay the little town of Karyai. This is the centre of the holy peninsular government. As we descended the cobbled streets, which seemed surprisingly full of people, not nearly all monks, I couldn't help wondering at the population. Owing to the exclusion of women, none of them can have been born here, none have wives here, and yet they had all the appearance of a settled population. Do they go away to the mainland and return with their sons, or do just confirmed bachelors and misogynists come to work here, tired of an evil world? It's a mystery to me.

I found the police up a rickety flight of wooden stairs, and the sergeant there bade me a friendly good day and gave me a chair and a cigarette, while he was writing out my form to send to the Council of Monasteries. Everyone seems to be imbued with the same spirit of kindness on Mount Athos, and in this completely unmaterialistic atmosphere the innate goodness of human nature is given a chance to breathe. Time has stood still here and the whole Sacred Mountain seems a relic of some era, aeons ago, when men lived in a sweet air of peace and goodwill.

One of the police led me along cobbled lanes till we arrived at the chapter house, where we were admitted by a heavily whiskered *kavass* in a flowing shirt, a black velvet kilt, tasselled cap with the silver badge of Athos, white stockings and pompom shoes. He looked splendid. All the monastery servants are similarly clad.

I was led into the council chamber, where an obviously important elder sat writing at a desk. He took off his spectacles to look at me, shook hands, and courteously asked me to sit down. He gave my papers to a young monk, including my beautiful letter from the Patriarch of Constantinople with its elegantly tangled calligraphy and handsome seals. We had a chat in French, and a *kavass* brought me the ritual coffee, liqueur and jam. The room was of interest, as it was obviously the official council chamber. A seat ran all round three walls, and above each place was a little brown plate, bearing the name of a monastery, and here the representative sits at the thrice-weekly parliaments of the little community. The Megisti Lavra was in the middle, as the senior monastery, and the others were all carefully graded according to precedence. On the fourth side stood an imposing throne on a dais, and a tall ebony staff, tipped with silver, a sort of emblem of office for the president.

Elders began to come in one by one, taking their places after crossing themselves three times before the ikon at the end of the room. (They cross themselves differently to the Catholics, making the cross-bar from right to left.) They all let their white beards and hair flow free and are forbidden to cut it. The surprising thing about them all is the complete integrity of their faces, which speak of a simple and happy life. They made a fine picture, sitting round in groups, talking together, in their deep seats, with the background, outside the windows, of the descending mountainside and the sea.

My friend read out the Patriarch's letter sonorously, and they all laughed at the adjective σπουδαῖος* which His Beatitude had applied to me in his letter. The abbot read it well, ending with the resounding formula: Ἡ δὲ τοῦ Θεοῦ χάρις, καὶ τὸ ἄπειρον ἔλεος εἴη μετὰ τῆς ὁσιότητος ὑμῶν.†

When my papers were ready, they all shook hands with me and wished me Godspeed.

---

* The word combines 'important' and 'learned'.
† 'And the grace of God and his infinite mercy be with your holinesses.'

I first went to the small post office and then, as evening was drawing in, bethought me of Father Giorgios's advice to spend the night at the monastery of Koutloumousiou, whose walls I could see not far down the hill.

Koutloumousiou is one of the smaller monasteries, and not so rich as some, but the monks received me very kindly and led me to a guest chamber, the luxury of whose appointment is in striking contrast to the austerity of the stone cloisters and chill passages outside. It is a relic of the time when Macedonia was under the Turkish yoke, and Constantinople its centre of culture. The long windows are curtained with rich stuff, and all round the walls runs a wide low seat, hung with cloth down to the floor and richly cushioned and spread with bright tapestry. The effect is exotic.

They immediately lit the stove, made up a bed on the divan, and laid the table for an evening meal. Of this I could hardly eat a mouthful, as it consisted entirely of vegetables, cooked and soaked in oil, so I ate lots of bread and sugar, and several oranges. Not wishing to offend the monks I wrapped most of it up in paper, and clandestinely disposed of it later.

The room is very snug and warm now, and I am sitting writing this before the open stove. It was a bit depressing sitting alone in the slowly darkening room as the sun set, watching the monks walk across to vespers in the chapel, their black cylinder hats hung with the sweeping veils they always put on for church. Later I could hear the deep plainsong chants, and strange Orthodox antiphony and, with the last streaks of daylight fading behind the cupolas and the red and white masonry of the chapel, I felt suddenly terribly sad. It was quite dark soon, with just the sombre outline of the mountain discernible. At such times I nearly always remember England, and London and the hooting of cars in Piccadilly, or soft English fields which (after a long absence) come so blessed in memory.

27th January, Iviron

I left Koutloumousiou early yesterday, and started off downhill, the road winding beside a rushing torrent, breaking over great boulders, and dashing on in a lather of white foam. The peninsula here is entirely forested with evergreens, so that it is difficult to believe it's only January; among the ilexes and oleanders are many olives, aspens, cypresses and cedar. The higher slopes are almost entirely fir.

Coming round a corner I saw a funny little grey-haired man sitting on the edge of an old stone well, with some big brown paper parcels beside him. He wished me good day in French, and giving me a cigarette, began to tell me all about himself. He was from Kavalla, and had lived on the Holy Mountain for four years, making maps of it, and copying the ikons on wood. He showed me a few of these, and they were good.

The sea soon came into sight round a bend, and the large monastery of Iviron, the high walls appearing above the trees. These walls are very lofty, and have the effect of being much higher than they are long, as they are divided into sort of rectangular bastions, rising sheer to quite a height without a single window, then suddenly branching out into an overhanging balcony, with undulating tiled roofs, and the plaster painted bright colours – red, blue, green, in crude designs.

Several monks were sitting on benches in the big, sunny cobbled courtyard, half asleep, stroking their beards. A young deacon, with scarcely a beard yet, took charge of me, and led me to the reception room, where the faded portraits of many kings hung on the walls: George and Constantine of Greece, Peter the Great, Czar Nicholas II, Edward VII, and several Romanov grand dukes in breastplates and helmets topped with the two-headed Russian eagle.

After coffee and the rest, I was taken to a big sunny guest

room, white-washed, with a deep yellow window-seat running cushioned before the yard-deep window embrasure. Outside was the tree-clad mountainside (it is called Golgotha here). Below, among the aspens, neat plots of the monks' gardens, and orange trees, with swordshaped, glazed leaves, heavy with golden fruit. Through the mountains and the treetops, whose highest twigs spread beneath the windows, a glittering triangle of the Aegean. The whole scene is so full of detail, it reminds one of the over-filled backgrounds of Italian primitives.

I read *Don Juan* all the afternoon, lying in the sunny window-seat; later on I heard the bang bang bang of the wooden beam, which a monk carries round the monastery, beating it to call the brothers to chapel; I went too.

The church was typically Byzantine, with a densely worked gold altar screen, the walls a mass of frescoes, all the figures having gilded haloes, shining among the fading paint and plaster. Candles twinkled in the half-dark with gold and silver ikons, before which the monks prostrated themselves, crossed and kissed, on entering the church. It was vespers, and I leant in my carved stall among the black- and white-bearded and veiled monks all with their elbows crooked on the armpit-high arms of their miserere seats. The office was all in plainsong, booming, mystical chanting, interspersed with the clang of censers, the blue smoke curling up through the coloured but fading sunbeams. All the churches here have the same reek of old incense, burnt oil, and stale beeswax. Hundreds of little brass sanctuary lamps dangled from the scarcely discernible vaults overhead, and huge elaborate candelabra. To me there is something at once marvellously mystical, and a bit sinister and disturbing about the Orthodox liturgy.

After vespers, an old monk took me round the library – masses of old Byzantine manuscripts, the parchment heavy with gilding and multicoloured allegories of devils, saints, virgins and martyrs, all wonderfully graphic. Psalters and bibles bound entirely with gold, clasped with rubies and diamonds, the gift of an emperor of Byzantium, sainted empress, or half-legendary voivode. The vestments too were of unimaginable splendour, cloth of gold stiff with precious stones, stoles studded with pearls, casket after casket full of chalices and holy vessels, crusted with amethysts and emeralds.

I spent the evening in my room with Byron, very appropriate in Greece. About supper time the deacon came to summon me to table; we ate downstairs in the kitchen. There were two Greek traders there, who spoke French, and several monks, and one Bulgarian. We had a very well-done fowl, and there was lots of red wine; it was a very jolly party; the monks were all excellent chaps, especially one called Father Sophronios, and before long we were all singing. They sang some splendid Greek peasant songs.

Later we adjourned to my room, and pulled our chairs up to the fire, and opened another demijohn of wine. Thus we spent a very happy evening, singing, smoking and drinking, and looking round at my comrades' faces in the lamplight, I could not help thinking how kind and good-natured they looked, instinct with their two great qualities of sweet reasonableness and appropriate seriousness: σωφροσύνη καὶ σπουδαιότης.*

28th January, Stavronikita
I left Iviron after an early lunch yesterday, the track running close along the shore, sometimes over the high rocks, sometimes over the pebbles and sand of the beach, and sometimes winding away inland, a little footpath between the trees. It was really a succession of Devonshire combes, but full of wildly growing evergreens, with now and then a squat stone hermitage standing on a ledge of the mountainside, surrounded by dark cypresses.

* Wisdom and earnestness.

The coast is really wild here, with jagged rocks and caves, inlets and little islands, with the sea breaking magnificently. I passed a tower built on a rock in the sea, the dwelling of a hermit; I've never seen a more desolate place.

Sometimes the wooded inlets were amphitheatres of vineyards, sloping down in strata to a semicircle of sand.

At last the monastery of Stavronikita came into view, wild, feudal and mediaeval in aspect, built on the crest of a crag overhanging the sea, its massive walls running up in lofty windowless bastions to the little windows and jutting balconies above. The rough, machicolated belfry of the chapel just showed above the walls.

A sailing vessel lay among the rocks, and some of the fishing brothers, their habits tucked about their knees, were drawing in their nets and grounding their boats. It was a scene from the Dark Ages, and showed how time has stood still here.

I gained the gates by a winding cobbled way that led under gloomy arches into a flagged, uneven courtyard, where the four cloistered walls of the monastery reared up like the sides of a well. A shaggy monk, who surprised me by speaking a word or two of French, led me up winding stone stairs and along flagged passages, to a small whitewashed room, at the highest point of the monastery, which looked on to a dizzy void, dropping to the foreshortened jagged rocks, and the white foam, slow and lazy with distance. The coast ran away to the north in a succession of rugged promontories and inlets, to the monastery of Pantocrator, perched on a small peninsula.

For supper I was given some fishes which were quite raw, salted and soaked in oil; how I managed to eat them I don't know, but I was so hungry I got through them somehow.

The shaggy monk who seems to be in charge of me is a fine chap, but he looks like a brigand.

It was marvellous, after the sun set, with the wind roaring round the monastery walls, and the sea beating wildly on the rocks below: a complete feeling of isolation, as if the ordinary world were something remembered from an earlier life.

After turning down the lamp, I lay a long time in bed, listening to the wind and the waves outside.

29th January, Pantocrator

The road from Stavronikita to Pantocrator was just as rocky and wild, running through a thick undergrowth of broom and briar, growing so thick at times that it was difficult to make a way through. When the path turned downhill a fast stream suddenly covered it so that the only way down was to spring nimbly stone to stone, carried on by impetus, so that it was impossible to stop till one reached the bottom.

Pantocrator is only about one and a half hours from Stavronikita, and, like it, stands fortress-like on a rocky headland reached by a winding, cobbled path, over crumbling bridges, and under wooden vine trellises.

One of the monks, after looking at my papers, led me upstairs into a charming sunny guest room overlooking the sea, and brought in coffee, raki and some Turkish delight, instead of the usual jam. The country all around is beautiful. Since it was early, I wandered about in the forested valley under the trees, smoking and feeling very happy. Up on an inland hillside perched the Russian skete of Prophiti Ilia, with its green, pointed Muscovite domes, so different from the squat Byzantine cupolas of the Greek monasteries.

It is a delicious valley, with a broad shallow, pebbly river scattered with boulders and overshadowed by olives and poplars. Wandering homeward in the gathering darkness, I frightened some of the belled monastery horses, who scampered away tinkling across the hillside.

On the flagged uneven space before the deep monastery gates, above the jagged rocks and not fifty yards from the breaking waves, stands a small tiled shelter, a sort of lychgate, with deep wooden seats, looking seaward. Several of the monks were sitting here, silently, or fingering their beads. I joined them, watching the red streaks of sunset over the blue Aegean, the foam breaking along the rocky coast, the turreted walls of Stavronikita away to the south, and in the distance the islands of Thasos and Imbros, and further still Samothrace. To landward rolled the coastal ranges of Macedonia. A wonderful peace seemed to possess everything, and we sat there in complete silence till the janitor called to us that it was time to lock the gates, as they are finally shut for the day at sunset, not to be opened till dawn.

In the little courtyard a pair of orange trees reached to the second tier of arches that frame the cloisters of the passages which run round the courtyard in all monasteries, sometimes five layers high.

I sat awhile in the room of one of the *epitropes** with several other monks, drinking coffee, and chatting with the one who spoke some limited French. I retired to my room later on, where the fire and lamp had been lit, and after supper spent a happy evening before the fire with Byron. Browsing through *Childe Harold's Pilgrimage* I came across a stanza which just captured the feeling when I was standing before the monastery gate at sunset, as he must have done a hundred years ago.

> More blest the life of godly eremite,
> Such as on lonely Athos may be seen,
> Watching at eve upon the giant height,

* *Epitropes*: the small group of monks who govern a monastery in place of an abbot – PLF.

That looks o'er waves so blue, skies so serene,
That he who there at such an hour hath been,
Will wistful linger on that hallowed spot;
Then slowly tear him from the witching scene,
Sigh forth one wish that such had been his lot,
Then turn to hate a world he had almost forgot.*

31st January, Vatopedi
What a day yesterday – one of those ones when everything goes
wrong. When I had packed my kit, and said goodbye to the
monks of Pantocrator, a depressing drizzle was falling and the
monks cried worryingly '*Avrio, avrio!*' 'Tomorrow, tomorrow!',
but I idiotically paid no heed and started off on the uphill road
overlooking the sea. It soon degenerated into a narrow footpath,
the going made difficult by the density of bushes and the overhang
of branches.

The way followed a water-course up the wooded slope for a
while and after a little level going began to go rapidly downhill,
so fast that it was difficult to keep one's balance, and one had to
catch hold of the shrubs to break the impetus. This got worse
and worse, till I was all but sliding on my backside down a muddy
serpentine track, which eventually ended up in a landslide of
boulders and pebbles on to the beach. Scrambling down this, I
started jumping from rock to rock, with the incoming tide lapping
round them, sometimes clambering along the cliff's face with
hands and feet. I realized that I must have taken a wrong turning
somewhere, but carried despondently on, hoping to find another
cliff-way up. This rock-climbing went on for quite a while, till
suddenly turning a corner, I saw it was quite hopeless. A sheer

* This stanza in *Childe Harold's Pilgrimage* (II, xxvii) is the fruit of imagin-
ation. Lord Byron never went to Mount Athos.

bank of overhanging rock rose, enormously high, with the water
beating round it. So I had to turn back. Then I saw a piece of
the black cliff sloping a little less steeply up, so tried to climb,
slipping on the rain-soaked rocks and hanging on to tufts of grass
and shrub. This also had to be given up, however, as the cliff rose
perpendicular, without a cranny or crack or foothold anywhere,
which I hadn't been able to see from below. Just near the bottom
I slipped on a bit of wet rock and skidded down the last twenty
yards or so, getting bumped and bruised and battered, my wrist
deeply cut, and finally ending up in a foot of water, where the
tide had come in, soaking one leg to the waist.

I tied up my bleeding wrist, and aching in every limb, retraced
my path over the rocks, and then, misery of miseries, clambering
up the cliff path again, with the strap of my rucksack broken,
and sweating like a pig. At last I found where I thought I'd gone
wrong, and started off on the right track, feeling more optimistic;
this went happily on for a mile or two, then I came to a clearing
full of white piles of chopped wood. The only path out of this
led downhill for a while, more and more steep and winding,
sometimes blocked for several yards by overgrown bushes, and
the tendrils of creepers, no thicker than a bootlace but strong as
wire. After following a downward path some distance I had a
horrible feeling I'd missed my way again, as the path was so
overgrown that it could not have been used for many years.

So, wearily and miserably, I decided I'd have to turn back to
Pantocrator, as the light was beginning to fail. After about a
hundred yards backwards I came to a dead-end, so thought I
must have taken a false turning again. I turned about, looking
through the bushes for the pathway, but found absolutely none.
Downhill it led to the brink of an overhanging cliff above a
leaden, angry sea, and uphill into an impenetrable thicket. Then
the cuts, the bruises, the tiredness and bafflement all seemed to

concentrate in demoralizing me, so that, putting down my sodden rucksack, I started running up and down the path, looking for a way out, all hope practically gone, and the rain and twilight filling me with a horrible despair, allied to an awful hunger, as I hadn't been able to eat much of the monastery lunch. The misery of being lost in a thick forest in the rain and the half darkness is unimaginable. Drawing my dagger, luckily razor-sharp, I started to try and hack a way uphill through the undergrowth in hope of coming to a path, but after a few yards it became so impenetrable, and my face and hands torn and bleeding, that I had to go back to where my rucksack was. I slashed a tree at each possible exit, so as to avoid trying the same place twice, the gash showing up white in the dusk. The gradient to right and left of the path was about one in one. Hell!

Then my guts seemed to drain right out of me, and a fit of panic came, thoughts of passing the night there, without food in the rain. Up till then, I had preserved a dimmish spark of humour, telling myself how I'd laugh about it later, and that though we read about such things in the papers, they didn't happen to one. Then hunger and fatigue-born panic seized me, and I sank on to my rucksack, and began to yell for help – a long 'hallo' at six-second intervals. It was echoed back by the mountains, the only other sound being the driving rain, and the sea below.

Then I gave up, thinking that nobody came that way in a year, and just sat awhile, dead beat, and as a last resort said a short but sincere prayer, feeling every kind of swine, because such times, real trouble, are the only times I do. But it was God's mountain, so I felt he had some sort of responsibility.

There was one thicket I hadn't tried, as it looked nearly hopeless, but I decided to try it; this involved crawling on my belly under some fallen yew trees, slashing at the creepers with my knife; it took about half a minute to get through. When I stood up on the other side I started to walk, and finding no opposing trees and brambles, struck a match, and holding up its sputtering, hand-sheltered flame in the darkness, saw (the thrill of relief was scarcely bearable) the pathway winding uphill in front of me. Getting my rucksack, I started running uphill, shouting and singing at the top of my voice, anything, as an outlet. If I'd had my revolver with me I'd have emptied the magazine into the air as a *feu de joie*; so I stabbed savagely at the bushes and trees, sinking my dagger into them with wild shouts. A stranger meeting me then would have thought I was a dangerous lunatic.

I passed through the clearing with the woodpiles again, and so along the road; until the blessed lights of the monastery glittered below, on its peak of rock.

Running downhill I found the gates were locked, and after hammering and shouting for a few minutes, gave up the attempt as the walls are several yards thick, and the wind, rain and waves were making such a din that it was hopeless.

There was a hut a little down the hill with some lights in the windows, so I walked down and tapped at the door. It was opened by a little black-bearded woodman, who hearing my trouble, invited me in, gave me a stool by the fire, produced a glass of raki and a cup of Turkish coffee, and, with his three companions, helped me strip off my trailing puttees, and squelching boots and stockings, rubbing my feet in front of the fire. They were so stiff and cold I could hardly move them. But all my wet things were hung up and, warm and dry, I was soon sitting in front of the blazing log fire eating a meal which the woodman made me, and drinking some splendid hot tea. They really were Greeks at their best!

One of them sat on a block of wood, honing the blade of his axe, the other smoking while the bearded one brewed eternal cups of tea or coffee in a little brown can which he parked amid the glowing cinders, piling the ashes outside almost up to the brim, stirring, sweetening and tasting like a witch over a cauldron. The fourth, a tall man with a long moustache, got down a Turkish *bağlama* from the wall and started to play. This is a sort of lute, with a very small, deep bowl, but with a very long shaft to it, and three or four wire strings, sometimes painted, and with a tassel or two dangling from the end. Although it is not played with a bow, it is not unlike a Bulgarian *gadulka* or *gûzla*, with a deeper bowl and very much longer shaft. The tunes played on it are the oriental ones, with a scale of about five notes, melancholy, monotonous and insistent but not without charm. It is to these that the *kütchek* is danced.

The other woodmen joined in that strange, wailing chant, clapping their hands together, and tossing their heads about like dogs baying the full moon.

So we spent a jolly evening, drinking alternate draughts of Greek red wine, Turkish coffee and sweet tea, till we were all tired out, our eyes blinking in front of the blazing logs. In spite of a spirited remonstrance on my part, one of the woodmen, the bearded one, insisted on giving up his bed to me, and covered me up with blankets on the padded bench, himself lying on the floor by the fire. A cricket chirped in the chimney all night.

1st February
After breaking our fast simply this morning with bread and tea, I put on my warm, dry kit, and saw that it had been snowing all night, and the mountainside was deep white. One of the woodmen had told the monks of my mishap the night before, testified to by the state of my face and hands, and they had sent along a horse with a padded wooden saddle: a docile, patient beast.

The bearded woodcutter accompanied me some way up the hill

to set me on the right track. I thanked him sincerely on parting, and knowing that it would be an insult to offer him money, as hospitality in the Balkans is a very real tradition, I gave him my Bulgarian dagger, which he admired so much. He was delighted with it, though loath to deprive me of so beautiful a weapon.

I clip-clopped up the cobbled road which continued far inland, and I saw by what miles I had gone wrong yesterday, a lost battle from the start. The snow covered my horse's fetlocks, and I realized how hopeless it would have been to stay in the forest overnight. A thought to shudder at.

It was a dreadful job thrashing through the branches, all weighed down with snow, and I got snow down my neck, up my sleeves and in every possible gap. Higher up, the snow got so deep that I dismounted and plodded along beside the horse. After what seemed ages – the snow had begun to fall again by this time, so that everything was muffled in a swirling white haze – I came to a crossroads, where two men were attending to a horse. I addressed them in Greek, but soon got out of my depth, so tried Bulgarian, which was much better as they told me they were Macedonians from Demir Hisar. On enquiring the way to Vatopedi, I discovered I'd passed it about five kilometres back; I'd seen the turning, blocked up with snow and bushes, and had thought it would lead downhill to the sea, like my two blind alleys yesterday. As there are no signboards anywhere, one has just got to know the way, or else get lost.

They told me they were off to Vatopedi too, and that if I waited for ten minutes they would be back with another horse. After waiting in the falling snow, walking round in circles, for nearer twenty minutes, I decided it wasn't good enough, so wrote deep in the snow with my stick: СТУДЕНО ТУКА. ОТИВАМ ЗА ВАТОПЕД! (Cold here, off to Vatopedi!) I began to retrace my steps. After about half an hour I found the track, unwinding endlessly downhill. At last the snow stopped and the sun managed to break through, showing a wide blue bay, the sea breaking white along the rocks. Round a corner, Vatopedi, with its high walls, its jutting balconies and many domes and towers, soared into sight, looming among the green fig trees and ilexes. Up the hill was the cloistered ruin of some former monastery.

Vatopedi is a village in itself and the flagged courtyards resound continually with the clip-clop of horses, mules and donkeys, and from my window as I write I can hear the cries of the fishermen drawing in their nets, and the woodsman's axe falling. One cloistered courtyard leads to another at different levels, with many pillars, arches, staircases and jutting storeys, creating the impression of a little monastic town.

A small, busy grey-bearded monk in the rosary-hung room under the entrance porch took charge of my papers, and appeared very impressed with the Patriarch's letter, and with a personal introduction to the *epitrope* Adrian. First he led me to a little refectory, and coffee, raki and *rahat loukoum* – Turkish delight – were brought, then I was given an extraordinarily good luncheon, with the first meat I have eaten on Mount Athos. It is the richest monastery and makes a point of entertaining guests as well as possible. You find the same spirit in all the monasteries, but here they have better means to indulge it.

I learnt that the busy little monk was an Albanian, which interested me. Albania, for me, is a land fraught with romance, especially since hearing about Baron Nopcsa.* After I had got out

---

* Baron Franz Nopcsa (1877–1933), Hungarian palaeontologist and an early, remarkable scholar of Albania. He was active in the country's liberation from the Turks in 1912, and during the First World War became leader of an Albanian militia. Many of his scientific theories were brilliantly innovative. Later, deeply in debt, he sold his fossil collection to the Natural History Museum in London. He committed suicide with his lover in 1933.

of my wet and snowy kit, and the cook (who is rather a character) had hung it up to dry, the little monk told me he had taken my letter to Adrian the *epitrope*, and asked me to follow him.

This part of the monastery is thickly and magnificently carpeted, with sumptuous curtains over the doorway, and the Turkish rug in the sanctum where the *epitrope* sat was adorned with the double-headed eagle and crown of Byzantium. He was a splendid old man, with a huge flowing beard, and grand prince-of-the-church manners, none of your starveling priest. He greeted me warmly, waved me to an armchair with a gracious sweep – 'be seated' – and over the ceremonial coffee, raki and *mezze*, we got on extremely well (considering my week-old Greek). He asked after mutual friends and showed some interest in my wanderings. Eventually he put me into the hands of another venerable monk, the librarian, who led me to the tower where all the thousand-year-old literary treasures of Vatopedi were stored.

The manuscripts were priceless – old monastic charts and geographies, written before the centuries were in double figures – gold and black Byzantine psalters, each initial a work of art, the gift of some almost mythical empress or voivode; wonderful calligraphies of the sultans, and lastly a precious chalice, the gift of one of the Comneni.

As I was coming along to my room after this pleasant half hour, the cook beckoned me into his little refectory for some tea, which was not made with leaves, but some berries in a sieve, and was a green colour. This cook had heavy moustaches and a little white cap, and twinkling eyes. Calling my attention, he did something I've never seen before: squatting on the ground, he took a big black tomcat in his hands and started to rub it hard up and down over the shoulders, talking to it all the time; then he set it down on the ground, and held up his arms in a hoop. The cat crouched a moment, then leapt neatly about a yard into the air, through the hoop and down to earth again. I could hardly believe my eyes, and he did it several times for my benefit, and also made the cat turn somersaults. How he taught him I don't know, but the cat seemed to like it too.

I wrote all the evening in my warm little room, till supper time, when the cook summoned me to the refectory, where about eight of us, four monks, the cook, a stranger, myself and a novice, supped together. It was rather gay as the red wine was good, and we seemed to be laughing the whole time. I managed to amuse them by giving an imitation of a muezzin calling from the minaret, and then a Muslim at prayer – ablutions, prostration etc. I must have been a little drunk, looking back, but it was quite a success. They applauded in Turkish – '*Eyi, eyi! Teshekur ederim! Chok güzel, Bey effendi!*'* (Naturally, many Macedonians speak Turkish, as the Bulgars do; it is not to be wondered at, the same as many Englishmen would have spoken French after several centuries of Norman occupation. Especially those speak it who are refugees from Asia Minor, after the Greco-Turkish War of 1919–22. There was one of these who came in later, a Smyrna man, who had a fantastic tale of being shot at by Atatürk's troops on the Asiatic shores of the Hellespont and swimming out to where some English and French warships lay anchored. Coming to the Frenchman, he shouted out to be hauled aboard, but they pointed revolvers at him and told him to clear off; so summoning his last breath (he told it so graphically) he swam alongside the British destroyer, the crew of which welcomed him aboard, fed him, gave him '*viski*' and lots of English tobacco, and arranged for him to be safely repatriated. I don't know if a word of it is true (his only English was a string of very bad language), but it's a good story. He can't speak highly enough of the English and England, clicking his

* 'Eyi, eyi! Thank you! Very fine, sir!'

tongue and holding up his fingers and thumb bunched together (the Greek gesture of enthusiastic approval) and exclaiming 'Θαυμάσια! ὡραῖα!')*

After supper, there was a short office of compline in a chapel, and the congregation consisted of the eight fellow diners: the chapel was very small, and lit by one taper, held by the Albanian monk over his breviary. We could just catch a glimpse of the haloed warriors and elders in the frescoes, the shine of the ikons, and the heavily armed forescreen of the altar. The service was soon finished, all crossing themselves, touching the floor, and kissing the ikons goodnight. We all bade each other a good night – Καληνύκτα σας – and walked with our candles to our cells, where I, for my part, wrote in front of the high-piled logs far into the night.

2nd February
On waking up, a young monk brought me a grand breakfast of tea, raki, bread and cheese and γλυκό.† After this I got up and dressed, and wrote all the morning till luncheon time. At lunch there were two more Albanians, compatriots of the little Father Kyriakos, and fine chaps they looked, tall, well built, with open faces, rather fierce eyes, and thick black moustaches. One spoke a word or two of French, and apparently they run a pub together in Karyai. These Albanians impress me enormously, and I'm hoping to see them in their own country.

I have made friends with two young monks here called Ephraim and Zachary, splendid chaps, one tall and thickly bearded, rather like Rasputin, the other small and fair, with a beard that scarcely is one. About four o'clock they summoned me to come to Mass

* 'Wonderful, lovely!'
† *Glyco*: traditional Greek fruit preserves.

in the big church. The sun was shining in the courtyard, and we could see the monk up in the belfry ringing the bells, which had a sweet tone and lovely peal.

All was dim, a twilight of gold ikons, rich cloth, marble and mosaic within the chapel. The altar screen is a mass of gilding, and a forest of little wrought metal lamps hangs overhead, like tropical creepers. I leant in a pew not far from the *epitropes*, a venerable body of men, shaded by the flimsy black veils worn over their cylindrical hats in church. Adrian sat among the most exalted. The deacon Ephraim seemed to do most in the service, wearing a wonderful vestment of gold and blue, a stole looped twice round him, once under the right arm, then over the left shoulder again, then down to the ground. He looked fine with his gold hair undone, swinging a huge brass censer, and holding in his other hand a sort of model silver church, a white lace cloth draped over his forearm. I didn't understand the service yet – lots of candles being carried round, censers swung, triumphal entries into the tabernacle, and the incessant, agitating Byzantine plainsong. The monks seem to doze much of the time, elbows propped on the arms of their stalls.

When all was done, and the monks were gathering before the main ikons, to kiss each of the little painted faces framed in silver before leaving the church, a monk asked me if I would like to see the treasures, and took me along behind the altar, and displayed the most wonderful gold-covered bibles, chalices, vessels and ikons and the finger of a saint encased in silver. A peasant was with us too; and as each was displayed, he knelt on the ground and knocked his forehead on the marble. At last the two greatest treasures were produced: a piece of the True Cross, and the Holy Virgin's belt, given by Emperor John Cantacuzene (forefather of the people I met in Bucharest) studded with gems and precious metals. I thought the peasant would never have done with his kissing and prostration.

After this Ephraim and Zachary and I went for a walk in the monastery grounds, pleasant well-watered gardens, full of olive and fig trees, and delightful to walk in. We saw the sun set over the Aegean, and in the twilight walked back to Zachary's cell, where we sat round the fire, brewing Turkish coffee till supper time.

After supper, we had our homely little compline in the chapel, and after that I wrote a while, warming my pyjamas before the stove, then went to bed and read *The Bride of Abydos* and *Lara* for ages.

3rd February
I worked hard all yesterday writing by the fire, and only making a break at luncheon time, and for the holy office in the after-noon. After Mass, I went for another walk in the garden with Brothers Ephraim and Zachary. Zachary officiated in the after-noon. He has a lovely voice, and looks magnificent in his glit-tering vestment, in lively contrast to the dozing *epitropes* with their white faces, snowy beards, and their long thin hands like skeleton leaves.

We had tea in Ephraim's cell, toasting bread and little sausages in front of the stove. It was all great fun, and very *gemütlich*. At supper there were a couple of Caucasians from Tiflis, and one of them spoke a little German, so we had quite a lively time. They were amazing-looking chaps, very dark with tight, wavy black hair, and a general wild look about them.

After leaving them, and attending compline, I went to my room, and wrote far into the night.

Today I finally quitted Vatopedi, and the farewells with Father Kyriakos, Brothers Ephraim and Zachary were touching. The bells of Vatopedi sounded after us up the valley. My two

Caucasians left at the same time, on horseback, and I slung my coat and rucksack on to the saddles, and walked alongside, talking with the one who knew German, and making myself understood with the other, he speaking Russian and I Bulgarian. We met nobody on the road except an old mendicant monk who begged for alms, a common type on the Holy Mountain, his robe all in rags, his cylindrical hat, which should be so stiff, a battered and shapeless pudding.

We took a completely different road from the coastal one which I had taken from Iviron to Vatopedi via Stavronikita and Pantocrator; this went several miles inland and climbed up the central spinal ridge of the peninsula, near to the actual watershed. The air was fresh and windy up here, and pleasant to walk in, jumping from stone to stone, and I didn't envy my Caucasian friends on their old armchairs of mounts. One of them met with a mishap when we were about half way, his horse stumbling on a loose stone, and finally turning a complete somersault and casting off its rider, who got a bad shaking up and cut his cheek on a pointed stone. This was the darker of the two. He told me he wasn't as fit as he should be in middle age, owing to having led an evil life in two great cities. He questioned me about the respective bedroom merits of the women in the different countries I had passed through and made up for my lack of communicativeness by regaling me with long and very amusing anecdotes of his wild youth. He said he was sorry for it, 'but we Georgians are made like it' – '*wir Grusinier sind so von Natur!*' As soon as we came in sight of the steeples and domes of Karyai, he took off his cap and crossed himself repeatedly, his lips moving in prayer.

We soon arrived in the narrow winding streets of that celibate little capital, and found our way into a little church, where Mass was just finishing. The piety of my friends was astonishing, the forehead-knocks and ikon-kissings innumerable. They got one of the monks to take us behind the ikonostasis, the carved screen that segregates the chancel in Orthodox churches. There was a special ikon of the Virgin there, and they spent a long time with it in obeisances. I felt an awful pagan and philistine standing by in insular immobility, but what is one to do? They asked the attendant monk for some of the oil from the lamp that burned before it, to take home to sick friends and relatives, so the monk soaked two bits of cotton wool in it, which he wrapped up and carefully tucked in their wallets.

I had decided to go downhill to the coast at Iviron again, and spend the night there before setting out for Lavra, and as they were going to Iviron too, we set out together. They had to leave their steeds at Karyai, and started with me on foot. The road is a steep and a stony one, with many twists and ups and downs, and by their pants and grunts and sweating even at the start I saw they weren't going to take to it kindly; their bad training was probably the result of the 'evil lives' of which the darker one had spoken. In the end, after taking about twice as long as we should, we arrived at Iviron in a dreadful state of fatigue and a muck sweat, with me carrying most of their kit, besides my own. They are both charming chaps, however, and with Russians one forgives everything, I don't quite know why.

At supper, they drank enormously, getting very rowdy and very amusing, and we all sang Slav songs together. They are both sleeping like corpses now in the same room I'm writing in, snoring in 'праведным сном'* as the song describes it. Russians really are amazing. Father Sophronios was terribly pleased to see me again, and we talked about Byron all the evening. It is very touching to see how Byron's memory is treasured in Greece – they

---

* 'Righteous sleep.'

all learn about 'λόρδος Βύρων' at school, and exclaim proudly that he was 'μεγάλος φιλέλλην'.*

4th February, Karakallou
My two Caucasian friends got up before me, in spite of their potations last night, and going down for coffee when I was dressed I found them chatting with Father Sophronios and some of the other monks. They greeted me noisily, 'Ah good morning, Mister Micha-el!', the only words they knew of English (this type are very boring; their vocabulary consists of 'All right' and 'How are you', the latter being pronounced as a statement, not a question). We had a jolly lunch together, a very good one too, of macaroni, tomato sauce and rissoles, with the usual Greek red wine that flows like water. Quite a worldly meal. Really, Father Sophronios is one of the best, and all the monks here improve on acquaintance. We have become quite good friends. One of the monks, a Brother Modestis, took us to his cell after lunch, and showed us a wonderful ship he had made of wood, with masts, sails, guns, everything, even to the little mariners lining the decks or scaling the rigging. It really was a work of art, and had taken him a year. His cell was very small, and everything spick and span, his little pallet and sheepskin rug rolled up in the corner, and on his wood-carving desk an ikon of the Holy Virgin half finished, the chips neatly brushed together. He himself was a delightful type, shy and retiring, absorbed in his work, and one of the simple practising Christians of which one sees so many on the Holy Mountain, and so few elsewhere. He had lived in his little cell for fifteen years.

I left the monastery soon afterwards, southwards along the rocky coast. It has been a lovely day, the sky and sea an unbelievable

---

* 'Lord Byron' . . . 'a great lover of Greece'.

blue, the stony peaks of Lemnos and Thasos shining in the sun, the huge white mass of Athos up above and the ridge of Macedon in the distance. The road skirted many wild and deserted bays and combes, the luxuriant evergreens coming almost to the sea's edge, shaded all the way by the interlacing boughs above, splashes of fretted sunlight falling on the flagged and stepped pathway. I came on a group of fishermen smoking in the sun before their squat, massive huts, who yelled me the way, along a little rock footpath, passing the Philotheou monastery far uphill.

Soon the road split at a ruined machicolated fortress jutting out to sea (they are common on Athos) and ran uphill inland to the monastery of Karakallou, whose high, slotted walls and rugged belfry were just visible. The road wound up and up, and a boy passed me whistling downhill, with half a dozen asses piled with wood. The road was the usual sort, of big flat stones, with a narrow bar of stone running right across every yard, to give purchase to climbing feet or horses, and, approaching the monastery under the criss-cross vine frames, having two sides sloping down to a channel in the middle, to drain it after rainfall and snowmelt. The janitor monk was blinking half asleep on the broad stone seat outside the ikon-topped monastery gates. (The Orthodox always reverently uncover and cross themselves when passing through.)

I was given the best room, high up in the cloisters, overlooking the old stone courtyard and the many-domed chapel, over the massed roofs to the rocky tree-clad hillside. After putting down my kit, I went for a walk among the mountains, the sun being still so bright that it was a crime to stay indoors. Soon I came to a little monastery, and saw it was a Russian one by the double crosses on the domes and the diagonal bar below, typically Muscovite.

A little Russian monk greeted me courteously when I entered the courtyard and said in Russian that I was just in time for tea

(I can understand a great deal, owing to its kinship with Bulgarian). He was a funny little creature, with a hump, very small, his frock discarded for chopping wood – as his axe showed – his trousers tucked into heavy knee-boots, wearing the Russian jerkin, buttoned at the side under the left ear, bound at the waist with a cord, and spreading down skirt-like below. His tall hat was battered about, and with his flat face, twinkling eyes and straggling brown beard, he looked like a gnome in woodcuts illustrating Grimm's fairy tales. He put down a block of wood to sit on, and soon brought me a glass of tea and some bread, and told me all about himself. He had come to this little monastery in 1904, in the same year as the battle of Port Arthur,* and for him the outside world must still be one of crinolines and high collars and billycock hats. Another, tall white-haired monk joined us; the talk turned to Stalin, and the newcomer quietly remarked in his silky voice, 'Сталин дьявол сатана!'† Russians are mysterious to me, but I adore their company – such gentlemen, even the peasants, such odd thought processes, and such sense of humour!

I had to run most of the way back to Karakallou, to be back before the doors closed, as the sun was starting to set; I got there just as they were closing the gates. It reminded me of racing the bell at school.

The abbot paid me a visit while I was having supper. He was a delightful old man and we battered away at a conversation consisting of no English on his part, and three weeks' Greek on mine. Later a Greek servant came, who had been in America, and said he would show me round the Holy Mountain and 'guard me like a brother'. His manner was sly and oily, and when I said

---

* The Battle of Port Arthur (1904) was the opening, inconclusive engagement of the Russo-Japanese War, when Japanese warships attacked the Russian Pacific fleet anchored in Port Arthur, Manchuria.
† 'Stalin is the most devilish Satan!'

I was a poor man like himself, his fraternal feeling began to wane, and he took his leave soon after.

The fire is almost dead. The wind is howling round the monastery, and I can hear all the trees in the forest creaking and groaning.

5th February, Megisti Lavra

The abbot came along to my cell before I was up this morning, and saw to it that I had a good breakfast. Later, when I was dressed, he presented me to the librarian who took me up the stone stairs to the library. He showed me the monastery's marvellous collection of hand-written gospels. In one of them each initial was a little picture made of intertwining serpents. He also unrolled a parchment scroll of the liturgy which stretched for yards, and all the work of one monk.

When my things were all collected into my rucksack, and I asked to bid farewell to the abbot, the monk led me along to the chapter room, where the abbot was on his throne, surrounded by the *epitropes*, all grandly stroking their beards. He wished me a happy journey, and hoped he would see me there again soon, and all the rest (it was a little embarrassing) joined in wishing me good luck.

The way from Karakallou to Lavra is one of the longest journeys in the peninsula. There are no intervening monasteries, owing to the rocky coast, and the great snow-capped mass of Athos is overhead and shining in the sun all the way. The road climbs up and down again over cliffs and headlands, and sinks into bays, combes, leafy valleys and dark gorges down which mountain streams dash, some of them so deep and narrow that one wonders if the sun ever gets there. I walked all day in the bright sun, only passing two people, a woodman with a laden ass, and the other a monk on his way to Iviron on a little horse.

When I asked them the time, I got incomprehensible answers, as on the Holy Mountain old Byzantine time, which has died out everywhere else, is still in use; the monk told me it was nine o'clock, although it was mid-afternoon: the sun sets at twelve, apparently; one gets used to it in a few days.

I came across a saddled horse wistfully cropping the leaves of a low bush, quite by himself, and on seeing me he trotted off down the path, looking back over his shoulder. There was nobody in sight. I don't know what he could be doing there, but for several miles, despite my efforts to get him to stop and return, he trotted on a few feet in front, breaking into a nervous gallop when I tried to catch his bridle. In the end, I managed to outwit him by cutting off a descending serpentine corner so that thinking me behind him, he suddenly saw me in front. He turned about and started back the way he had come, sped by a whack on the hindquarters.

The birdsong was glorious, as it is forbidden to kill wild animals on the peninsula, and they all roam free over the mountain. I saw a hawk hovering up in the sunny haze overhead, and a large eagle too, sailing on outspread wings round the peak of Athos. A couple of white-sailed fishing boats sped over the sparkling waves now so far below.

The path seemed endless. It had degenerated into a rocky track made of a blood-red, earthy stone, coated with bright green moss and shaded by the smooth leaves of rhododendron and ilex. At last towards sunset, the grey walls of the Lavra appeared above the trees, perched above a spiky, surf-fringed bay. It is the oldest of the monasteries of Mount Athos, and the chief one, and as I drew near, its crumbling and venerable walls, its ramshackle tiles and its peeling frescoes seemed to speak of the dawn of Christianity: a hallowed place perched between the white crag and the stormy sea, like an eagle's nest.

One of the fathers came out and took my rucksack and coat,

and soon I was sitting before a fire in my room. I went for a walk around the courtyard, where the monks, their hair coiled up under their cylinder hats, and their hands hidden in their flowing sleeves, had come out for a breath of air before the sun set. They nodded gravely and said good evening as I passed. Poised near the tip of this wild peninsula, and only approachable by the rockiest and most difficult of paths, the Lavra has an air of utter remoteness, and a stronger feel of age-old survival than any of the other foundations.

A young brother brought me supper, and said that the roads from here are quite impassable owing to snow, and that there is great danger from the wolves: he said the word – 'λύκοι' – several times, his eyes popping out of his head, baring his teeth, and making rapacious passes with his hands, and appeared delighted at my comprehension. He took great trouble for my comfort, piling logs high in the stove, and asking me if there was anything I wanted, before saying goodnight. It is very moving to see the solicitude of the monks towards their guests.

My growing proficiency in Greek, day by day, is an added delight. I have written enough for today, and I can scarcely keep my eyes open, after my long march, so I'll go to bed.

6th February, Megisti Lavra
I woke very late. When I asked if I could see the library, they told me to wait a couple of hours, as the librarian had been to Karyai for a few days, and was expected back that morning. It was a lovely day. One of the monks told me that a Rumanian monastery or skete was only three quarters of an hour from the Lavra, so I walked over the wooded hillside and soon came to the monastery, where a porter greeted me in Greek with 'Καλημέρα σας κύριε' and was taken aback and delighted when I gave him '*Bûnä diminea̧ta, Domnule*' and broke into Rumanian. Then he started

chattering away in Rumanian. He led me upstairs, and produced a few of the brethren, who were very pleased with my few words of their language, and questioned me exhaustively about my wandering in Rumania. There were two of them from the part of Transylvania I know – or rather the Banat – one from Temesvár,* the other from Turnu Severin, and they all asked me what Rumania was like. None of them had been there since many years before the war, and they remembered only the twin states of Moldavia and Wallachia, recently elevated to a kingdom, and would be surprised at the enormously expanded country it is now, with the annexations of Transylvania's Banat, Bukovina, Bessarabia and the Dobrudja. They were very friendly and hospitable, with quick Rumanian faces, and eyes that missed nothing, and very different from those Russians I saw the other day. They have a great charm.

I enquired after a young monk from Lugoj, whom the grocer's son near Orşova had spoken of as a friend, but nobody seemed to have heard of him. It was great fun talking Rumanian again. I like the language, and wish I knew it better. I'm soon out of my depth, but I can fake it up a bit.

I ran most of the way back, as it was downhill and it is great fun jumping from stone to stone, with one's heart in one's mouth. I discovered it was quite late; I was just in time for vespers, and I abandoned the idea of leaving Lavra today. The singing was very fine, and the singers seemed to rock themselves rhythmically in their stalls, leaning on their elbows, in perfect time. How they sing it all so accurately is a wonder, as the tunes sound extraordinarily elaborate and irregular, and if they didn't sometimes sing it all together in perfect unison, one might take it for improvisation. The notation in their prayer books is quite extraordinary, looking rather like Arabic, with squiggles and curls above the text,

* Temesvár: modern Timişoara.

and quite unlike any other score. The musical line returns continually to a single deep backbone note, ascending and descending
elaborations, and amazing half-tones, in unaccompanied voices.
It makes an effective and rather unsettling impression at first. The
ceremony is already becoming familiar and I am beginning to
know at which points the candelabras will be lowered from their
obscurity to be lighted or extinguished, when the officiating priest
will cense the community, and when the monks will begin to
leave their stalls for their long ceremony of prostrations, ikon-
kissing, and multiple signs of the cross, before going out.

The library, like the monastery itself, is the largest and oldest
on the Holy Mountain. It is in a little building by itself, and full
of manuscripts of great interest. One, of the fourth century, is
the chief treasure of Mount Athos, and written in the same
century as the Codex Sinaiticus. The cloth of gold and embroidered vestments are numberless, and there are whole cases full
of archiepiscopal staves, topped with a cross and two intertwining
serpents; whole rows, too, of abbots' mitres, glorious gold and
jewelled headdresses, in shape something like an imperial crown
or the high priest's hat of bible illustration. The man who showed
me them was rather a character, with bright, sparkling eyes and
knowing a word or two of English. He proudly showed me a
card, with a picture of the codex, from Sir Arthur Hill, director
of the Botanical Gardens at Kew.

Brother Paul accompanied us round, and invited me to tea,
when it was through. He had been a doctor, born at Trebizond,
and fled Turkey under Atatürk. He inveighed feelingly against
the Young Turks* and their treatment of the Armenians, as well

---

* The Young Turks were a junta of fiercely patriotic army officers who took
power in Turkey in 1908, and instituted a policy of modernization. They entered
the First World War alongside Germany, and were responsible for the infamous
genocide of the Armenians. Their leaders went into exile in 1918.

as of the Greeks. He was rather a surprising, cultivated man, very oriental, with olive skin and hooked nose, soft eyes, a long silky beard and a deeply stooping back. He seemed abstracted from worldly things, however, and spent his time writing an enormous journal, thirty or forty pages a day; he had kept it up for five years; he pointed to row on row of uniform and neatly written volumes, all carefully numbered and catalogued, the pages already in five figures. He told me he would leave them to the monastery, as it was a review of the times as well as a minute record of his own life. His firmest ideal was the reunion of all Christians into a single Church, and a great deal of his work was devoted to it. He spoke in a very soft voice, as if he wasn't quite aware of my presence, and might almost have been talking to himself, as he pottered among his papers. His walls were covered with replicas of old ikons and manuscripts and prints of the monastery, all traced neatly and accurately. He rather surprised me, when I left, by giving me a long rosary of glass beads. I will always remember him, in that odd, untidy room overlooking the rocky Aegean coast.

I sat all evening in the little shelter outside the monastery gates, watching the sun set over the waves, and breathing the mountain and sea air. The young monk who is looking after me brought me, to my amazement, a plate of limpets for supper. Apparently they are a usual dish here. They tasted like nothing on earth, and I had to eat them, to save his feelings, as he stood and chatted while I swallowed them. He is so kind and thoughtful that I should hate to offend him. Afterwards, I spent the whole evening with Byron in front of the fire. Then bedtime. Outside my door is a gallery overlooking the courtyard, its chapels and rambling cloisters, walls and balconies interspersed with yew and cypress trees. I'll just walk round and smoke a cigarette before sleeping.

7th February

I was woken this morning by my friend, one of the two laymen
I drank so deep with at Iviron. He is an amusing type, a great
cynic, and speaks excellent French: he asked me where I had
been since our last meeting, and hearing that I was setting out
that day for St Paul's monastery, he invited me to accompany
him by boat, as he was sailing to Daphni. He is an amusing
chap, and we laughed a good deal together. As soon as I was
dressed, we set out down the hill, to his little dwelling by the
pirates' watchtower. Our lunch, in his little house among the
rocks by the tiny harbour, was very snug and civilized, with a
blazing fire, armchairs, and a gramophone. We had an excellent
meal, served by a servant who does everything for him. His name
is Vrettas, and he is a sort of general trader for the monasteries
in wheat and other supplies.

The boat was a little wooden one, sailed by a heavily bearded
skipper, and when we were out of the bay it began to pitch like
a leaf in a mill race.

The scenery we passed was amazing for its wild masses of
jagged rocks, round which the waves thrashed themselves into
white foam. These rugged, grey and red cliffs are much higher
than elsewhere in the peninsula and as we rounded the cape the
most astonishing hermitages came into view, each perched on a
perilous ledge of rock, looking scarcely big enough for a bird's
nest. They are the wildest, remotest and saddest-looking dwellings
I've ever seen, and the thought that people spend their whole
lives in them baffles me. There are not even paths leading up to
them, only rungs and pegs driven ladder-like into the rock, and
food is sent up to them every week or so, in baskets on the end
of ropes. Each of these little eyries appeared more fantastic than
the last, some at an enormous height on the mountainsides and
overlooking sheer and jagged chasms.

Rounding the cape into the Sithonian Gulf, I decided to sleep at Dionisiou, not at Agios Pavlos, and when we drew near, the boat curved inland, and I jumped on to the little quay as we were about to sail past it. The road to Dionisiou winds up and up behind the monastery for some minutes, as it is built fortress-like on an overhanging crag, and its huge windowless walls, jutting battlements and machicolated tower smack of the Dark Ages.

I passed through a tunnelled archway into the courtyard, and saw, to my consternation, that the huge ironbound doors were closed. Looking over the parapet, I saw the little boat rounding a headland, already tiny in the distance, and so I started knocking and shouting at the gate until a black-capped, bearded figure appeared at the window-slit, and popped back again. After a long time, probably involving a conference with the abbot, a light appeared through the chinks under the doors, and soon, after unbelievable clanking and shooting of bolts, a small rectangle of the wood swung back, and a monk with a lantern peered at me through it. It was scarcely big enough to get through, and when I was the other side, all was locked and barred again, and the monk, his swinging lantern casting fantastic shadows on the walls, led me up some stone stairs, and into a lamp-lit room, where several monks were seated.

I was welcomed warmly and given a seat, and after coffee, γλυκό and raki, they told me that a special exception had been made in opening the gates after sundown, as I was a foreigner. I produced a letter of introduction; it was for one of the monks present, a jovial, heavily bearded, Friar Tuck-like monk, who spoke Rumanian, and kept the table in constant peals of laughter. He saw that everything was fixed up, and after supper, chatted awhile, then left me to my work. My window overlooks the Aegean, gleaming under a new moon, which looks very frail and slender, surrounded with fidgeting stars.

8th February, Simonopetra

The road from Dionisiou was the roughest and steepest I have seen yet on the Holy Mountain, going up and down like a switchback over bleak and rocky headlands, and down into green, leaf-shaded canyons. This coast faces the afternoon sun, and the cactus and prickly pear give it a tropical air.

I came across a group of men squatting among the rocks round a little wood fire, blinking in the noonday sun like lizards. We exchanged greetings, and they made room for me. They were an odd crew, two of them elderly, silent men, with stiff black beards sprouting from beneath their cheekbones, the other two young and voluble, displaying their tattered clothes. They told me they were communists, saying that so were all the poor in Greece. One of them had a fine voice, and sang some Greek songs in one of those deep, easy, effortless voices which are such a delight to listen to. They were a nice lot, and their poverty very depressing. A little later, I fell in with a Macedonian from Strumitza, who didn't seem quite certain whether he was a Greek or a Bulgarian. He spoke Bulgarian with a strong Macedonian accent, the first time I've really noticed it. A melancholy, bearded chap, he grunted and wheezed at every step, most unlike the hardy Bulgarian mountaineers I met among the Rila mountains, or the Rhodope or the Stara Planina. He soon dropped far behind.

Descending, I could see over the roofs on to the courtyard of St Gregory's monastery where the foreshortened monks were moving to and fro; I had a chat with some of them; they gave me a cup of tea, and seemed surprised that I was going on further that day. One rather embarrassing thing was a monk who insisted on holding my hand and pressing it affectionately. I didn't want to seem churlish by snatching it away, so I pretended to slip on the cobbled pavement, disengaged myself, and on recovering buried my hands deep in my pockets. This is the first time I have had the slightest inkling on Mount Athos that abnormality exists, though in a permanently celibate community it is pretty likely that it must.

The first glimpse of Simonopetra is magnificent. It is perched high up on the mountain, looking as if it grows straight from the peak beneath it, the brick blending as imperceptibly with the rock as a mermaid with her tail; it is the most unlikely-looking thing, shooting up to a dizzy height sheer above the rock in a magnificent sweep, tier after tier of wooden balconies running round the upper parts, supported above the drop of blank wall and the rugged bastions by diagonal props, seeming to spring from the wall's face like the branches of a tree. Robert Byron compared it to the Potala of Lhasa, and he was quite right.

The climb is a long and weary one, rocks all the way, the steep pathway twisting again and again up the mountainside till it leads under the low archway of great thickness, opening out into the uneven flagged courtyard. Vespers were not quite over when I arrived, sweating and exhausted, so I got in for the last few minutes. Many of the brothers seemed very poor, bowed with age, their monastic robes in tatters and their black caps collapsed out of all resemblance to rigid cylinders.

As the evening softened to sunset, I stood on the wooden balcony, gazing out to sea, where the sky, sea and the promontories of Sithonia and Kassandra melted into a soft water-colour blue. The evenings on Mount Athos, with their touch of melancholy, are of an unimaginable quietness and serenity.

To look down brought one's heart into one's mouth. There was a drop for several hundred feet on to the jagged rocks and boulders; the tops of trees showed underneath too, and a little stream, white with foam and dashing among the rocks, seemed – optically delayed by the distance – to move sluggishly. I might have been looking down on it from another sphere, and I remembered Rossetti's lines about 'the flood of ether as a bridge . . . where this earth spins like a fretful midge' – it was just such a feeling.

A year ago, at this time, within the day, I was standing on the ruined keep of Dürnstein, the dungeon of Richard Coeur de Lion, looking at the rugged mountains of the Wachau, the blue sweep of the Danube far below, and the just discernible spires of Gottweig monastery in the distance. It seems a long time ago.

Yielding to a childish impulse, I got a piece of paper from my pack, folded it into a dart, and threw it from the balcony; it soon got into a tailspin, and corkscrewed into the treetops. The second, however, floated out slowly, and began to descend in wide circles, trembling on the breeze, and sometimes seeming to stop in mid-air altogether. It was wonderful to watch it, descending the void so leisurely, down, down, down, till at last, tiny with distance, it vanished among the leaves.

The whole monastery is hushed and asleep now, since the monks have retired early, as long before dawn the hammer striking the beam of wood, which usually replaces the church bells here, will rouse them from their beds, to shiver in their chapel stalls for an hour or two, while I am still sound asleep. Sometimes, half asleep, I hear the signal, and am never sure next day whether that, and the awareness of movement near me, were a dream or not.

10th February, St Panteleimon
I slept very late and lay a long while in the sunlight in a rare and delicious state of semi-consciousness.

The winding road over the cliffs was pleasant walking, shaded from the sun by olive trees, among which occasional flocks cropped the grass to the piping of their shepherd. After an hour, the roofs of Daphni appeared below, and beyond, each smaller in the distance, the monasteries of Xeropotamos and Panteleimon.

Daphni, that sunny, dead little village, seemed fast asleep with only the lapping of the waves on the pebbles to break the silence. The few members of the population visible were all sleeping with their caps over their eyes. I found my way to Vrettas's abode, just such another whitewashed room, with two windows facing seaward, as at Lavra; and there was Vrettas lying on his back in his shirtsleeves, smoking and reading a Greek satirical weekly. He seemed pleased to see me. I lay on the spare bed, and so we chatted and read all the afternoon, and towards evening walked down to the diminutive quay, where we watched the sun setting, then went on into the inn and found the chief of police and the customs officer – 'la fleur de la société de Daphni', as Vrettas sarcastically dubbed it – and drank glass after glass of raki, with cheese and olives. We all got very amusing, especially Vrettas and I, who were feeling slightly tight by the time his servant came along to tell us dinner was ready. This was a jolly meal, with Vrettas and me and another sprig of the Daphni elite. We were all in good form, laughing a good deal, and drinking lots of some Macedonian wine that reminded me of Tokay. In the end, we all sang.

Vrettas and I talked far into the night: he is a real cynic, and sneers at everything. He says the religion on Mount Athos is a farce – 'elle n'a aucun rapport avec le Bon Dieu!'* I didn't agree at all. On hearing I was off to Panteleimon in the morning, he told me of its present poverty compared with its affluence in the days of Imperial Russia – champagne and caviar every night, he said, which I take with a huge pinch of salt. He referred to Father Basil, the governor of the Caucasus's son, of whom I had heard so much, and he said he was astonished how such a man could become a monk. He told me he spoke perfect English, Greek,

* 'It has nothing to do with the good Lord.'

German and French, and was very intelligent. '*Mais*', he finished, '*il devient mystique, ce type-là, et quand un Russe est ainsi, je vous assure, c'est trop pour moi!*'*

We slept very late this morning. Then Vrettas and his pal and I had luncheon in the open behind the inn, under a trellis of brown leaves. Afterwards, chairs were set on the quay by the low, broad sea wall, and there we sat chatting with a few village cronies over Turkish coffee and cigarettes, relapsing into frequent silences, the only sound beyond that of the waves being the rattle of beads, as somebody flicked the amber beads of his *komboloi* between his fingers.

I got the impression that all the inhabitants of Daphni are bored to extinction, the same faces and conversation every day, being jarred by the same things continually, with a choice of twenty or twenty-five inhabitants, of whom most seem odd in some way, blockheads or halfwits. I don't know what Vrettas does, being an intelligent chap, with such company year in year out. When I left, they were still contemplating the sea in silence, playing with their beads.

For some time my track followed the one I had taken on my first day on Mount Athos, branching off towards Xeropotamos about half way. From there the road got more desolate and melancholy with every step. The wind through the trees, and the very streams among the rocks seemed to murmur in sorrow. Underfoot the bruised leaves of the evergreens filled the air with an aromatic flavour. Just such scenery as I have always pictured for the Mount of Olives and the garden of Gethsemane. The wind brought the tinkling of the bells of St Panteleimon, and

---

* 'But that fellow's become a mystic, and when a Russian's like that, I assure you it's too much for me!'

soon I saw rambling walls by the sea, green Muscovite domes, and glittering Russian crosses above the treetops.

I soon saw the monks. Many were tall, and unlike all the others they were clothed in blue frocks, and wore heavy knee-boots, and underneath their black hats and wild hair their pale Slav faces appeared childlike and simple, many with the slightly slanting eyes and high cheekbones that one's mind probably wrongly associates with Siberia. Some of their beards straggle like those of Macedonians. They bowed their heads in greeting, and one led me to the *arhondaris*, who has all strangers in his care. His face was a mixture of guilelessness, sadness and quiet humour. He led me to my whitewashed room, and brought some Russian tea, with a slice of lemon floating in it.

After I had drunk it, he led me across the huge courtyard to see the Father Basil of whom I had heard so much. We went up flight after flight of wooden stairs, and eventually tapped on the door of his cell. Father Basil was almost invisible, owing to the darkness of the cloisters and the fading daylight, but when he addressed me quietly in English my heart bounded with joy. It was balm after the jerky cacophonies of returning émigrés from America, and each word of his soft unearthly voice was music.

We went for a walk down by the sea. I don't quite know what Vrettas meant when he described him as a mystic; but the tall, pale forehead, the high-bridged, formally classical nose, and sculptured, sensitive features discernible through his auburn monastic beard did seem fraught with sadness and mystery; and the surprising thing about him was his youth, that waxen face without a wrinkle, yet touched with the sorrows of the world, as though my presence had brought him out of a dusky forest of meditation.

His English, like that of many white Russians, was perfect, and his German and French too. We spoke of Western Europe, and people we both knew – the charming Professor Whittemore, and Mark Ogilvie-Grant,* who came here some years ago with Robert Byron† and David Talbot Rice‡ when they were preparing their book about the Holy Mountain. His company was delightful to me, famished as I was, after an uninterrupted stretch of peasant company, for some shades of human intercourse subtler than saying I come from London, and giving the number of inhabitants, and answering enquiries then about my father, mother, sister (people seemed sorry I had no brothers) and as to whether I had done my military service.

It was an evening full of charm. After returning, we had a second tea in my room, then went over to the chapel where vespers were ending. The monks were singing in a ring, among a forest of candles and gilding, in deep, Slavonic voices. I saw my two Caucasians kissing the ikons with a self-conscious devoutness that was very noticeable amid this slow-moving, abstracted company. When it was finished, I met the deputy abbot (the abbot himself was ill in bed), and then, bidding goodnight to Father Basil, ran across the flagged courtyard, to a good supper of borscht, boiled eggs (from the mainland, I suppose), oranges and a very dark wine.

It is late now, and my window is directly above the advancing and retreating sea; its subdued murmur will go on all night. A few minutes ago, there was a noise in the passage; an old monk, bowed with age, and dragging his heavy knee-boots, was shouting

---

* Mark Ogilvie-Grant (1906–69), botanist and aesthete, one of the 'bright young things' of 1920s London. He later settled in Greece for many years.

† Robert Byron (1904–41), prodigious travel writer and art historian, author of *The Station* and *The Road to Oxiana*. He died at sea in the Second World War.

‡ David Talbot Rice (1903–72), eminent Byzantine art historian, author of several standard works and of the ambitious *The Birth of Western Painting* with Robert Byron in 1930.

cryptic condemnation, talking of powers unseen and waving his heavy stick at the air; his blue slit-eyes blazed, and his mouth worked under his wisps of beard. Several monks turned up, and laughing softly like children, persuaded him back to his cell.

11th February, my 20th birthday, St Panteleimon
Woke up this morning, the weight of my twenty years heavy upon me, wondering how many people at home were wishing me many happy returns and whether the waves of their well-wishing would reach me through the air. The *arhondaris*, with whom I have made great friends, brought me tea and jam and bread. He seems to have taken me under his wing, as I'm his only guest.

After dressing, I was just setting out in quest of Father Basil, when I met him on the threshold, coming to visit me. So we sat talking in my room, and then we set off to look round the chapel, where the ikons and frescoes were all new, and though not unpleasant, not very interesting. The gilding in the upper chapel is all recent, and some of the stencilling on the wall awful, and luckily not very obvious. The two-storey library is enormous, with long, pleasant rooms packed full of books in expensive cases. It is very poor in manuscripts however, except for one with the gospels for each day of the year, which has fascinating illustrations, a Nativity where the interest and adoration in the eyes of the animals is really wonderful, and another of the Baptism of Christ, naked in Jordan, with the devil, or some evil water sprite, in a posture of submarine thwartedness. The soft-voiced librarian spoke affectionately of Professor Whittemore, and consented to my taking Robert Byron's *The Station*, which Father Basil had presented, back to my cell. Then I bade Basil goodbye, and he returned to his cell, I to mine, he dragging his heavy boots behind him, and giving the impression, in his youthfulness, of a schoolboy dressed up in a flowing beard and hair, tall hat and long robes.

The rest of the morning I read *The Station*. It's a splendid book (the fly-page bears the words 'to Father Basil, with best wishes from Colin Davidson,* 64 Curzon Street, London W1'). I kept breaking into laughter, making the cloisters echo with solitary mirth, and it was amusing to read a description of Father Charalampi, while he laid my lunch before my eyes. The description of Basil under the name of Father Valentine is a masterpiece, and the types and the spirit of Athos are caught brilliantly all through.

I remembered Father Giorgios and the Abbot of Xeropotamos, who had been so nice in presenting me with his book; so, taking the staff that the woodman at Pantocrator had given me, I started off over the rocks and stones, and up the steep path to Xeropotamos, less than an hour distant from Russiko.† The wind was like a gale, and the climb uphill was a hard struggle. The Albanian janitor was pleased to see me again, and addressed me as before in Russian, knowing I knew Bulgarian better than Greek; he led me inside and gave me a raki and coffee, not the official welcoming one, but a personal nip. Asked if he remembered 'Mr Byron' he shook his head, but his face lit up with recognition at the second, Mark Ogilvie-Grant‡ – 'ὁ Μάρκος!' – and he held forth what a nice young gentleman he was, and how well he dressed. When I asked after Father Giorgios, he led

---

* Of Colin Davidson, PLF writes: 'A delightful, civilized man I got to know years later. I'd met Robert Byron a year and a half before in a deafening, smoke-filled, nearly pitch-dark night-club – the Nest? The Nuthouse? Smokey Jo's? – where everyone was pretty tight.'

† Russiko: the popular name for St Panteleimon monastery.

‡ PLF writes in a footnote: 'I had set out on this journey with a rucksack he had given me – the year before last now – the very one he himself had carried when accompanying Byron and David Talbot Rice in the great Athos journey *The Station* describes. It was stolen in a Jugendherberge' (in Munich, in January 1934).

me to his cell. From the sounds along the passage, I could hear he was practising. He greeted me warmly, his French bubbling over, his mobile eyes dancing and his gold teeth flashing. His cell was bare and small, every available table and chair cluttered with sheet music, his bed unmade since jumping out of it for early Mass, and many oranges ranged in the window to ripen.

He said he had had a very entertaining time reading the *Contes drolatiques*, which I had given him, and said he would leave the monastery, if only he could get hold of a piano. I wonder if, through my agency, Balzac has planted these improper desires in his breast. He seemed a bit forlorn, sitting on his bed, his bearded chin cupped in his hands, recalling better days in Paris – '*Comme j'ai gaspillé des sous, hé-hé!*'* He gave me a couple of oranges despondently. Then we went to see the abbot, who had been so kind on my last visit, giving me his autographed book. He was in conference with an archimandrite from the mainland but appeared delighted to see me, and over *glyco*, coffee and raki, asked me all about my activities, what monasteries I had visited, and what my impressions had been. He and Father Giorgios besought me to stay the night in the monastery, but as it would have been a bit awkward at Panteleimon, I excused myself as best I could. When I got up to bid the abbot farewell, Giorgios whispered, '*Baisez la main, baisez la main!*'† and I bent with a flourish over the Abbot Evdokios's hand. The old man appeared charmed at this apparent knowledge of ecclesiastical manners in a barbarian, and his benedictions followed me from the room. Father Giorgios came a little along the path, his monastic frock blown up like an agitated balloon by the gale-wind. Holding his hat to his head, he bade me goodbye, beseeching me to write, which I promised to do.

---

* 'How I wasted money, he-he!'
† 'Kiss his hand, kiss his hand!'

Aided by the wind, I ran most of the way back, feeling fleeter than Hermes, and waving my long peasant's staff overhead like the Mercurial caduceus. Over stones, streams and rocky clefts and valleys I sped, and the grey-white leaves of the olive trees streamed with me, like a silver head of hair. It was nearing dusk when I reached Russiko again, and I found my way up to the cloisters and Basil's cell. He was there in the dusk, poring over a huge theological tome, looking like an etching of a mediaeval necromancer seeking the philosopher's stone. When I was seated, he removed the chimney of his oil lamp, and set a match to the ragged wick, dispelling the twilight in a soft golden light, shaded by a green shield. As we talked, he prepared cups and saucers and the samovar, and soon we were chatting over Russian tea, and looking round his simple room, with its plank bed, and his desk piled high with a disorder of huge dictionaries. His life seemed an enviable one. He reminded me of those pictures of St Jerome in his cell. We talked of the coenobitic and anchoritic lives, I saying that surely the latter was preferable, owing to the clashes, jealousies and squabbles inevitable in a large community. He seemed to agree with me, saying that he considered the life of a coenobite monastery a stepping-stone to solitary eremitism, as it was a large jump to make all at once. Thence his conversation led to Jerome, Augustine of Hippo and St Simeon Stylites.

I felt slightly depressed as the conversation continued, owing to the realization that I was talking to someone for whom all the vanities and selfishness to which I am prone were non-existent. I had an unusually strong desire to be at my best in his presence, and suffered agonies when I thought that I said anything jarring or with a false ring. It was immediately apparent to me against the quiet conversation of Father Basil. He has a most peculiar personal charm, and his company here is a blessed stroke of good fortune. I eventually bade him goodnight, as he had to go to his abbot's chamber to read vespers, and I took my way to the church.

Today is the vigil of the *prazdnik* celebrating SS Basil, Gregory and John Chrysostom (the Three Hierarchs), and I came into the chapel at the beginning of the all-night service of eight hours, which heralds the holy day. Basil, before leaving, led me to a throne-like stall, quite alone before a pillar. The chapel was in almost complete darkness, save for the candles and oil lamps, twinkling like glow-worms before the ikons, their reflections reiterated a thousandfold in the gold and silver encrusting the altar screen and the holy pictures. The monks in their stalls were black shadows in the gloom, the whole church sunk in silence, broken only by the occasional entrance of a brother, the scrape of his huge boots on the floor, making his obeisance before the Virgin; a monk flitted ghost-like round the church, a taper lighting the insides of his cupped hands as he tended the hanging silver lamps.

All was still at last, and a stoled priest issued from the sanctuary, swinging a censer in his hands. He turned his back on the people, and gravely censed the ikons of Jesus, the Virgin and Child, St John the Baptist and then the saints one after the other, all round the church, silent save for the clang, clang, clang. In the obscurity of the nave, all that was visible was the glowing fiery bowl of the thurible, and the iridescent blue clouds that issued from it; then he censed the monks one by one, each bowing gravely in his stall, finishing with me, when he returned to the tabernacle, leaving the church again in deep silence, which was soon broken by soft, unearthly singing, harmonies of a quality and weirdness that set my pulses throbbing. Gradually the chanting grew in volume, and several of the monks, all black in their veils and gowns, filed up both sides into the chancel where they stood in a group about a many-faceted lectern under a hanging lantern, joining their voices to the harmony, with a volume, richness and mystery quite new to me. All my landmarks were lost, it was as unlike the familiar Bulgarian, Rumanian and Greek liturgy as it could be, and looking at the inscrutable, expressionless *moujik* faces, it condensed for me the spirit of those snowbound steppes, conjuring up visions of the many-domed Kremlin, of Siberian villages among the pines and the lullaby of howling wolves.

Slowly the church lit up with the burning of tapers, and the masses of goldwork and the twirling columns lost all their garishness in the kindly light. Another robed priest issued from the tabernacle, the choir formed a semicircle, the singing changed, mounted, descended, always preserving its unreality. Ceremony succeeded ceremony, the ikon of the three saints was displayed on a veiled tripod, the service shifted from one wing of the church to the other. All this time the wind howled outside, sometimes echoing the thunder's pitch as it roared through the wires of the crosses overhead. The singing became a litany, and three fantastic harmonies sank to an infinitely sorrowful and exquisite 'Lord, have mercy, Lord'.

How many hours I leant in a semi-trance in the darkness I don't know, but I was roused by a touch on the shoulder, and turning, saw Father Basil, a candle in his hand. He advised me to go to bed, as it was late and he said the litany would continue for many hours longer, and there was a great Mass tomorrow which I could attend. Reluctantly I descended the cloister steps with him, the singing growing faint in the distance, and the wind gaining mastery. I left him at the head of the steps leading down to the courtyard, and there below, the domes of the chapel gleamed in the night, and the branches of a palm tree lashed wildly in the gale. Suddenly, for no reason, I felt that prickling which we call hair standing on end, and took to my heels across the flagstones as fast as I could go, never halting till I was in my cell.

It has been a wonderful day, and I could not have wished for anything better for my birthday. Just a year ago, I was in a *schloss* in upper Austria, sleeping after a dinner and evening with Count and Countess Trautmannsdorff.

12th February, St Panteleimon

I sat up so late last night that I quite failed to rise in time for the Mass of the Three Saints, the absent-minded Charalampi bringing my tea, bread and *sladkoe* an hour after it was finished. Looking out of the window, I saw that the gale last night had brought on a snowfall, as the whole beach was deep in white, and the windowsill outside piled high. It was a depressing scene, the leaden, rough-surfaced sea and the white flakes swirling down in fierce whorls and eddies. It was out of the question to leave Russiko that day.

Buttoning my coat high under my chin, I set out across the six-inch deep courtyard, the falling snow capping my head and covering my shoulders with white. I had hoped that I might be in time for the tail-end of the Mass, and seeing a little procession issuing from the church, bearing candles that were immediately blown out, I followed them through the huge doors under the belfry just opposite, and to my embarrassment found myself in the monks' refectory, where hundreds of monks sat about their tables. I beat a hasty retreat back to my cell, where Charalampi was laying the table for lunch. He helped me out of my snowy overcoat, repeating over and over again his word 'снег' – snow. He is an excellent man, the only monk besides Basil who has ever knocked on my door before entering, and he doesn't bombard me with endless questions about my family, and how much money my father has got, and the size of London, respecting my privacy as much as I his. There is a twinkle in his small eyes, that shows that though few words may be spoken, we understand each other very well. A change from the garrulity of the Greeks.

Basil paid me a visit not long after lunch, and Charalampi brought along tea as we sat talking. We spent most of the time over my maps, planning out my route in Greece. I have decided to visit the monasteries of Meteora, near Kalambaka, and Basil also advised me to visit Osias Loukas near Delphi, and Daphni near Athens.* We went over my past route together too, in which he seemed interested, and passed a few hours pleasantly enough, discussing foreign countries, and comparing their inhabitants, our views being practically the same on most of them. I was sorry when he went. Later on, I went over to the chapel in the cloisters, where a simple vespers was sung, drinking deep of the Russian singing, which I will not hear so often hereafter, things being what they are.

My supper was excellent, the fresh boiled eggs and the borscht being a constant delight, and the un-oily soup a pleasant change. Charalampi has the trick of arranging it in an appetizing way, always with a spotless table napkin, cutlery from which one is not forced to scrape a month's coagulated slime, and his sweet oranges placed in artistic juxtapositions. The snow seemed to grow stronger and stronger, touching the windowpanes with a muffled patter and, melted by the heat of the room, running down the panes in a hundred little streams which, before Charalampi drew the curtains and lit the lamp, distorted the

* The monasteries of Meteora ('the monasteries in the air') in Thessaly are built on natural pinnacles of rock, and date from the fourteenth century. The important Byzantine churches of Osias Loukas and Daphni are famous for their eleventh-century mosaics, Daphni above all for its great Christ Pantocrator in the cupola.

bleak world outside like a freak mirror at a funfair. I went to bed early, reading the whole of *Marino Faliero, Doge of Venice*, before I finally fell asleep. I am growing fonder and fonder of Byron; I can't see why our odd nation sets no store by him, to the amazement of Europe.

13th February, Xenophontos
The snow had stopped when I woke this morning, and the sun was trying to shine through banks of grey cloud, which hung threateningly above the greyer sea. A thaw had set in, and everywhere the snow was melting in chill streams that flowed everywhere. After a brief walk outside, I retired again to my warm room, where Charalampi, replacing my empty cup for a full one, hoped that I had had a 'спокойная ночь',* which I assured him was the case. I worked all the morning, my table and chair drawn close to the stove for warmth, feeling very depressed, partly owing to the weather, partly to the prospect of leaving Russiko, the monastery of all the monasteries of Mount Athos where I have been happiest. I look forward to coming back again, before the world gets many years older. Sadly, I eat my borscht for the last time.

The afternoon was pleasant enough, however, as Basil came over to tea, and we sat long, talking of Virgil, Horace and Catullus. I showed him the little Elzevir Horace that his compatriot, Baron Liphart, gave me a year ago in Munich. He talked of the Englishmen he had met at his monastery, a few of whom I knew – Professor Whittemore, Robert Byron, Mark Ogilvie-Grant, David Talbot Rice and Balfour and Captain Stuart-Hay. The last he advised me to go and see in Athens, as he was a very amusing character, and had been forbidden to come to the Holy

* 'A peaceful night.'

Mountain, owing to some clash with the monks of St Gregory. I promised to bear his greetings. When all my things were packed, I said farewell of him and Father Charalampi, who seemed sorry to lose me. I was very sad to bid farewell to Father Basil, as I felt I had made a friend; I promised to bear his salaams to such of his friends as I might happen upon in my travels.

The rocky path from Russiko to Xenophontos was miserable, owing to the melting snow on the lower slopes, and the solid banks of it, ankle deep, higher up. It was of that sort with a brittle, sticky crust, and I have never cursed it more than I did today; it looked firm enough, but gave way at once, with the noise of breaking wood, and my feet sank into the soft snow beneath, sometimes knee deep, and my boots, ruined by a fortnight's springing gazelle-like from rock to rock, soaked in the damp like a sponge, so when I arrived at Xenophontos, I was a miserable case.

Xenophontos makes the impression of a large ecclesiastical group of rambling farm buildings. It is right down on the sea shore, within a yard or two of the water's edge, and its lack of rock-girt grandeur, such as one sees in many of the other monasteries, gives it a normal workaday look. The eaves are low, and there are none of those stacks of balconies which are seen on the other monasteries. A little caravan of asses, laden with firewood, was clattering about the yard, and a few ragged fowl were pecking jerkily among the wet cobbles. The *arhondaris*, a sad, dark-bearded figure, led me to my room down one of the longest, gloomiest passages I've ever seen. The windows overlooked the waves which broke a few yards below, and there was a Turkish cushioned window-seat running across the wall, the usual white-columned plaster stove, and an ill-fitting door which admitted a chilling draught. Above the windows hung a picture of Joachim III, Patriarch of Constantinople, an energetic old man with a streaky beard, his bosom hung with ribbons, crosses and archiepiscopal insignia the size of jam tarts, and his black frock crusted with stars and orders.

I put in an appearance at vespers, where the church is light and whitewashed and hung with a profusion of ikons, many of them very beautiful, especially one in the southern transept, of two saintly warriors in the thorax, lorica and greaves of classical soldiers, the depth and richness of colours in the red-golden armour and halo being delicious. The two mosaics spoken so highly of in *The Station* are really remarkable too, for feeling and execution. The service however was tame after Russiko: the usual antiphony of two solo voices, their cues being given by a deacon who crosses from one side of the nave to the other, bearing the psalter and placing it on a high table, usually of Turkish or Arabian inlay. He sings each verse through rapidly, the monk slowly and elaborately, the deacon starting the next verse before he has finished. It has an oddly harmonious effect.

The *arhondaris* did his work as guest-master as if it were an unpleasant infliction, and each little service that Charalampi had done so promptly and with such a good grace was done with the expression of a martyr, making me feel extraordinarily uncomfortable. Seeing me shivering in my overcoat, he asked me lugubriously if I wanted a fire, and on my reluctantly admitting that it would not be unwelcome, he went about it, his head bloody but unbowed.

After supper, as I was busy writing by the fire, two *epitropes* paid me a visit and I jumped up and gave them chairs. It seemed a sort of official visitation, and commonplaces were exchanged for a long time, and when these were exhausted a long and embarrassing silence ensued. I tried to bolster up the failing conversation by showing them drawings, writings, trying to get them interested in maps and routes, but everything failed at last, and helpless I

sat down, and let the swamping silence envelop everything. To
break it, at intervals, I ejaculated 'hey ho!' or 'ἡ ζωὴ καλὴ εἶναι',
'life is good', trying to coin the sort of platitudes that one emits
in England at such times. That failing, I pretended to relapse into
a brown study, gazing abstractedly into the flames but really in
an agony of embarrassment. At last, after I don't know how long,
one of the *epitropes* heaved a sigh and said 'λοιπό!' and the two
greybeards rustled to their feet, wished me goodnight, and left
me to continue my interrupted work. This word 'λοιπό!' is very
useful, the equivalent of 'well' in English, '*eh, bien*' in French,
'*also*' in German, '*haidi*' in Bulgarian.

Since their departure I have been writing, feeling depressed at
my leaving Russiko and regretting Father Basil. I think my depression has rather jaundiced my outlook tonight against perfectly
ordinary and reasonable beings.

14th February, Dochiarion
Luncheon was awful today, uneatable vegetables soaked in oil,
which looked too much like that in which the wicks burn before
the ikons to be palatable, so I flung it to the wild waves, and
lunched off bread and wine, and white cheese. The *arhondaris*
seems quite a nice chap, and I got a wrong impression of his
melancholy last night, mistaking it for surliness. I got off fairly
early, avoiding a second intrusion by the *epitropes* whom I saw
coming down the passage, so I bade a hasty goodbye en passant,
instead of the alternative agonizing hour in my cell.

The way from Xenophontos to Dochiarion was pleasant and
leisurely, in spite of the melting sun, which turned the pathway
into a rivulet. The two monasteries are scarcely an hour apart,
and the going is easy all the way. Dochiarion soon came in sight,
reminding me somehow of an Italian scene, with the cypresses
and yew trees, the gently sloping cobbles, a tiled lych-gate shelter

built over the way and the pathway approaching the deep gates through orange trees. The gates are a broad, mounting tunnel, the porter's room built in the wall's thickness up a few steps. He was a genial Pan-like little fellow, who handed me a thimbleful of raki as soon as he set eyes on me, then led me along the steeply slanting courtyard to a walled flight of whitewashed steps, and then wooden-banistered stairs on to a terrace overlooking the well of the courtyard and the chapel and the irregular, chimney-peopled roofs of the lower parts of the monastery. The *arhondaris* was chopping wood in the sun, his gown tied about his knees and his sleeves rolled back, displaying muscular hairy forearms. He resembled an early ascetic, with his spreading fan of fine silver beard, hollow eyes, and lined face. He vouchsafed a smile to me, and led me to my room, a big white one, facing the sea and the south, so that the afternoon sun poured in. It had the first open fireplace I have seen on the peninsula so far, and after my host had tendered me his guest's ratification of welcome, he kindled a great fire there, piling up logs of enormous girth and soon making the chilly room as warm as toast.

The sun was still shining brightly in a cloudless blue sky, reflected in the tranquil Aegean and flung back by the gleaming snow, so I sat on the stone seat running along the parapet, and made a sketch of the leaded roof of the church, the irregular tiled roofs below, with their groves of slender white chimneys. The charm of Dochiarion, for me one of the most appealing of the monasteries, is the hill on which it is built, so that the roofs sloped down and down under my eyes, seawards, the tall cypresses jutting over the walls, and with the foreshortened monks, peasants and beasts of burden in the steep courtyard below, under the church's shadow, suggesting some peaceful little town of Arthurian legend.

Vespers in the church amazed me by the shirtsleeves

atmosphere, none of the monks seeming to take it at all seriously, the young beardless novice who took the service grinning like a chimpanzee at one of his comrades; there was a constant undertone of whispering between two of his *epitropes*, and the priest who came round to cense the congregation (using a strange, jangling, chainless hand-thurible) had the air of a retired publican coming out to water his roses on a summer evening. As if to complete the evening, a greenfinch flitted in at one of the windows, and for the rest of the office flew round and round the church, sometimes up into the central cupola, where a frescoed Christ the All-Powerful blessed mankind, the thumb and fourth finger of his right hand joined in benediction; sometimes the greenfinch perched opposite a host of saints and martyrs, the serried ranks of their haloes diminishing in the distance, and interlapping as neatly as fish scales. The eyes of everyone followed it round and round the roof, twittering and chirping, pointing and drawing it to each other's attention. At last the service ended, and as the congregation trooped out, one of the brothers walked round with a fan of turkey's feathers, extinguishing the candles with one sweep of his hand.

The sunset over the sea was lovely, as the globe of the sun was purified to one of those clearly defined orange balloons that in winter set so prettily over the Serpentine. I sat on the window-seat, thinking of home until it was quite dark, the room being lit with the leaping flames of my open hearth. I was sitting, looking meditatively and contentedly into its glowing depths, when a horrible little man came in, sat himself talkatively down beside me, soon abandoning his stereotyped bombardment of questions for his own life story. He pulled a medicine bottle filled with raki from his pocket, took a gurgling swig at it, and sighing contentedly proffered it to me. Affected at length by my slightly churlish unresponsiveness, he took himself off, and left me to my own devices, which were to sit quite happily and alone in the twilight. I think one of the greatest blessings of this life is its solitude.

It is very late now, and I supped long ago off rice and sardines, and sat before this glorious fire, drinking my red wine for a while, and feeling like some mediaeval traveller alone in his chamber over a bottle of sack or mead – Denys in *The Cloister and the Hearth*, for instance.

Outside now, the moon and stars are shining brightly on the snowy roofs, and making a silver track across the inky sea. I do so wonder what everyone is doing at home now.

15th February, Konstamonitou
The guest-master made up my bed on the broad Turkish divan running round the room, and after turning down the lamp I lay a long time in the flickering firelight, listening to the hissing of the damp logs and watching the sap bubble from them. At length sleep came, and it is morning. I basked a delicious hour or two in the southward-facing window, level with my cheek as I lay. Outside the world was sunny and inviting, the Aegean flashing back the sun's rays, and beyond the roofs, chimney-pots, leaded cupolas and cypresses below, the coast of the peninsula curving away into the misty distance.

The way lay downhill, under the deep arch of the monastery gates, and past two orange trees, laden with heavy, golden fruit against a background of pointed leaves like glittering green sword blades. I soon found myself on the beach, the path running over the pebbles, and the foam of the breaking waves never more than a few yards off. Arriving later up the hillside, among the cultivated ledges of land, terraced one above the other and shaded by groves of olive trees, I found a taciturn Albanian sitting on a rock, looking out to sea with the sorrows of Prometheus on his brow. Turning his sad eyes on me to tell me the way, he pointed uphill with his staff, past a field where two grimed charcoal burners were busy round their glowing pyres. This road, climbing steadily and gently, was shaded all the way, and owing to the increasingly rugged and uninhabited aspect of the country, it seemed I had been misdirected, or had missed the right path. So before going further, I decided to wait until a passer-by could redirect me; I amused myself meanwhile by rolling snowballs down the slope, watching them grow bigger and bigger until they broke against a tree, and pressing hard snow in a knob at the end of my stick, so that by twisting it in softer snow I could collect huge unwieldy ammonites. Someone rounded the bend in the road as I was doing this, and I felt very guilty, somehow. After finding the right way, I slunk off feeling his eyes riveted on my back, as if he had found me manufacturing bombs instead of snowballs.

Konstamonitou, reached soon after, lies in a cup of the mountains, and has a forlorn and neglected air. I waited quite a while in the courtyard, and at last a doddering greybeard came and took me to the *arhondaris*, a jovial man with opulent beard and glowing cheeks. He gave me a pleasant little cell with the divans down both sides so broad that only a yard and a half's space was between them; another open fire too, which was soon full of blazing logs, my boots dripping greasy pools of melted snow on the bricks before it.

A French-speaking monk was produced, a meek young Father Paul, with black beard and hair, and melancholy eyes; he was intelligent however, speaking good French and a little German. After a few minutes' conversation he asked me if I believed in miracles, and receiving a non-committal reply, he launched into a long lecture about them, and the strict humbleness and poverty which his coenobite monastery enforced on its monks. He led me down to vespers as soon as we heard the clanging wooden beam in the yard, and leading me from ikon to ikon, told me their histories. Coming to an old one of St Stephen, which the Turks had once tried to burn, he pointed to it as proof of his homily of an hour before. At one point during the service, the monks left their stalls, and started a succession of crossings and obeisances, bending and touching the floor repeatedly with both hands. I naturally remained stationary, for fear of dropping some brick, but an old monk came up, and with fury in his eye muttered 'ἔξω! ἔξω!'* to make me do likewise. Father Paul arrived in time, telling him I was a heretic and knew no better.

The rigours of their life seemed to have told on most of the monks, as a more decrepit, broken-looking group of men it would be hard to find, drooping in their stalls, their gaunt frames draped with tattered and rotting robes, and a misery and apathy in their sunken eyes that is indescribable.

After vespers, Father Paul – it seems odd to call him Father, when he is only a few years older than me – led me into the refectory where all the monks were seated at long trestle tables down one side of the chamber. The abbot, an imposing, full-bearded man, with his black staff of office by his side, exchanged bows gravely with me, and Paul took me to sit at the table. After a long grace, we sat down, all the monks still draped in their veils, and set about vegetables and sardines, raw and swimming in yellow oil, with the stone-hard loaves and the metal jug of wine next to our places. Not a word was said all the meal, as one of the brothers read from the Bible in a singsong voice, the monks frequently laying down their forks to cross themselves. Finally, he came on his knees and kissed the abbot's hand, who gave him a ceremonial crust of bread. Then we all stood up for a grace after the meal, and processed from the refectory, the abbot leading, his staff carried like a fasces in the crook of his arm.

* 'Get out! Get out!'

This evening, all the monastery seemed to congregate in my room, sitting round on the divans, and so, to the best of our ability, we chatted away. The *arhondaris*, kind man, didn't consider the refectory fare sufficient for me, and brought a plate piled high with fried potatoes. For the army of guests, raki was produced, over which we grew quite gay and noisy. They were good souls and in spite of their ascetic look, men and brothers.

16th February, Zographos
I slept latish this morning, as my guests didn't leave till far into the night. The *arhondaris* woke me with a cup of tea, raki and a slab of *rahat loukum*. He really is a kind old man, and besought me to stay another day at Konstamonitou, but I felt restless and said I had better get going. He seemed really sorry. While I was dressing, along came Father Paul, and talked about miracles and mortification, and the significance of Christ's wounds. I am sure he would show his humility by kissing lepers' sores like St Francis. Father Seraphim, who has a wonderful carved belt-buckle representing the Trinity on his capacious paunch, introduced a gayer note, when he came in beaming over my lunch tray. I learnt that the usual way to the Bulgarian monastery of Zographos was blocked by snow, so I had to go down the valley of a long steep canyon to the fir trees on the shore, and then inland again. Quite a group of monks escorted me to the gates, pouring out last-minute instructions.

In the gorge the snow was deep, as no sun could penetrate the woods to thaw it, but soon the path climbed up one of the slopes, through the trees, and emerged on the crest of a hill. It was splendid in the sunlight, and I lay awhile on my overcoat soaking it in. The grass slope sank to the waves in stone-buttressed olive terraces, and the sparkling Aegean was framed in the silver-grey leaves. Further downhill, a shepherd sat piping to his tinkling flock. At the sea's edge, the square top of the arsenal of Zographos stood beside a round one like a martello tower. The breeze came fresh through the woods, heavy with the smell of bruised leaves. The scene might have come straight out of Theocritus.

At the bottom, in the group of fishermen's huts that always cluster round these pirate-proof little fortresses, there was a sudden clatter of hooves, as a muleteer drove his timber-laden beasts down to a waiting dinghy. Otherwise the whole village seemed asleep, so I took the obvious path, leading uphill through olive trees. Big, stratified and veined rocks reared up on the left, and as the way wound deeper up the valley, the lichen-covered roof of a mill appeared, a clacking wheel, a turmoil of white foam and, further up, its still, clear pools. The forest closed in with a jungle of olive, yew, oleander, broom, laurel, rhododendron and holly. A blackbird told of the nearness of spring, and set me thinking about home.

Even in the distance Zographos amazed me by its size. It looked a bit like an Austrian *schloss* or hunting lodge of indeterminate style, huge and bare. But inside it was better, with two tall yew trees in front of the church. The porter seemed pleased with my smattering of Bulgarian, and led me as a curiosity to the *arhondaris*, who gave me my coffee, raki and *glyco* in the sunny kitchen, talking rapid Macedonian Bulgarian. I couldn't understand much. The view from the windows is fine, with the leafy treetops of the valley rising to an answering height the other side, and lifting up a one-storeyed, rambling hermitage painted in blue and white. Beyond, rocks and hills roll away in waves, tufted with tall, twisted pines.

The way to the hermitage lay along an avenue of tall cypress trees, hung with their little tight cones. The hermitage seemed deserted at first, except for a sandy kitten, who awoke at my approach and glared suspiciously. Hearing voices down the passage, I looked round the door and saw a tiny wire-haired monk in a cobbler's apron, with a half-mended shoe in his lap, and a big monk sitting on the sunny windowsill, balancing a spoon on the brim of his teacup. They told me to come in, and learning my nationality they launched into warm praise of the English. They told a story about the French and Greeks trying to break into the monastery to set fire to a portrait of Czar Ferdinand,* but John Bull stepped in and saw fair play. They gave me a cup of tea, and asked me all about Bulgaria, on learning I had been there so recently. They seemed quite out of touch, and had no idea of the Giorgieff† *coup d'état* last May, so I told them what little I knew.

It was just time for vespers when I got back, so I went in and listened to the singing, which is practically the same as the Greek, except that in the latter there are hardly ever more than two voices singing at the same time; here the whole community kept up a droning monody on a low note. The monk who took the service was a fine type with strong hard features, deep-set black eyes, high cheekbones, a firm mouth and a bristling iron-grey beard. His voice was deep and powerful. Most of the monks were Macedonians: that melancholy, warlike people. I spent most of my time, head flung back, gazing at the frescoes, which though not old, were amazingly graphic. One of the best was a group of martyrs, their eyes lifted to heaven in a forest of tilted haloes, on the top of a tower, round whose base scarlet and crimson

---

* Czar Ferdinand (1861–1948), founder of Bulgaria's revived but short-lived royal dynasty. After the defeat of Bulgaria in the First World War – more than sixteen years before PLF's journey – he abdicated in favour of his son, Boris III.

† Kimon Giorgieff (1882–1969), leader of a right-wing military faction, effected a bloodless coup against Bulgaria's coalition government in May 1934. He was removed in a counter-coup by Czar Boris eight months later.

flames were licking, stoked by a dastardly Pope in cope and tiara. In another a heathen king was consigning the faithful to torture. A white-robed youth stood before his throne and reasoned with him, but in the background waited the wheel, the gibbet, and a smoking cauldron of boiling oil. One of the youth's comrades was already being hauled up the gallows, a halter round his neck, and an infidel was making a feint at a second with his scimitar. Two were already despatched, their still haloed heads lying some feet away from their gushing trunks, the hands remonstrating in ghastly *rigor mortis.*

The most macabre frescoes are usually those on the outside walls under the arcade, showing the afterlife of the damned, with an intricate network of ladders and chutes from the hall of judgement to the bottomless pit, where swarms of little black and red demons await them, with forked tongues, and pigs' and wolves' heads, serpent tails and eagle claws; they pile the wicked among the flames with tridents and pokers, or fling them to lions and bears and dogs, a scene in which the beasts go ravening round a dismembered corpse, with legs, hands and heads in their teeth, or halfway down their throats. The delight and cunning in the demons' faces show they have their hearts in their vocation, thrusting firebrands into the navels of the fallen, or, crowning indignity, defecating upon them from above. Over the sulphurous cloudbank sits Christ the All-Powerful enthroned and robed, his face expressionless, the hand raised in formal blessing, while round his feet cluster the army of the saved, smug in gleaming new robes and haloes. I scan these scenes of beatification or damnation with a zest that can't be altogether healthy.

As we left the church, a monk with whom I'd previously exchanged a few words asked me if I spoke French or German, and on my admitting I did, took me to a venerable-looking monk, whose bright eyes and full white beard somehow lacked the monastic stamp. He spoke to me in French, later shifting to German, as being more at home. He spoke it perfectly, and, on my inviting him to my quarters for tea, unfolded a queer tale. He had owned a large cloth factory in Gabrovo, and with growing age and wealth, travelled all over Europe becoming as familiar with all its Western capitals as with Sofia. At Monte Carlo, bathing, a couple of years ago, he had so narrowly escaped drowning that he attributed his life to God's intervention, and his wife being dead, and his children provided for, decided to embrace the monastic life for his remaining years. He had had the utmost difficulty in joining the community at Zographos, owing to the Greek reluctance to admit foreigners on the Holy Mountain (the same story as the Russians) but had finally managed it. Since then he had lived perfectly contentedly as a monk. He showed me a picture of himself a few years ago, very worldly and ceremonial, in evening dress, his breast a mass of medals and orders, and one strung round his neck on a ribbon, which King Boris had given him on quitting Sofia. He had served the state in several diplomatic capacities, and had been German consul in Gabrovo. He had a prosperous look, despite his garb, but seemed perfectly contented with his lot. He wore underneath his black gown a wonderful embroidered jerkin, patterned with crosses and, lower down, a skull and crossbones. He was charming company, and although nearly eighty, full of life and talk. We both waxed garrulous in reminiscences of Bulgaria, and he led me to the big reception salon of the monastery where the pictures of Czar Boris and Queen Joanna, familiar from every café and pub in Bulgaria, hung on the walls. There, too, was the picture of Ferdinand which the French had wished to destroy, regal in his imperial beard and plumed kalpack. Father Viniamin (his worldly name was Karaghioseff) told me of the few-days-old changes in the cabinet in Bulgaria, when Giorgieff had been dismissed in favour of General Pentcho Zlatoff, the former war minister. The presence of two active generals and one colonel in the cabinet displayed the growing strength of the military dictatorship.

Before I had supper, he brought me several back numbers of *la Bulgarie*, and also (this with a great air of mystery) some butter, the first I have seen on Athos, and some Bulgarian *kashkaval*, so vastly superior to the oily white cheese of the monks. He left me repeating how friendly the English always had been to Bulgaria, citing the examples of James Bourchier and Lord Buxton – he pronounced it 'Bookston!' He is a delightful old chap, and extraordinarily kind.

After supper I read the news of Bulgaria's governmental changes. They are an energetic little folk, and, with Hungary, have suffered more than any as a result of the war.

17th February, Chilandari
Today is a *prazdnik* – a feast day – and the monks sat up all last night for the *agrypnia* vigil; after breakfast, I went down for the tail-end of the Mass, and when we came out my friend Father Viniamin suggested that I should have lunch in the refectory, as it was a fine one, and the ceremony interesting. We went to the abbot's table (his name was Alexander and I kissed his hand on introduction). Viniamin sat next to him, then came me. I felt very honoured, as it was a semicircular table, only seating the abbot, in the middle, and the eight superior monks – the *starets*, or 'old men'. The rest sat down the refectory along three rows of trestle tables. The hall was a fine lofty one, its whitewashed vaults arching high above. The procession entered from the church with a jangling of censers, headed by a monk bearing an ikon and flanked by two novices holding candles, shielded in coloured lanterns from the wind, and the thurifer brought up the rear. After grace, the monk with the fine voice who officiated last

night climbed into the high pulpit, and read from the eagle lectern while we ate. After he had kissed the abbot's hand and received his crust, all stood up in rows by the tables, and then a monk brought round a platter of white bread, and we all took a morsel. Another followed with a hand-thurible, and each monk held his crumb a moment in the sanctified smoke, then swallowed it. (This last rite is absolutely mysterious to me.) Then we processed silently out, the abbot leading, holding his black staff.

I set out soon after, led to the gates by Father Viniamin, who parted with the following words: '*Gute Reise, und gehen Sie mit Gott. Wenn sie Zeit haben, wäre ich Ihnen sehr dankbar für eine Briefkarte manchmal. Kommen Sie bald wieder zurück, und wir werden noch einmal von Bulgarien redden. Alles gute!*'*

As I set off, I couldn't help feeling depressed at the lot of the minority foreign monasteries here. Zographos has been especially impoverished by the confiscation of once-Bulgarian lands in Macedonia. Formerly it had many more monks, and a flourishing hospital, all of which Father Viniamin showed me. It seems the Greeks have been very hard in all their dealings with foreign monasteries on the Holy Mountain. Zographos is luckier, however, than Russiko, in that it has a country which still grants it enough to get along on. King Boris is extraordinarily kind in these things, and takes a great personal interest in the monastery, sending frequent gifts. Next to our own, I think he is probably the most loved monarch alive.

The land changed a lot between Zographos and Chilandari. The evergreen valleys have been left behind and replaced by heather-clad highlands, shaded by fir and oak woods, and the rock underfoot has turned to sand and gravel. The whole scene

---

* 'Have a good journey, and God be with you. If you have time I'd be grateful for a postcard sometimes. Come back soon, and we'll talk about Bulgaria again. All the best!'

reminded me of Scotland. The day was wonderful, not a cloud in the sky, and the birdsong was filled with optimism and the promise of spring. A bright-winged jay screeched at my approach, and a whirring cloud of woodpigeons burst from a giant ilex. High overhead a hawk hovered, casting his wavering shadow on a stretch of bare sand.

The pathway nearly always followed a water-course, and sometimes the going was torment, as the recent gales and snow have mangled or uprooted innumerable bushes and saplings. This meant crawling underneath on all fours, or clambering over mountains of shrubbery, no easy task when each twig is festooned with a mesh of spined brambles and creepers as strong as wire. That hallowed neighbourhood soon re-echoed to savage blasphemies. Perspiring and aching, I climbed at last to a higher point, commanding the surrounding country, and there below, basking in the noonday sun, lay the Serbian monastery of Chilandari, the faded tiles of the lichen-coated roofs appearing above feathery treetops; in one wall a tall battlemented tower overlooked the courtyard, with the four leaded Byzantine domes of the church and three cypresses, almost as high as the tower itself. Fold on wooded fold descended into the valley, like a wide staircase, and not so far away the blue sea glittered. A dilapidated tower was just visible among the trees by the water's edge. A few yards out the sea creased lazily round a tiny island of white rock. Haze obscured the horizon and hid the lower slopes of the snowy island of Thasos, which hung in the sky like something from another world.

In the courtyard of Chilandari everything seemed asleep, the wind-mellowed walls bathed in the sunlight. Only a cat stepped secretly across the grassgrown cobbles. Time seemed to have come to a halt in that soundless courtyard, and I sat down on a wooden bench and closed my eyes against the sun, letting the sky filter through the joined lashes in a nimbus of prismatic colours. A tap on the shoulder roused me, and the little Serbian guest-master, Father Damascene, presented himself. Almost a dwarf, with oddly growing beard and moustache, his face was filled with hospitality and goodwill; he picked up my bag and stick and preceded me up two broad flights of stairs into a sunny room, with a large bay window overlooking the courtyard. While he was away preparing my coffee, I looked round the portraits and photographs on the wall – Peter of Serbia,* the four-months dead Alexander, Queen Marie and her three sons, prints of former Obrenovitches and Karageorgevitches, Prince Milosh† with high collar and cravat à la Wellington, and most interesting of all, endless engravings of famous comitadjis and voivodes, in their little pillbox hats, embroidered waistcoats, and sashes stuck full of brass-bound pistols and yataghans; yet their faces looked mild enough, with deep thoughtful eyes and drooping moustaches. There was a picture too of Montenegrins doing the sword dance, to the time of clapping haiduks, and one of the bloodthirsty battle of Kosovo,‡ with the infidels, their turbans smitten to the ground, rolling in their gore, the victorious Slavs on horseback prancing gaily above. No one would have thought they had lost the battle.

It is amusing to think that Count Hunyadi, the nephew by marriage of the last Obrenovitch king, lives in Transylvania within a few miles of Xenia Czernovits, the cousin of the present

---

* Peter I Karageorgevitch of Serbia, the popular soldier-monarch, was proclaimed King of the Serbs, Croats and Slovenes (the future Yugoslavia) in 1918. Of the recently widowed Queen Marie's three sons, the eldest became Peter II, last king of Yugoslavia.

† Prince Milosh Obrenovitch (1780–1860) is widely considered the founder of the modern Serbian state, and was its liberator from the Ottoman Turks.

‡ The Battle of Kosovo (1389) between a Serbian alliance and the Ottoman Turks virtually wiped out both armies, and remains an event of dark heroism in Serbian folklore. It opened the way for Ottoman domination of the Balkans.

Karageorgevitch, on perfect terms of good neighbourhood. It only occurred to me now, and what a coincidence it is my knowing them both.

I spent the rest of the afternoon wandering about the buildings, putting in an appearance towards the end of vespers, and after that, going for a walk among the woods above the monastery. Coming to a clearing among the pines, above the steep hillside, among a tangle of saplings and undergrowth, I got a wonderful view over the monastery, the powerful upward sweep of its buttressed walls, the irregular lines of its balconies and roofs, and, beyond the church, the cobbles of the courtyard. The evening was delicious, and I wandered long among the trees, till I felt it was time to return, when I sauntered back along the dried-up bed of a brook; the janitor was waiting for me, and admonished me with wagging finger and twinkling eyes.

The tower is one of the highest on the peninsula, and not used, as in the other monasteries, as a library or treasury. The threshold has only rusted hinges to show where the door had once swung. Its interior is dark and mysterious, with rickety wooden steps leading up into its highest recesses, where a bat flew squeaking out of the window on my arrival. The top of the tower is roofed over with tiles, and finding a trapdoor jutting from there, I sat looking out for a while at the courtyard where the monks had come out like rabbits in a warren to catch the evening sun. The long shadows of the cypresses sprawled across the flags, and the walls took on a beautiful golden hue. The glow was fading fast from the stretch of sea just visible over the treetops from my crow's nest, and the sparkling crest of Thasos grew every moment dimmer. As evening set in, I wandered sadly down, contemplating my impending departure from the Holy Mountain with gloom.

Father Damascene cooked a splendid supper of fried fish and potatoes, and some good soup too, which he dished up with great aplomb, watching me eat it with great pleasure; just as he was bringing my coffee, a noise came like a dog scratching on his door, then the window began to rattle. Father Damascene and I looked at each other in bewilderment as the floor beneath us began to tremble and heave with a noise of subdued thunder; somewhere some china broke, and as it was subsiding we realized that there had been an earthquake. Damascene winked archly and knowingly, as he put my coffee down, and grinned at me with a chuckle, as if it was a little joke arranged by him to give me a turn. It's the second earthquake I have experienced within two months, the last time being when I was having tea with Miss Kent in Constantinople.

I reread parts of *Don Juan* all the evening by the stove, still finding it wonderful.

18th February, Esphigmenos
I got up rather earlier than usual today, soon after my morning tea, of which Father Damascene gave me two cups, and putting on my soft Bulgarian moccasins, as it was a glorious, sunny day, prepared to spend the morning up on the hillside. Delving in the bottom of my rucksack for the *A Shropshire Lad* my mother gave me last birthday, I found an envelope full of Capstan Navy Cut. This was a real find, and getting out my best pipe (unsmoked for nearly a month) I stuffed it full and set it alight. I'm sure the good God never breathed incense with more delight than I felt then. Pipe tobacco, after a month's cigarette smoking, is an ecstasy too deep for words.

I found the same clearing as the day before, looking over and into the monastery, and beyond at the sea, and spent the morning there lying on my overcoat under a Scotch fir, reading *A Shropshire Lad*, and finally falling asleep. The bells of the monastery roused me later on, and running all the way back, I found Damascene in a great twitter about my lunch, which he had managed to keep warm. My moccasins caused quite a stir among the monks, who grinned and shook their heads in a knowing way (the Greeks call them τσαρούχι).* After packing up my rucksack, I said goodbye to Father Damascene, who told me to be sure and come next year: the janitor had made a wonderful little sketch map of the road to Esphigmenos, and filled me with directions as to the way – 'Turn to the right when you come to the cross,' said he, 'and above all, don't go down to the tower on the seashore.' As the road had a little shrine with a cross almost every fifty yards, this proved rather difficult, but at last seeing the tower of the arsenal on the shore, I took the other path, leading along a cultivated valley where the monks were hoeing their fields, their loins girt and their long hair bound in little pigtails or buns. A Macedonian who was chopping wood showed me the road after that, which led over several stiles, through a few fields, then sloped down to where the monastery of Esphigmenos lay in its little bay. Crossing the bridge to the monastery, a voice shouted from somewhere, 'You English fullow?' and looking round, I saw a venerable-looking monk with a curly beard beaming at me. 'Where you come from?' he went on in deepest American. 'I know America, England, Japan, China, France – oh, many countries!'

He took me along to the *arhondaris*, and, for the last time on the Holy Mountain, I was given my raki, coffee and *glyco*; meanwhile Father Velisarios, my travelled new friend, produced some cuttings from *The Times* sent him last year by Sir Arthur Hill, the director of Kew Gardens; choosing something representative, Sir Arthur had sent some photos of the Derby, which had so affected Father Velisarios that he had written back suggesting they should club together for a sweepstake ticket; judging by Sir Arthur's

---

* An outdoor leather slipper with a pompom on the toe, still worn by the ceremonial Evzone guards.

reply, he was very surprised at receiving these proposals from a monk of the Holy Mountain, and admitted that he never betted. Father Velisarios couldn't let the sweepstake idea go, however, and instructed me to write from England as soon as the next sweepstake came round. He admitted he had been a great gambler in his secular life, and the evil spirit seems to have been reawoken by the botanist's pictures. Velisarios was a delightful chap however, his face full of goodwill, his eyes in their network of wrinkles a-sparkle with humour. Father Ignatios, the cook, was a great friend of his, and though an equally delightful type, completely different: more ascetic and polished, with the kindest face over a long brown beard. He and Velisarios between them took enormous pains for my well-being, giving me the best room, several storeys high, and directly above the sea, which lapped on the walls below; Ignatios kindled a bright fire in the big white-pillared stove, brought me extra bedclothes, and set fresh water in the carafe by my bedside. He was a model monk, taking a real pleasure in service, and for whom no trouble, if it was within his power, was too much. All the while, Velisarios sat with me at the table, entertaining me with amusing and racy remarks on life.

He took me down to vespers, stopping at his cell en route to don his veil and gown. For the last time, with an emotion that surprised me, I listened to the solemn liturgy, watched and anticipated each stage of the ceremonies grown so familiar, and looked at the halo-gleaming frescoes, where the Risen Christ poised above the earth in a star-studded sky, his legs crossed, as if taking the first step in a grave celestial minuet. The thurifer, censing the people, gave me my own personal two swings of incense, for which one inclines the head in thanks, and I snuffed it up as never before; the hard stall, always so irksome till now, seemed oddly comfortable: the mainspring of all these feelings being my departure, which seems harder than one would think possible.

Ignatios, Velisarios and I leant on the wooden balustrade opposite the kitchen door, watching the sun set, while the monastery and the church, with its characteristic double Byzantine stripe of red bricks in the white plaster, the bell tower, and the lemon trees with their tiny spring fruit, gradually faded into the dusk. The evening had a stillness and melancholy completely Athonite, and silently we turned indoors to the big white kitchen, where Velisarios dissolved our low spirits with a bottle of raki which he produced from a dark cupboard. The monastery kitchens are mediaeval in appearance, vaulted and massive, with vast stoves under a deep blackened arch of chimney, the walls hung with different-sized bronze casseroles for coffee and tea, and the earthenware pots and dishes are all thick and painted in bright colours. Generally an ikon or two hangs on the walls, and sometimes there are big white amphorae a yard deep, in which the water is kept deliciously cool and oil safely lidded. The kitchens are always cheerful and sunny. I have spent many pleasant times in them, over wildcat swigs of raki, talking with the monks, while the cook, his black gown laid aside, and his sleeves rolled back, busied himself at the eternal task of coffee-brewing, pushing the blackened pannikins among the glowing charcoal.

After supper, Velisarios paid me a visit in my room, sat himself down with a whirl of draperies, and seemed quite changed from his former worldly mood. He railed against the Catholics and freemasons, and then went on to sinners in general, saying that they may have a good time now, but when they are dead, 'God'll see to 'em, God'll fix them fullows up OK?' Then he launched forth on saints and miracles and peripatetic ikons, fascinating tales of which, owing to his strange English, I could not grasp the full tenor. One phrase sticks in my mind: 'His woman, she made him three boys.'

Hearing that I was setting off for the mainland tomorrow, he drew a little sketch map of the way, and said he would talk to Ignatios about making up a lunch packet and wrote a note to an innkeeper there, explaining that I was going to the Stathatos estate,* and to help me as much as he could.

After he went, I wrote awhile, and then smoked the last of my tobacco, listening to the sea under my window, the waves breaking with a crash then sucking backwards with a rasp of pebbles. Looking at my jolly room, with the clean sheets and everything arranged so neatly, and at the glowing stove piled high with logs, I feel a great deal of regret at leaving this quiet and happy life. This last month will be an unbelievable memory when I'm back in England. I wonder when I shall be here again?

THE END

---

* Peter Stathatos had invited PLF to stay at his estate at Modi, near Lake Volvi.

Acknowledgements

It was Patrick Leigh Fermor's friend Olivia Stewart who reignited his interest in what he always called 'Vol III', and our first, heartfelt thanks go to her. Not only did she have the first draft of the book typed up and put into digital format; she also encouraged Paddy to take up the project he had abandoned for so long.

We are especially grateful to Dr David McClay of the John Murray Archive, and the Trustees of the National Library of Scotland for all their assistance, including permission to reproduce the Mount Athos section of the Green Diary; and to John and Virginia Murray for warm hospitality.

Rudi Fischer reviewed the Rumanian passages, as did William Blacker. Professor Peter Mackridge's help was invaluable with the Greek, as was Thomas Kielinger's on the German and Sophie-Caroline de Margerie's on the French. Our thanks also go to Edvard Gurvich and to the Bulgarian Cultural Institute; and to Howard Davies for his sensitive copy-editing.

Index